Toastmaster's Treasury

Books by Edward L. Friedman

TOASTMASTER'S TREASURY

THE SPEECHMAKER'S COMPLETE HANDBOOK

Toastmaster's Treasury

by Edward L. Friedman

DIRECTOR, NATIONAL REFERENCE LIBRARY

A Complete Guide for the Toastmaster,
Master of Ceremonies, and Program Chairman

HARPER & BROTHERS, PUBLISHERS, NEW YORK

*To my mother and father, who found in humor
a way to enjoy life more and ease the pains of adversity.*

The author wishes to express his thanks and grateful appreciation to the many distinguished and busy men and women who offered their help, suggestions, and—in many cases—actual manuscript writing as a contribution to this book.

Contents

Preface

In Biblical times it was the custom of man to raise his voice and sing for joy. Today, man is content merely to smile, laugh a little and utter a few pleasantries as a demonstration of his happiness. That is why a toastmaster is selected, not on the basis of his singing voice but rather on his ability to tell a humorous story well, entertain and keep a gathering of people in good humor, no matter how many times in one evening they may be subjected to the iniquities of public speaking and speakers.

The greatest singers of all history seldom, if ever, wrote their own music. They borrowed the music from another and gave it meaning through the use of their voice and talents. In the same way, the greatest toastmasters who ever lived seldom, if ever, wrote their own humor and jokes. They borrowed liberally from the great storehouse of man's accumulation of jokes and witty comments.

This treasury of humor is another such storehouse where toastmasters may borrow what they need so that, with their voice and talent, they may fulfill the obligations they assume to take charge of a meeting and make it successful. It is the author's hope that the *Toastmaster's Treasury* will be more suitable and helpful for toastmasters and speakers than other storehouses. Efforts have been made to select each bit of humor that is most becoming for such use and rewrite it, revise it and distill it down until it is essentially a sparkling and polished gem specifically and exclusively for use by toast-masters and speakers, as distinguished from humor in general circulation—humor having no particular purpose or application in some other form or field outside the limited range of a toastmaster's special needs and requirements.

Toastmaster's Treasury

1
Duties of a Toastmaster

THERE are many banquets and dinner meetings held where the presiding officer is the president of an organization which may be host to the guests present, a program chairman or other officer selected for the honor of opening the meeting and presiding. In such case, this presiding officer has the responsibility of calling the guests to the table, establishing order, introducing the minister or other person who will bless the food and being first to speak up when the dinner itself is concluded. Directly after the dinner, the president may welcome the guests and then introduce the toastmaster, who will take over for the rest of the evening. On the other hand, the welcome remarks may be left for the toastmaster. In this case, the presiding officer would merely bring the gathering to order after the dinner has been concluded and then introduce the toastmaster. The toastmaster would begin his remarks with a welcome for all the guests and then go on to introduce the speakers or announce musical entertainment or acts which may have been arranged as part of the program.

The toastmaster very often will run the whole show. He will call the people to the table and urge them to be seated. After he has everyone seated and the noise of the conversation begins to subside, the toastmaster may speak a few brief words of welcome and then introduce the minister, or anyone else who has been selected to deliver a short prayer before partaking of food. Everyone is asked to stand and bow heads

1

during this religious observance. After the dinner itself has been concluded, the toastmaster begins the entertainment with some humorous remarks to warm up the audience and get them in a receptive mood to welcome the speakers. Then he will introduce each speaker and, when that speaker has finished, he will comment on the talk. Compliments are usually in order, although a certain amount of mild rejoinder is permissible as long as there is no sting. However, whether the toastmaster's comments are flattering or jocular, they should be apt and appropriate to the occasion. Above all, they should pertain directly to what the speaker has said and represent a commentary on the speaker's remarks. This is done for the amusement of those present and not intended to stir up any enmity or ill feeling between the toastmaster and speakers.

The popular custom of kidding the speaker and having the speaker come back at the toastmaster with some sharp and pointed remark is strictly for the "home town boys." This is all right when the speaker and the toastmaster are both residents of the city where the meeting is held, members of the same organization sponsoring the banquet or otherwise familiar figures to everyone present. This type of friendly antagonism is not to be carried on between a toastmaster and a guest speaker from another city or one not well known to everyone present. In this case, the toastmaster should show the invited guest utmost respect and never tell jokes at his expense. Unwarranted humor involving a guest not familiar to everyone present would be considered rude and inappropriate for the occasion. The toastmaster must be polite and considerate at all times.

A successful toastmaster has—usually unfairly and without due credit to the abilities of the individual—been frequently described as an individual with a low I.Q. and a high P.R. (personality rating). He can get along all right if he doesn't try to impress anyone with his own importance and mental attainments and if he avoids making a clown out of himself. The toastmaster should always speak slowly and distinctly. He should not run his words together. Every word is important in his remarks and should be clearly conveyed to each member of the audience.

Any occasion which requires the services of a toastmaster is one designed for entertainment and dedicated to good fellowship and good humor. Serious meetings call for a moderator and discussion panel.

Meetings which require the services of a toastmaster are intended to contribute nothing more than a good time for all who are present. For this reason, anything which may be regarded as controversial or creating antagonism should be avoided. Nothing should transpire which might be regarded as objectionable or personally distasteful to any person present.

The toastmaster does not, as a rule, have an opportunity to arrange the program and select the speakers. Sometimes he has this privilege which simplifies his job. Usually, he has to take the program as it has been arranged by others and do the best he can to create a unified program which brings everything together to fit harmoniously and in some semblance of order.

If the toastmaster has charge of arranging the program, he can build it around an appropriate motif or central theme. If the occasion is to be a testimonial dinner, the speakers must concentrate on the honored guest. To speak of other things might be considered rude. In arranging the program, never overbalance with entertainment features and especially never seek entertainment which will overshadow the speakers and make them take second place. If you have an important speaker scheduled, do not place him on a program where the audience will be anxious for him to conclude his talk so they may witness the performance of popular and highly regarded entertainers.

The toastmaster should consider that his responsibilities toward the speakers begin even before the meeting is held. He should make sure that each speaker who is to appear on the program has been invited. He should tell each speaker exactly when and where the meeting is to be held. He should remind the speaker before the meeting and urge him to be present. This will help insure the presence of the speaker and also flatter him. It shows that his presence is considered important and he will endeavor to do the best he can.

SHOWMANSHIP

The toastmaster is the band leader who runs the show. Every instrument is under his command, and through his skill and talent he brings out the best in everyone who participates in the program. The band leader usually engages in certain antics to hold the attention of the audience. The music in itself is not sufficient to dramatize the effort of the musicians for the audience. The toastmaster must understand something about showmanship.

Showmanship is a term used to describe the technique that accounts for success in any public entertainment. If an entertainment is successful, it has been so because of good showmanship. If the entertainment fails, it was a poor show. Showmanship is supposed to be a rare talent possessed by professional entertainers and those who arrange and promote public performances. Actually, showmanship is nothing more or less than the ability to hold the attention of others and is frequently possessed by small children and adults who have never considered themselves talented as professional performers. If you can hold the attention and interest of others, then you understand something of the principles of showmanship.

Frequently good showmen cannot explain why or how they

manage to succeed. People come by these things naturally. Others, who possess some skill and natural talent for entertainment, endeavor to improve themselves and study the principles and techniques of showmanship. There is always room for improvement for everyone, and the person who wants to do a better job in the field of entertainment should undertake a serious study of the principles of showmanship.

INTRODUCTION OF GUESTS

The introduction of all of the guests of honor or those individuals seated at the speakers' table usually precedes any other part of the program immediately after the dinner has been concluded. The person who has this responsibility stands at the center of the speakers' table and introduces all of the guests to his left and to his right. It is a popular custom to begin the introductions with the last person at the extreme left of the table and then the next person until all guests to the left of the presiding officer are introduced, with the exception of those who will be called upon to speak. They will be introduced at greater length later. When all guests seated at the main or speakers' table to the left of the person acting as chairman, toastmaster or presiding officer have been introduced, then the chairman begins to introduce those to his right, starting with the person at the extreme right and following an order which leads directly up to the center of the table, omitting speakers who are to be introduced later. The speakers should sit directly next to the chairman at his right and left, so that they will be immediately available when called upon to speak. The chairman ordinarily requests that the audience withhold all applause until every person has been introduced. As a novelty, the chairman may request that after each person is introduced and stands up briefly to be seen, the audience applaud with one clap of the hand—no more! This lends a little variety and amusement to the routine procedure of introduction.

APPLAUSE

Applause is the only reward for amateur entertainers, which includes speakers at dinners. Applause is the most sought after gratuity of the professional entertainer who receives money as his reward for his performance. Money in itself is not his only compensation. Some performers put applause even above money, and all entertainers place applause next to money as the second best possible compensation for their efforts. The toastmaster should encourage liberal applause throughout the entire program. He should try to encourage enthusiastic applause after each introduction and at the conclusion of each speech.

ANNOUNCEMENTS

Frequently, there are announcements to be made during the course of the evening. Some of these are prepared announcements concerning future events and require considerable time for description and full detail. A person making an announcement regarding some future event may be especially enthusiastic regarding it and personally responsible for the event's success. Therefore, he may be moved by a desire to elaborate on his announcement and turn it into a sales pitch which requires more time than the program schedule has allowed. The toastmaster must assume control and make sure that announcements do not exceed the time provided for them and do not destroy the continuity of the entertainment for the evening. Where possible, it is best if the toastmaster personally makes all the announcements and does not call upon some individual to speak for this purpose. When the toastmaster makes an announcement, he is in full control over the length of time consumed and the content of the message.

WATCH THE TIME

Nothing kills a program more completely than disregard for time limits. Each speaker should be informed of the amount of time which has been allotted to him for his speech, and he should be cautioned about not going beyond the limits set. The most difficult job the toastmaster is called upon to do is to keep the program running on scheduled time. It should open at the time anticipated and conclude at an hour previously determined. The toastmaster can time his own remarks perfectly, but he has a great responsibility in keeping all speakers to their assigned time limit. Also, there may be long applause and other interruptions which will disturb the time schedule. The reading of bulletins and announcements frequently takes up time not provided in the program. As a timekeeper the toastmaster must be polite but firm with the speakers.

DRUNKS AND HECKLERS

The toastmaster must deal with hecklers, drunks, those who disturb the meeting by being loud and noisy, some who shout questions and demand proof from the speaker and the ever-present and most embarrassing circumstance when people begin to walk out of the meeting. All of these things require tact and diplomacy. There are no rules to prescribe because every situation requires a different method of treatment. The toastmaster must maintain order without creating any antagonism or distracting from the program itself. The disturbance in the audience can become the main show, if the toastmaster permits it to get out of hand. He must be prepared for these eventualities and have a plan of action to pursue in advance, in case he must meet a situation of this kind.

It is best to ignore hecklers and interruptions wherever possible, in the hope that the disturbance will subside of itself or persons seated close to the heckler will bring him under control. If a question is shouted at the speaker, the toastmaster may interrupt to announce that questions will be called for later or in some other way put an end to this type of interference. In extreme cases, the toastmaster must call for stern disciplinary action and may even go so far as to order the offender to leave the room.

ORDER OF THE PROGRAM

Often there is some doubt about the order in which speakers should be presented on the program. Generally, the main speaker is called upon last as the climax and concluding feature of the entertainment. There may be good reasons why this conventional arrangement should be changed. This is particularly true at an occasion when it is expected many of those who will attend plan to leave early before the program is concluded. In fairness to them, when it is impossible for them to stay for the entire course of the evening, and in fairness to the principal speaker, his position on the program may be advanced ahead of other speakers so that everyone will have an opportunity to hear him and he will be able to speak while there is a full attendance present. When there is no principal or guest speaker, and all speakers rank on a par as to their importance and their contribution to the program, other considerations may be used. The appearance of speakers may be in an order to lend the most variety, according to their personalities, their vocation or other established classifications. They may be scheduled on the program in order according to the subject of their talk. The titles or subject matter of the talks may be of such nature that certain ones are best if heard at the beginning, while others are more suitable for the middle or end of the program.

INTRODUCTIONS

The speaker might be regarded as a rocket or missile which the toastmaster must launch. A good start is important for the speaker. Since the speaker must make his impression upon the audience in the first hundred words of his address, anything which takes place just before he gets up to speak becomes extremely important. The toastmaster launches the speaker into his orbit by means of the technique known as the introduction.

The toastmaster should avoid the dull, drab, disappointing type of introduction which presents the speaker in an unfavorable light or brings him on as an anticlimax rather than a climax to the toastmaster's remarks. The toastmaster must encourage laughter at all times. He should try to get the audience to laugh through his own efforts and at every humorous allusion of the speaker. Laughter is evidence of good humor and may be used as a standard of measurement to determine how well the program is going over with everyone present. The toastmaster always stands while introducing a speaker and generally continues to stand until the speaker completes his salutory greetings to certain individuals and all the guests present.

Introductions should be carefully planned and worked over long in advance. Some toastmasters leave everything to the last minute because they regard introductions as short and easy. A good introduction is difficult to prepare because every word counts. The purpose of the introduction is to present the speaker favorably in a few well-chosen words. The speaker should feel well pleased with the introductory remarks and the audience should be stirred so that everyone wakes up and listens. Be careful to face the audience when you introduce a speaker. Too often the toastmaster will face the speaker and talk to the speaker so that the audience misses the name or other important facts. Be particular to get names right and also cities, titles, speech subjects and other vital facts connected with the speaker being introduced. It is better to be accurate than funny. Being inaccurate is funny, but in the wrong way.

The introduction often follows a theme or central idea which ties together the whole program. Otherwise, each introduction is a complete unit by itself. The introduction conducted from the speaking platform has exactly the same purpose as the introduction when a person will present a friend to someone he happens to meet. The purpose is to make people acquainted with each other. In addition, the introduction for speakers is to inform the audience concerning the subject which the speaker will discuss. The matter of the subject is frequently as important as the individual himself. The audience wants to know about the subject they are to hear discussed, and why they should be interested in it. They want to know why the speaker is interested in this subject and what are his qualifications to discuss it.

The length of the introduction varies with the circumstances. Generally, the rule of three is a good one to follow— brevity, clarity and simplicity. Another good rule is that the more important the speaker and the better known he may be to everyone in the audience, the shorter is the introduction. The toastmaster should avoid tiring the audience with his own remarks before the speaker is introduced. However, there are times when more time should be taken by the toastmaster. His introduction is often part of the entertainment. If the toastmaster feels he should talk for a longer time than actually necessary to present the speaker, he should avoid talking on the speaker's subject. He should devote his remarks to non-related topics and not give the speaker's speech for him.

There is always a problem of how much biographical data a toastmaster should include in his introduction. A good rule to follow is that those who have gathered for the dinner meeting need not know all about the speaker. However, they should know everything which pertains to the occasion of his visit, the reason for his selection as a speaker at this particular meeting, something about his qualifications to speak on the subject selected and why the people gathered should consider it an opportunity and privilege to be present and listen to what the speaker has to say.

The person who must introduce a speaker should avoid

overpraise. People just can't be that good! Remember, you are not delivering a funeral eulogy but talking about someone very much alive, who is richly endowed with the usual human faults and frailities.

The toastmaster should keep in mind that the only difference between a pat on the back and a shove is the amount of force involved. This is true in his introduction and compliments for speakers when they have concluded their talks. A gracious and moderate amount of praise is a pat on the back. Too much praise and elaborate, flowery compliments are the same as a shove. This is disliked by the speaker because it makes him look ridiculous and causes the audience to snicker and laugh at him rather than with him. A little praise is a good thing, but the toastmaster should bear in mind at all times the possibility of spoiling his efforts when he disregards the old proverb about too much of a good thing being worse than not enough.

The comments after the speaker has finished and words of thanks and praise for the speech are important and should not be neglected. It is here that the toastmaster has an opportunity to carry on with a graciousness which will endear him to the speaker and the audience.

2
Typical Banquet Program

THE following represents a complete banquet program, including the after dinner speeches as well as the toastmaster's remarks. Most dinners have a special purpose, which this does not. The purpose may be to honor a person, and is known as a testimonial dinner. In such case, all speeches are intended to laud the individual being honored. Generally there is a main speaker, a distinguished personage or close associate of the guest of honor. Also, there is usually a gift presentation toward the end of the program, and then the guest of honor is called upon and given time to respond to all the words of praise and good wishes bestowed upon him.

Banquets also are frequently held to mark the end of a year for an organization and to install new officers, for fundraising purposes, at the conclusion of a series of events such as the end of a bowling tournament and for many other specific purposes. When a banquet is arranged for a specific purpose, the various speeches should touch upon the purpose of the banquet and follow a pattern of harmonious sequence.

The typical banquet program offered here has no specific purpose beyond providing entertainment. It serves as an example of a standard format to follow.

PROGRAM

Toastmaster begins his duties by seeing that everyone is seated at the tables and then he calls for order. There will be a prayer to bless the food before eating. The toastmaster may speak briefly as he presents the clergyman for the invocation.

1. Toastmaster—The poet laureate of England, John Masefield, once said that God warms His hands at man's heart when he prays. And tonight, at what we hope will be an occasion memorable for gaiety and camaraderie, it seems wise, to the man who will try to steer the evening into a great channel of happiness, to ask all of you to join me in an invocation. Every joyful event is one more gift from the great Giver. Will you reverently stand while I call on our friend (insert the clergyman's or layman's name here) to give the invocation. (They rise as asked.)

2. Invocation—Our Heavenly Father, we know that from Thee must come all the great pleasures we enjoy—friendship, glad reunions, the making of new friends, the chance to laugh and sing and look up at the stars. We ask Thee to bless us with the thrill of companionship, the blessing of bodily nourishment and perhaps the renewal of old dreams that may—in the stress of our strange times—have lost some of their luster. We thank Thee for every gracious hour of our lives. May this one become memorable as we leave behind our cares and distractions and live this little hour of relaxation and rest and happiness. Amen.

Toastmaster sits down and begins to eat, setting an example for all others. When it appears that eating has been concluded at all tables and the process of clearing the tables is going forward, the toastmaster arises, calls for order and begins the program for the evening.

3. Welcome Remarks—As your toastmaster for this evening, I am glad to welcome you to this meeting. I hope that you will enjoy yourselves. This is more than I can say for myself, for whoever heard of a toastmaster enjoying himself? Nobody ever treats a toastmaster with the respect and dignity to which he is entitled. I don't know how a toastmaster ever gets involved in such a situation except, possibly, the same way that a fish ends up being served on a platter. Every time I think of a toastmaster I recall seeing in the office of a friend a large mounted fish. Under it was this significant bit of wisdom: "If I had kept my mouth shut, I wouldn't be here."

I should have followed that same advice. As it is, here I am and I shall try to help you enjoy this meeting. I shall follow the same formula for success as used in government circles. This is: "Shoot the bull, pass the buck and make seven copies of everything." Well, we will skip over the seven copies tonight, but I expect we will lean heavily upon the rest of the rule to shoot the bull and pass the buck.

4. Introduction of Special Guests—As toastmaster for this evening, I have a special opportunity and pleasure to which I have been looking forward for a long time. I am very much in the same position as the maid in the home of a society woman who was making the final arrangements for an elaborate reception.

"Bridget," she said to her old servant, "for the first thirty minutes after six o'clock I want you to stand at the drawing room door and call the guests' names as they arrive."

Bridget's face lit up. "Very well, ma'am," she replied. "I've been wantin' to do that to some of your friends for years."

I have an opportunity to call the guests' names. It is a real pleasure for me to welcome them to our meeting, and as I call their names I will ask each to stand and be recognized.

TOASTMASTER CALLS UPON SPECIAL GUESTS TO RISE AS THEY ARE INTRODUCED. This part of the program is performed as quickly as possible and the number of persons to be introduced should be limited.

5. Compliments for Those Who Arranged or Served Dinner—We are more fortunate tonight than the rookie at a military camp. When passing the mess hall, he asked the cook, "What's on the menu tonight?"

Back came the reply: "Oh, we have hundreds of things to eat tonight."

"What are they?" asked the rookie, consumed with curiosity and high expectations.

"Beans," said the cook.

No, we haven't had "hundreds of things" to eat tonight, but for what we did have we owe a good round of applause to the banquet committee. Let's hear you show your appreciation for this splendid dinner.

6. Introducing Song Leader—Of all the wartime slogans, that of the Sea Bees probably was the most expressive of the wonder-working power of intelligent thinking and a determined fighting spirit. "The difficult we do now," declared their slogan. "The impossible takes a little longer!"

I am going to call upon a man who has expressed a willingness to undertake a difficult or impossible task. He is going to get us to sing. Knowing the musical ability and type of voices of some who are present, this appears to be a difficult undertaking. He is, however, ready to do his best. I am sure all of you will be good sports and try to help him out. If you can't sing, at least you can make some loud noise which will show everyone that you are happy. I take great pleasure in presenting to you our song leader for this evening. (Introduce song leader by name.)

7. Limiting Speeches—In order to keep our program within schedule, we are limiting the length of speeches. I know that our speakers will co-operate. I know that our speakers will understand the necessity for this rule and be guided by the fact that if God hadn't intended us to listen more than we talk, He would have given us two mouths and only one ear.

8.   *Announcing Program*—We have arranged an excellent program for this evening. In arranging this program, those who had charge of this meeting had in mind the story about the Tennessee couple. A doctor was called to examine the young wife of an elderly, deaf mountaineer. "Your wife is pregnant," he told her husband.

The mountainteer, hand behind his ear, queried, "Eh?"

The doctor shouted, "I said your wife is pregnant."

"Eh?"

Finally, the doctor screamed, "Your wife is going to have a baby."

The man walked to the edge of the porch, spat out a mouthful of tobacco juice and drawled, "I ain't a bit surprised. She's had ev'ry opportunity."

In the same way I feel confident that all of you are going to have every opportunity to enjoy yourselves tonight. I know our speakers will do their best to entertain you and make this meeting successful.

9.   *Explains Purpose of Meeting or Type of Entertainment Planned*—It has been said that the very best after dinner speech ever made was simply this: "Waiter, give me both checks." But your toastmaster hopes to steer for you a course threaded with laughter. Truthfully, I hope I will not bore you with my own remarks—we have banquet speakers who may do that even better. And we heard of a rather dumb waiter who was serving at a large dinner, when the bread ran out. Said the waiter, "Well, what if the bread did run out—let's serve 'em toast." And now I will serve you some toasts. So forget that you normally take a nap after your meals. Let's all wake up! Will you stand to your feet? (Waits for audience to arise.) Now let's stretch toward the ceiling—

now up—up—and UP! Will you sit down now and applaud your own noble effort? (Toastmaster leads the hand-clapping.) Feel better? You look better. Now a big grin. Thank you— thank you very much. Before the tedious talks start up, I want to explain the general topic for this occasion. I decided it might be smart to have a topic. Probably our gifted speakers will leave it—but it is nice to have it around, like a family Bible that is never opened. The topic, ladies and gentlemen, and I hope I do not exaggerate in so addressing you, is "Who Are the Most Necessary People in the World?" Our first speaker believes honestly that men are. Well, he has a hard chore ahead of him. But let's sit up and try to laugh if he thinks he's funny and give him all the encouragement we hope he'd give us—if we were in his place. All hail the first daring speaker. (Give the name of the speaker and tell something about him to meet the requirements of a satisfactory introduction, using biographical information available.)

10.   *First After Dinner Speech*—Ladies and gentlemen, you who have paid your dues, you who have eaten far too much to give me very keen attention, and you who have probably forgotten to turn off the faucet in the kitchen. I address you now very earnestly in my defense of the male animal as the one most important person in the world. First of all, when the Divine Maker thought in terms of people, of whom did He first think? Now take your time. Think carefully. Even if you haven't opened your Bibles since the first baby came, take your time. That first creation—both alert and listless listeners—was a man! Well, not such a perfect specimen, but he was a man. I have never learned anything but his first name—Adam. Maybe Adam Smith or Adam Jones or Adam van DerHoven. He was the first. And he did right well in the Garden of Eden until the Almighty took a floating rib and brought on Eve. She messed things up a lot, didn't she? But the world was at least started.

Now let us turn to modern times. Man is the most important of all modern creatures. He should wear the pants in his home and would, except that his high school daughter and wife want to. Why all of us men know just how wonderful and patient we are—don't we? We want to run off and play golf—but do we? Well—anyway, not all of us. We never ask the Little Woman if she has overdrawn the budget—do we? We don't have to—we know. We work our fingers to the bone and never complain. And do our wives suggest that we have a good time with the boys? Do they look for us while reading detective stories? Do they have the cigarettes and slippers ready for us? Do they see that the children are kept quiet while we recuperate from a long, long luncheon date or ask us please to bring home the pretty typist for dinner? Certainly you who are men know that answer! Men in their utter nobility see that their wives and daughters have all the clothes their little hearts desire. Men bring home candy and flowers even on anniversaries! Did any of you gentlemen before me ever forget a wedding anniversary? Did you ever forget to post a letter or bring home a can of baked beans—which was fiercely demanded of you?

The famous playwright August Strindberg once said, "Only the man feels true maternal love." Think of that! We have even gone into the mothering business! Women do not stay home long enough. How gently we arise and get a drink for the baby! How beautifully we dole out the allowances to our children! How unselfishly we leave the dinner table to do the dishes—and how gloriously we are misunderstood! Is there a male present who will not back me up in that? If such there be, he is only a plain coward and does not belong to those who call ourselves Men.

My point is—if you were sleepy and missed it—that we not only do our jobs faithfully and bring home the money—but we are even better than women at their own duties. Want a good steak dinner—you either go to a well-known restaurant where there is a male chef, or go out to some stag party where a man—mind you—a man broils the steaks on an outdoor fireplace. If we came home what would greet us? A humble little meatball or an overdone hamburger. But we men know we are not only supreme in our own fields of work, but we are superior to any housewife. May I add that any of these statements may be applauded by any of my sex.

It is our great minds and souls that really matter. A scientist has said that our bodies would bring less than a dollar in the open market. A man's body has enough lime to white-wash a chicken coop, enough potassium to explode one toy cannon, magnesia enough for one dose, phosphorus enough for two thousand matches, iron enough to make one eight-penny nail, sugar enough to fill one small shaker and fat enough for seven bars of soap.

No, fellow banqueters, we are not superior in body. But if you will carefully examine all the data I have brought you, you will soon acknowledge man is the most superior of all God's creations. We do not even need to prove it—we admit it. And I earnestly hope you ladies leave this banquet table to give real and merited praise to the men who so generously pay all your bills. To the toil-worn male that asks so little and bestows upon you so much; look up to him! Praise him! Be tender and gentle and sympathetic! See that meals are on time! Greet him with deep affection. For he longs to hear you say, "O wonderful protector! O miracle mate! O dearest of all God's creatures!"

My fellow gentlemen, I wish I had the oratorical power to make your case much stronger. But I now give way to another who probably has been forced to stand up for the weaker sex. I have done my poor best for my, the stronger sex.

11. *After Speech Comment*—We keenly appreciate this forensic spasm. Our speaker has given us many good reasons why men should be considered the most necessary people in the world. I am convinced. I hope the ladies present are also convinced. I can tell from the reaction that they did not agree entirely with what our speaker had to say, and that is putting it mildly. If I try to speak for the ladies, I'm sure they would say that this speech to which we have just listened demonstrates to us how greatly our country and the people in it have changed. Yes, there have been many and great changes since the days of 1776 when those ragged but heroic patriots formed our Union. In those days men were different from what they are now. Just as an example of how this country is progressing, we recall that history tells us back in the old days George Washington couldn't tell a lie. Now everybody can, and one of the best at this is the speaker we have just heard.

12.   Keeping Order—Please try to be a little more quiet. There is so much noise in here that we can't hear the speakers and the speakers can't hear themselves—even though they may not be as sensitive as a well-known souse I could mention.

This habitual drinker was suffering from one of his daily hangovers. "May I fix you a Bromo-Seltzer?" suggested the waiter.

"Ye gods, no!" moaned the souse, "I couldn't stand the noise."

While I haven't got a hangover, I can echo this fellow's remark and say, "Quiet down! I can't stand the noise."

13.   Introducing Second Speaker—Our next speaker was warned several days ago that he was to be called upon, and furthermore he was told that he had better be good. As the safety director says, it's a good idea to "stop, look and listen," but it's not necessary that you talk unless you really have something to say. I hope our next speaker has taken this warning to heart, and when he gets up to speak he will really have something to say.

Before I present our next speaker, I want to qualify any

of my remarks with a brief statement. Here it is: Any toast-master has a perfect right to tell any story he may wish—whether it be true or false—about any speaker on the program.

The reason? Why, no one expects a good toastmaster to tell the truth about a speaker—especially if he decides to tell a story about the person he is to introduce.

Now I hope you'll remember this—but—I am told our next speaker's wife was talking with one of her woman friends the other day and this friend asked, "How do you keep your husband from staying late at his work?"

And she answered, "Why, my dear, that was easy. When he first started coming home later and later each night, I hit upon a perfect remedy. One night when he came in late, I called out, 'Is that you, Harry?' "

You see, her husband's name is Robert. And ever since then he comes home early. (Change names to fit case, of course.)

If he doesn't make his defense of the ladies good tonight, I don't know what sort of disciplinary action his wife will take —but he better not come home at all. (Give some information and facts about the speaker to be introduced.)

14. Second After Dinner Speech—The eminent cynic and greatest of modern English authors, George Bernard Shaw, once said: "Woman's greatest delight is to wound man's self-conceit, though man's greatest pleasure is to gratify hers." And that was the truest dig imaginable. The one supreme human being in the human race is a woman.

The last speaker did try a lot of humor—laid on stickily at times in order to cover up probably for lack of preparation or lack of logical thinking or maybe just plain old-fashioned, yard-wide stupidity. I, my gracious listeners, on the other hand, will try to build a real case. I may not be funny, mind you, but I'll be there with the dry goods—if you can possibly label womanhood that. Was there ever a superior to Jane

Addams of Hull House fame? Is there a keener person than
Rosalind Russell, or a greater personality—off the stage or on
—than Helen Hayes? How far would a President get without
his First Lady to smooth the social path? Ever hear of Clara
Barton, Eleanor Roosevelt, Madame Curie, or Jenny Lind?
Did any half-baked male artist ever get the fame that has
been heaped upon Grandma Moses—or even Whistler's
mother? It was a good thing for his career that he had her!

Why, when Cicero spoke up and praised the loveliness of
woman and the dignity of man, I wonder if he realized that
every woman is lovely and you can't locate a dignified man
at this banquet. Without woman, we would have no human
race. Maybe the world might have been just a little better
off—but the males know that wives and daughters and sweethearts are the only kind of sex that will keep a man at the
grindstone—trying to earn his thin dime—when he actually
longs to be out on the fairway with his golf clubs or in his
club, having a grand time chewing the rag. One wonders if
all those chewed rags laid end to end—but that doesn't mean
very much.

In short, women are tops! They bear children, cook, sweep,
dust, wash the laundry. Why they excel at everything! Where
can you locate a better gossip—I ask you? Who is more loyal
to her card club? And, speaking of cards, a minister we know
said to his leading deacon, "We want a series of prayers;
Deacon, will you lead?" The drowsy deacon, who was rudely
awakened replied, "Pastor, it ain't my lead—I just dealt."

Women are not secretive. A Biblical proverb declares:
"Woman conceals only what she does not know." And that
truth extends from the church sewing circle to the summer
beach. Marie Corelli once said that women who use the
power of their intellects are more to be respected than those
who merely display their legs; but that men preferred the
latter. But of course we will at times run into a recent wit
who said of woman, "Her body is Vogue; but her mind is

vague." But as famous George Eliot, the woman novelist, once declared, "I'm not denying that women are foolish; but God Almighty made them that way to match the men."

And it is queer how the sexes differ. A man keeps hoping his lean years are behind him; while a woman vainly hopes that her lean years are ahead of her. And blessed is that male who does understand even one woman! Beau Brummel was asked his secret of success with women. He replied, "I treat charwomen like duchesses and duchesses like charwomen."

Members and guests, women have fully ten character traits to one found in even any decent man—well, say like the esteemed toastmaster—or even myself. They are found to be sturdy as oaks; yet forever love to consider themselves merely a clinging vine. It has been said, you recall, that there are no ugly women; only those who do not know how or take the time to look pretty.

Listen! Women may be lazy; but men are lazier. Women may display temper; but males are more tempestuous. Woman may not know a lot about handling money, but it is quite as much as most men know about getting it in to handle. Women sometimes fail in handling children; but watch how a man turns monster when he gets home after a busy day and runs smack-dab into mischievous children. Maybe women do like to use cosmetics to too great an extent; but watch the glamorous maiden her husband tries to sit with on the bus home. Maybe women talk too much; but a tape recorder in any male haunt would reveal quite a bit of gab coming from the stronger sex. She may be a flirt; but she is the one that is surrounded by ten men who outdo her.

Women are the ones who make any home-sweet-home. Home may be a man's castle; but she carries the keys to all the rooms. She bears her mate all his children—even when very often she can't bear him. She is tireless; he is tiresome. She is loyal, charming and a better manager than he is of his office, store or factory. Therefore, Mister Toastmaster, I contend that even if we cannot get along with 'em, by the same token we cannot get along without 'em.

God made women human, for they'd have to be so to forgive their human mates and their offspring. God gave them a woman's heart which is the most forgiving one in all the universe. Go to your church and who does the raising of funds? Ask the Legion what it thinks of the Legion Auxiliary. Ask the boss how he could get along without his secretary. Ask the schools what we would do with all-male faculties. A friend of ours was asked what he thought of clubs for women. And he replied that this seemed a little less brutal than hatchets. And women's various clubs have done more for most communities than any male organization around the place.

My toast to the ladies. They merit every bouquet they ever got, every good-by kiss they ever received. They are the only creatures that make life worth living. God bless every mother's daughter of them!

15. After Speech Comment and Introduction for Next Speaker—That speaker did a bang-up job. And your applause easily shows it. Which reminds me of a neighbor's boy who came in from school and told his daddy that he had just done well in an examination in Latin. "Great, son," exclaimed the father. "Why I used to make 105 in Latin. You're a chip off the old block. What was your grade, son?"

The lad hesitated. "I don't quite know what my grade was—but I was good! Why, Dad, I got an encore—and I'm going to take it all over Monday!"

Oh, I'm just packed with yarns. Clever ones, too. But I'm here just to shove the speakers up and put them through their paces. Sometime I'm going to get rid of all the downright clever things in my mind, all waiting to be said. Remember the fellow who was timid and had only one yarn he could tell—a hunting story? He kept waiting for the appropriate place to get it in—none came. Finally, he banged his foot to the floor and said gaily, "What's that?—sounds like a gun—and speaking of guns," and he then told his hunting story.

A distinguished Japanese author, whose name I would murder if I tried to pronounce it, once said: "If a woman has been loved, hated and envied, she deems that her life has been worthwhile." She works with living things, husband, children, friends, relatives, acquaintances. So she has to be a spark that kindles warm fires of the heart. Mercy, I think I am playing favorites—so on with our third speaker. It is my pleasure to stop my inconsequential remarks and put the question of whether men or women are the most important people in the world up to our next speaker. (Give name and biographical information about next speaker.)

16. *Third After Dinner Speech*—Neither men nor women are the kings of this life we live! Men and women blunder. They make mistakes—yes, even I do! I nominate for the world's supreme creation: Children—"for of such is the Kingdom of Heaven."

Where would the hurdy-gurdy be without children for its patrons? Where would the movies be without its little patrons who sit through show after show? Where would education be without a lot of youngsters who need to learn? Where would circuses go without children to give their eager parents an excuse for attending?

Life isn't much of anything without a tot right in the center of it. Who uses the telephone, the TV set, the cookie jar, the yard and basement? Why do you even try to find any other answer? It is the American youngster!

They know the makes of every car; they can spot the type of airplane five times faster than you and I can. And they know you! They wheedle out of you the money they need by virtue of knowing your weaknesses—yes, and mine, too. Maybe they will be very loving—that method is a push-over

when used with Daddy. Sometimes they will be real diplomats—better brand than go as delegates to the United
Nations. Sometimes they work on your sympathy. Sometimes
they scare you to pieces with bursts of deep feeling. They
will debate, argue, plead and even blubber—until they get
what they want. Even the President can't do that!

This is the day of the child. Maybe he is a little philosopher
like Sammy. You see, Sammy and Tommy were talking
very seriously—coming out of nursery school. Said Sammy,
"Tommy, which would you rather be in—a colleesion or a
esplosion?" Tommy thought for quite a while, but could
not quite make a choice so he put it back in Sammy's lap
with, "Which would you?" Sammy was right on the ball.
"Why, a colleesion, o' course." "Why," asked Tommy,
"would you want a colleesion?" Philosophic Sammy answered
slowly, "Y'see, Tom, in a colleesion—there you are; But in
a esplosion, where are ya?"

They are good traders, too. When little Bill asked for a
dime, his father said very soberly, "Billy, don't you know
you are getting too big to ask for a dime?" Then Billy came
back with, "You're right, Daddy—may I please have a dollar."

Young kings and queens of our homes! What man or
woman present would dare to stand up and state that he
was superior to the dirtiest youngster on your block? Our
biggest mistake probably is that we sometimes fail to understand that they are literal. They take our word for what it
is worth. So when we say that the policeman will come and
get them for not getting off the street, they believe us. But
we have lied. No policeman ever comes—so they go back to
playing in the street. Children expect promises to be ful-
filled. When they are not, then the grown-up loses standing
with even a tot. A college professor promised ice cream to
his two-and-a-half-year-old little daughter. He was caught
up with faculty matters and had to stay and eat at the college

that evening. Next came a long dramatic session where he was training a class for a college play. When he arrived home, his wife said that little Isabel had gone to sleep crying and saying that Daddy had said he'd bring her ice cream. And the weary college teacher went down to a delicatessen where he knew the owner; he awakened the owner who lived on a floor above, got the ice cream and rushed back, wakened the baby girl and said, "See, Daddy didn't forget." Maybe that was a cockeyed thing to do. But forever after that child believed in his word.

A child lives in the present. We foolish oldsters find that a hard thing to do. We think of the past—coats-of-arms and family trees and just who our grandfather was—and why. Or we save and save and skimp and plan for a day that never actually comes—and before long a worried doctor says, "Old boy, you got to slow up—it's the old ticker, you know—you've been working too hard." Imagine a boy doing that! Why, boys are the laziest creatures God has yet created. They'll work harder getting out of doing some task than it would take to do the task. Children live today! They play hard—for when the sun goes down, it may be raining tomorrow. And what sages they are. They'll make the sunlight last until they can't see the ball. And what a lesson to many of us. When Benny's mother reprimanded Benny for not beating the rug, his explanation was sound. Said he, "Mother, you told me to put the rug up on the line and beat it. So I put it on the line and then beat it."

Children are supreme. Men—well, they are pretty fair. Women—well, frankly, they are fairer. But the whole of the world was created for boys and girls. We tax ourselves for their schools. We pay ministers to help them lead a good life as they grow older. We build courts of law to protect them. We load them with every invention—for their pleasure or education or growth.

And if we have love to give, we'd better be at it! If we have tenderness to bestow, we'd better be on our toes. For just two or three short winks—and lo, a daughter comes and tells us that she is in love—maybe shows us a beautiful diamond solitaire. Yesterday we were playing tag with Sonny. Tomorrow Sonny is talking about college and day after tomorrow he wants us to help him get a job. How quickly the years come! We do our funny little courting. Before we know it, our children are bringing home their children for a visit!

Discipline? Undoubtedly that is a good thing. Maybe it has dropped out of most American homes. But a famous educator once said to a body of teachers that there was no problem of discipline—if they would love their children enough. I wonder why we don't love 'em more and more wisely. Probably giving the brats everything they ask for is not love at all. It is a sort of promise for the small amount of time we give them.

Money? Well, maybe yours can have more allowance than mine. But if we look around at the children of the super-rich, we find a pretty spoiled generation. All of them hell-bent for a new sensation. All trying to spend more than the other.

Maybe our children are just starved for us! Maybe we can give up an afternoon of golf—for a long walk with a boy who wants to tell about his tiny little problem—but one that is big for him. Maybe we can stay home from a card club—if it means getting very much closer to a little girl's tender heart, touched with a first case of puppy love.

Children are the tops! And a very few of them are going to the dogs. Even those dogs often belong to mature people who have forgotten just how wonderful a child is.

My salute, if you will, to every tot in town! Women are wonderful—men are marvelous—but again I say it, children are tops!

17. Call for Order—I am sorry that I will have to interrupt our proceedings to ask some of those present to consider where they are and act accordingly. Their deportment can be compared to that of Tom in this story:

A minister met Tom, the village ne'er-do-well, and, much to the latter's surprise, shook him heartily by the hand. "I'm so glad you have turned over a new leaf, Thomas," said the good man. "I was delighted to see you at prayer meeting last night." "Oh," said Tom, after a moment of doubt, "so that's where I was."

Judging by the way they are carrying on, some of those present tonight do not seem to know where they are. I must request them to quiet down and help keep this proceeding orderly.

18. After Speech Comment—I am now in the position of the .140 hitter at the lower end of the batting order who came to bat just after a slugger had slammed out a home run with the bases loaded. Anything I may say is an anticlimax after the entertaining and interesting address we have just heard.

Having to get up and say something now is like having to get up and wash the dishes after a perfect dinner. I feel like the commercial slide which follows the feature movie in a small-town playhouse. I don't doubt that I make Mr. ——— look better by contrast, although he certainly doesn't need such assistance.

His talk was most entertaining and convincing. I am sure that we all agree that our children are the most necessary people in all the world. We love our children and respect and admire the speaker for presenting them to us in such a favorable manner.

Toastmaster—Thanks to all of our brilliant talkers. I'll not call them speakers for they speak for themselves. And I am

sure you have all greatly benefited by their wonderful
thoughts—and by hearing me. But if there is anybody who
feels at this festive table that he could do better, I will gladly
give him or her a chance. (Pauses.) I am very happy that you
are satisfied.

Extra Speaker (Member or Guest by prearrangement)—Did
you say satisfied? I'm not! I could do better by standing on
my head.

Toastmaster—We are not equipped at the moment for you
to stand on your head. But I'll gladly yield you a few minutes
—and I say few—for you to add some real thought to this
occasion. I want all of you to go home happy—at least to go
home. So I'll ask you please to come forward—give your
Social Security number—and try to better the product or
add to the gaiety of the evening.

19.   Extra Speaker—My name—(gives it)—my home—(gives
address)—my business—rotten. I think a speech, ladies and
gentlemen, should contain some meat. Some downright interesting facts. These other speakers merely blew their tops
and had for you no great chunks of truth. Am I right?
(Waits.) Yes, I am. Do any of you know the salary of a United
States District Judge? I'll wager not one of you do! It is
$22,500. Does he earn it? Well, we had better not press that
point too far. Do you know how many square miles there
are in the Arctic Ocean? There are 5,440,197 square miles—
marked down from 5,440,200! See what I mean? Why yap
about men and women and kids—when you can give a thinking audience—and I am flattering you—some real mental
nourishment. Now you think that Pike's Peak is the tallest
hill in the whole U.S.? That's because it advertises. But
Mount Whitney is almost 400 feet taller—or 14,495. Isn't
that something to remember? Verily it is. And listen, I'll ven-

ture to say in all modesty that I'm the only person here who can give—offhand, mind you—the amount of forest land in this country. How can you stand up and sing the National Anthem and know deep in your heart you do not know the total acreage of timber? Well, hereafter you can sing our hymn without a blush. It is 459,541,000 acres. Now you can go home feeling that you have a new sense of the vast resources of your native land. Hear me seriously: Did you know that the average elevation of Arkansas is only 650 feet above sea level? How can you sleep without knowing that? Did you know in May of 1953 our population was estimated at 160,000,000? But that was incorrect. The exact population was only 159,260,000! Did you ever stop to realize that the immigration from Albania in 1952—

Voice from Audience—Aw, shut up! Tell him to sit down!

Extra Speaker—I can see my intelligence is not appreciated here. I will not waste any more of my time trying to give you the benefit of my wisdom and knowledge. (Sits down.)

Toastmaster—Our guest who interrupted our program with his short speech delivered a very illuminating address. However, with the wonderful dinner served, I have already had more than I can digest. The speaker who just finished should get some consolation from the observation of a wise man that many a good idea has been smothered to death by words. This fellow never took that chance with all his ideas. They may die, but they will never die from being smothered with words. I wish he had had a little more to say, but we must be thankful for small blessings and consider ourselves fortunate to have heard as much from him as we did.

Voice from Audience—Are you giving a speech?

20. **Toastmaster**—I'm not giving a speech, but there is something I must say before I conclude this meeting. We have had a very enjoyable meeting and I want to thank the speakers for contributing so much to the success of our program. I know that you will agree with me that their efforts were of the highest order. There is so much good humor in evidence tonight that we could go on indefinitely, but all good things must come to an end. I would like at this time to express myself as did a member of our Armed Forces during the war.

A Marine air observer on Iwo was overjoyed to discover an exposed Japanese gun position; several hundred artillery men were sitting right out in the open. He radioed to a cruiser offshore: "Target area so and so. There's a whole swarm of them . . . looks like a meeting."

The cruiser's guns fired as directed. A moment later, the observer reported cheerfully, "Meeting adjourned."

In the words of this gallant Marine I say, "Meeting adjourned."

3
Toastmaster's Remarks

THE following selection of short remarks will be helpful for the toastmaster:

21. *Opening Remarks by Toastmaster*—Ladies and gentlemen, these are great days for banquets—and public speakers—and toastmasters. In fact, they are such great days for occasions like this, that trained toastmasters are becoming almost a necessity.

Nowadays a school child is given hours and hours of special instruction in public speaking, for educators assume eventually they will have to do some public speaking.

And if the boy or girl goes to college, well, there is more public speaking—perhaps even a two-year course in the subject, with radio speech thrown in for modern emergencies.

But when I was young, my father gave me a good lesson in public speaking—especially good for toastmasters—in just three points.

He said, "If you are going to give a talk, remember this, 'Stand up; speak up; and shut up.' "

22. *Toastmaster's Introductory Speech*—My minister was telling me today about a service he attended not so long ago. It was a big conference, with a large audience, and the minister who was giving the invocation prayed in this fashion: "Oh Lord, be with the speaker of the evening and give him power to move this audience; and be with the pastor of this conference and help him to guide his flock; and Lord, Lord, have mercy on the first speaker. . . ."

Well, I'm it!

But even if I do have to break in on the neighborly conversations that are going around the table, I know that you can look on me as merely a promise of something better to come. In fact, I sort of feel like Fido, the not-so-good pup who was entered in the dog show, not because of his chance of winning a prize, but because there he would be with such very nice companions! But if I am Fido, then I'm going to fool my master (I couldn't brag and say mistress there!) and get a prize for myself. Not for what I am, but for what I'm going to do. . . .

Ladies and gentlemen, it is my privilege to present to you the various speakers of the evening. . . .

23. Delayed Welcome—By the way, I haven't even welcomed you! Ladies and gentlemen, you are positively welcome! To the guests a very homely Howdy-do, to our own pure and untainted fold a deep salaam—which please accept in the warm friendliness with which it goes from me to you. To everybody who helped put on this shindig, may you do better next time in choosing your toastmaster! The situation is something like that of a social occasion where a movie extra crashed the gate and came up to the eminent John Barrymore, slapping him on the back and saying, "How are you, ole fellow?" The distinguished "profile" turned to the stranger and said, "Aw, don't be formal—call me kid!" Anyway, you are welcome.

24. Welcome to Visiting Club Members—Since science and invention have contracted the size of the globe, a new interpretation has been given the word "neighbor." There was a time within our memory when our neighbors were confined to those just beyond the line fence, or at least those within easy horse-and-buggy driving distance. Today, we think of South America as our "Latin American neighbors"; we regard Europe and Asia within that category.

Tonight, it is our privilege to extend the warm hand of welcome to our neighbors in (name of organization). Bound closely by the common purposes of our organization, we anticipate keen pleasure in sharing with you the hospitality of our laden board. Mr. President, we are happy to have you and your club associates with us tonight.

25.   *Greetings to Ladies*—My companion on my right just whispered to me, "Shall we let our friends enjoy themselves a little longer, or had we better have your speech now?"

Well, I decided you could enjoy yourselves a little later, and a little longer, if I got my part of the program over with.

First, I want to welcome our guests, the ladies, those fair magicians who can turn a man into a donkey and make him think he's a lion.

We are lucky to have you with us tonight. In fact, we're lucky to have you at all. We'd really rather tell you that than have you tell it to us.

Now I don't want to be a hog about the time I'm taking; my real job is to introduce to you the speakers of the evening.

I've sort of got the idea that being a success as a toastmaster is rather dependent on the same two things as success in life— luck and pluck . . . luck in finding someone to pluck. And I've had that luck, ladies and gentlemen, and it is my great pleasure to present to you some very fine speakers who have consented to take part in our program.

26.   *Limiting Time*—We have several different speakers who are going to talk to us this evening, and in fairness to each of them it is necessary to set a time limit for each talk. For this reason I am going to request that no one speaks longer than —— minutes. I would like to remind our speakers for the evening of the old proverb to the effect that brevity is the soul of wit. I hope they will keep their remarks brief enough to embody the soul of wit.

27. Avoiding a Subject—Our next speaker is a man of decided opinions, and since he decided these opinions himself the decision is his and I might add that the opinions are his own. Since they are his own I suggest that he treasure them and guard against even sharing them with others. A philosopher once observed that it is a wise man indeed who can withhold an opinion on any subject you care to mention. We are not asking our next speaker to be that wise. I am going to request him merely to withhold his opinion on only one subject. It is a subject which is very dear and important to him but is not so vital to others. For this reason I say to him, treasure your opinions, keep them close to your heart, but for Pete's sake don't share them with others—at least, not here tonight!

28. Announcing Extemporaneous Speakers—As a part of our program this evening we are going to call upon some of our members and guests present. They will be asked to deliver what is known as an extemporaneous speech. We have given them no advance warning that they would be called upon because we were afraid it might affect them as it did the lions who were set to devour a Christian in the ancient days of Rome. In the time of Nero, sport-loving Romans crowded the Coliseum to see Christians tossed to the lions. For one victim who had given the authorities untold trouble, Nero had eleven of his most ferocious lions starved for a week.

When the first lion made a beeline for the Christian, the spectators wet their lips. But the Christian calmly bent down and whispered in the beast's ear. His tail between his legs, the lion slunk out of the arena. Six more half-starved kings of the forest followed the same performance, and the crowd started hollering for its money back. Then Nero summoned the Christian and said, "If you will tell me how you make those lions act that way, I will grant you a full pardon."

"It's very simple," explained the Christian. "I whisper in their ears, 'Remember, you'll be expected to say a few words after dinner!' "

This warning that they were expected to say a few words after dinner drove away the half-starved lions. We have not taken similar chances with the lions of our banquet table. We have not given them the opportunity to run away. For this reason they are being called upon without notice. I hope that you will enjoy their efforts. At least, you can enjoy their confusion and discomfort.

29. *Introduction for Extemporaneous Speech*—Gentlemen, the pleasure is ours. Tonight we have with us a speaker whose renown is something less than world-wide in scope but who is unique in many respects. He is not going to tell us what is wrong with the world—he hasn't time tonight. He isn't going to tell us what's wrong with politics. In fact, he isn't going to tell us what's wrong with anything.

Our guest of honor tonight is a devotee of the lighter things of life, a man who won't challenge your gloomy prognostication that things are going to be worse before they get better, but who prefers to think of how much better they're going to be. Or how good they are now, for that matter. He's a member of that fast-dwindling clan of sunshine dispensers, the association of incurable optimists.

Our speaker is one of those rare individuals loved alike by men and women, children and graybeards. His best friends never stab him in the back without feeling a pang of regret. The stranger who glares after bumping into him on the street always feels a little like a heel. If he were a pianist we would laugh when he sat down—and then feel ashamed of ourselves for pulling the chair out from under him. He knows he is among friends—the most merciless kind of audience. His guardian angel should be on duty and getting time and a half for overtime right now.

Unaccustomed as he is to public speaking, he has no idea that he is to be called upon tonight. As yet he has not even begun to fumble for the notes for his extemporaneous address. He is enjoying the digestive processes of the conscience clear, a blissful state soon to be shattered.

Fellow revelers, the privilege is mine, the pleasure is shared by all of us. Gentlemen, I give you Mr. ———.

30. Introduction for Speakers—Ladies and gentlemen, doubtless you feel much better now, after the fine food and the pleasant conversation with your neighbors. I'm wondering if you feel good enough for me to come on the program.

Why the committee picked me for this job I can't quite understand. Not unless they felt like the lawyer who had just won his suit. The cripple who had been his client had just been presented with his bill and he thumped his crutch angrily at the size of it. "Your bill is outrageous," he thundered. "It's extortion. You've taken four-fifths of my damages."

The lawyer answered quietly, "I furnished the skill, the eloquence, the legal learning to win your case."

The client objected, "But I furnished the case itself."

And then the lawyer sneered, "Anybody could fall down a coal hole."

Of course, this isn't a coal hole, but this is the whole goal—that you all have as fine a time in your own way as the gal who writes her diary a week ahead of time.

The committee knew, however, that I'd had some experience at public speaking—I once talked on the phone in the country over a party line—so I could stand on my record. But as the political boss told the candidate, the right way to campaign was to jump on the other fellows. And that's what I'm doing, friends, when I land on our speakers for the evening.

31.   *Age of Wisdom*—I am happy to introduce to you a man who has reached the age of wisdom. The age of wisdom is that time in life where we begin to realize that we should find happiness and enjoyment as we go along. It is said that at twenty a man tries to save the world. When a man gets to be middle-aged he is content merely to be able to save a part of his salary. When he gets along in years he forgets all about saving and begins to really enjoy himself and look for the good things in life. Such a man is the one I am going to call upon.

32.   *Adult*—The person I would like to introduce is one who reminds me of a definition I once heard of an adult. An adult has been described as a person who has stopped growing at both ends and has started growing in the middle. This person has grown very well in an adult fashion. So that you can see for yourself what I mean, I call upon ———.

33.   *Real Compliment*—In presenting the next speaker I would like to say a few complimentary remarks about him. One of the most valuable things about a compliment is that it is something which is given free. A real, sincere compliment cannot be bought. It must be given free and without request in order to be the real thing. Many millionaires live their whole lives without receiving an honest compliment. Many poor men are complimented almost every day of their lives.

The man I am about to introduce to you is one who is accustomed to receiving many sincere and flattering compliments. I know that you will agree with me that they are well deserved.

34. Difficult Name—The next speaker is a man who is remembered because of his odd name. People who have an odd name usually get more attention because their friends make it a special point to remember the name, knowing that it is unusual. I, myself, do not trust any system for remembering names. I am warned by the story of a preacher who was introduced to a Mrs. Hummick. He tried to remember her name by rhyming it with stomach. The next time he met her he greeted her cordially by saying, "How do you do, Mrs. Kelly." That proved to me that it is better to try to remember the name than what it rhymes with. I am sure everybody remembers ———.

35. Sound Advice—I would like to call upon a man who has served us well and through whose efforts, knowledge and experience our organization has benefited. His advice has been helpful to us on many occasions in the past, and we know that we can depend upon him in the future. It has been said that good advice is something old men give young men when they can no longer give them a bad example. Advice has been described as a commodity sold by a lawyer, given away by a mother-in-law, but something difficult to dispose of yourself. Our honored guest, upon whom I am about to call, has never had any trouble disposing of his advice because it has always been good and sought after by his fellow club members.

36. Deeply Religious—The man I would like to call upon has led a life devoted to religion and he has been guided by the Biblical virtues. His devotion to God recalls to my mind the story told about the naturalist Thoreau at the time he was near death. A very pious aunt came to visit him and asked in deep concern, "Henry, have you made your peace with God?" "I didn't know that we had ever quarreled," was the reply. In the same manner I would like to call upon a man who has never quarreled with his God.

37. *Having a Good Time*—Among our speakers we have a man who has lived foolishly. When I say that this man has lived foolishly I am thinking of the sailor who, when asked what he'd done with his money, answered, "Part went for liquor, part for women and the rest I spent foolishly." By the same standard we can say that this man has lived foolishly.

38. *Secret of Old Age*—I wish we could all live to attain the age of the next speaker I will introduce to you, and at his age have the same vitality and energy. I will not ask him to tell us the secret of his successful old age, because he will no doubt give us as little satisfaction as the fellow who at the age of one hundred years was still going strong. He was interviewed by newspaper reporters, who asked him to what thing he attributed his marvelous vitality. "I don't rightly know yet," the old man said as he blew smoke lazily. "I'm dickering with two breakfast food companies right now." I suppose we would get no more satisfaction if we would ask this robust old-timer what is his secret of successful old age. Anyway, I will call upon him and see what he has to say.

39. *Content*—Our speaker is a man who can give us a lesson in contentment. His life has been an example of contentment and satisfaction. He reminds me very much of the man who was once asked if he would rather have a million dollars or twelve daughters. This man replied without hesitation that he would rather have twelve daughters than a million dollars. He explained that if he had a million, he'd want to have two, three, ten or a hundred million more. But if he had twelve daughters, that would be enough. This man knew the meaning of contentment. Our next speaker also knows the meaning of contentment, and his life is an example of that kind of living.

40. *Introduction for Distinguished Speaker*—We are most fortunate, ladies and gentlemen, to have our next speaker with us on this occasion.

When the program committee was arranging this array of talent for us, they sought to bring one who would be of outstanding prominence and ability in his own line as well as an excellent speaker for the evening.

Now this speaker recently was attending a conference in the leading hotel of one of the larger cities of the nation. The bellhop repeatedly annoyed him by referring to him as "Colonel" or "Major."

Finally, the bellhop was taken aside and told that our guest was neither a major nor a colonel but a (state vocation).

"O.K., boss," said the boy, "I didn't know just what he was, but I sure knew that whatever he was—he was one of the face cards."

I present our next speaker, one of the face cards, who will speak to us on the subject ———. (Fit titles to suit occasion.)

41. *Before or After Talk by Man Who Plays Golf*—You all know this speaker as an enthusiastic golfer, but I don't believe you ever heard what happened to him one day when he was invited to play with a friend in a neighboring city.

Taking his stance at the first tee, Mr. So-and-So gripped his driver, brought it back in what appeared to be perfect form—and then missed the ball completely in a wild swing.

"By George," he said to his host. "It's a good thing I found out early in the game this course is at least two inches lower than the one I usually play."

I present Mr. So-and-So who will speak to us on the subject ———.

(NOTE: If used as comment after a speech by a golfer, change the ending after the story as follows:)

But that was a golf game, and this was a speech. I am sure you will agree with me that Mr. So-and-So not only hit the ball tonight, but has been playing the game on a course that is higher than we all are accustomed to—giving us new inspiration for the days to come.

42. *Thanking Speaker*—A little optimism is good for all of us in these days when pessimism comes all too easy most of the time. I often think of the village philosopher in a certain small town who refused to be ruffled by adversity even in the dark days of the 1933 panic. From his favorite chair in the village store he could just see the tops of the tombstones in the village graveyard a quarter of a mile away. One day when the Calamity Joes were moaning a little louder than usual he smoked his old pipe in silence until they paused for breath. Then he said, "Well, things ain't so good, but we're still a lot better off than them folks over yonder in the stone orchard. We can still move around, but they're mighty cramped." He has his own tombstone now, but he lived a mellow life and enjoyed it to the end.

Life is that way. We can fight it, or we can accept it and enjoy it, and it depends pretty much on ourselves. Tonight we've been enjoying it. The pleasure is ours, and our sincere thanks go to our guest of the evening.

Mr. ———, we salute you, wish you Godspeed and pray that you return ere many moons wax and wane.

43. *Reply to Razz*—I have just heard some very uncomplimentary things said about me and it grieves me to have listened to them. I was particularly disturbed because so many of those present seemed to enjoy the dastardly remarks and laugh at them. No doubt this speaker has many persons present who are obligated to him or seek to humor him. His performance reminds me very much of that told about the late Governor Folk of Missouri.

The late Governor Folk of Missouri, accompanied by a

friend, arrived at his office one morning to find a number of men waiting for him in the anteroom. He paused as he passed through and told a very ancient joke. In the Governor's office, the friend said, "That was an awfully old chestnut you pulled out there."

"I know it," the Governor replied, "but I wanted to find out how many of those fellows were here to ask favors."

"And did you?"

"Oh, yes," said Folk. "They were the ones who laughed."

Those who laughed at the speaker's old jokes were probably trying to keep on the good side of him. I know that they could not in any way agree with the statements he made concerning me.

44. Presenting a Gift—On this occasion we wish to honor an individual who is well known to all of us. He needs no one to vouch for his fine character and reputation, and his circumstance here tonight is just the opposite of that of a man who needed a friend.

They were trying an Irishman, charged with a petty offense, in an Oklahoma town, when the judge asked, "Have you anyone in court who will vouch for your good character?"

"Yis, yer honor," quickly responded the Celt, "there's the sheriff there."

Whereupon the sheriff evinced signs of great amazement. "Why, your honor," declared he, "I don't even know the man."

"Observe, yer honor," said the Irishman, triumphantly, "observe that I've lived in the country for over twelve years and the sheriff doesn't know me yit! Ain't that a character fer ye?"

The man to whom I refer would have no trouble identifying himself and his fine personal qualities. Because we hold him in high regard and want to honor him we are presenting to him this gift.

*45.   Thanking Entertainers—*I want to thank those who have taken part in this program and who have done so much to make this evening most enjoyable for all of us. We appreciate their efforts and we want to express our thanks. It was kind of them to give up their evening to do so much for our entertainment. Let's give them a hand.

*46.   Concluding Remarks—*More than 2,500 years ago the ancient Greeks developed a formula for the good life. I might say that this formula was so satisfactory that never in the 2,500 years that have passed since that time has it been improved upon. A formula for the good life which can endure for 2,500 years and be as suitable now as it was then has surely been a great contribution to human knowledge. I am sure that you are all familiar with this formula, but for those who may have forgotten it I will refresh your memory by reminding you that this famous ancient Greek formula for the good life was as follows: "Nothing in excess." Yes, there is a rule of life which should serve as a guide to all our activities—nothing in excess. I think it would be a wise idea to follow this ancient rule once again and bring this happy and enjoyable evening to a close.

Dear friends, members, guests, everybody—our good times should become more frequent. And there should be no regret or sadness in our parting. A poet once put it far better than I could. And with his words we are adjourned:

> Hail and so long—
> There's no time for adieu.
> Life is best lived
> With old friends and new!

Good-by and God bless all of you.

WELCOMES

47. Sincerity—We bid you welcome and we do so in a spirit of generosity and a desire to entertain you as royally as possible. We want you to go ahead and enjoy yourselves to the utmost.

I want you to know that our welcome is most sincere. We do not look upon our guests in the same way as a Mrs. Cakelbush who was telling a guest at her table, "You must have some more of my delicious cookies. Won't you please take a couple more?"

The guest smiled in a friendly fashion. "I would love some more of your cookies, Mrs. Cakelbush," she replied with a sigh, "but to tell you the truth I am embarrassed. I've already had six."

"You already have had ten," Mrs. Cakelbush corrected and then added, "but who counts around here?"

48. Nothing Spared—We want to welcome all of our guests and members to this elaborate and delicious dinner and program. I can say honestly that nothing has been spared—except money.

49. Ladies' Day—We are very happy to welcome our special guests, the ladies, to this meeting. It is not often that we have ladies present.

Our club follows the same principles as the professor of mathematics who was bitterly opposed to coeducation. It was his belief that it was difficult and often impossible to teach a boy mathematics if there were girls in the class.

Someone who opposed this theory said to the professor, "This may be true of some boys, but there are exceptions to that case."

"There might be an exception," the professor snapped back, "but he wouldn't be worth teaching!"

50. Enjoy Yourselves—We are happy to welcome our guests and we hope that we have provided a program which they will enjoy. I realize how difficult it is to please everybody.

I keep thinking about the story of a man who was in the habit of leaving his home early every evening and going to a tavern. He would not return home until many hours later. This made his wife very unhappy, and one evening she determined to go herself to the tavern and see what he was doing there.

At the tavern she found her husband sitting at the counter and drinking some liquor. She walked up and sat beside him. She asked him what he was drinking and he told her bourbon. She ordered some bourbon from the barkeeper.

The glass of liquor was set beside her. She drank a large gulp. Then she made a face and gave every evidence that the whiskey was most distasteful to her. Her husband noticed her expression and said, "And you thought I came here every night to enjoy myself."

Well, I hope all of you came here tonight to enjoy yourselves, and we will do everything possible to offer our best entertainment.

51. Recipe for Fun—I want to say that the success of this evening must depend upon our guests. One cooking authority has stated that no real dinner is complete without nuts. Well, we made an effort tonight to invite some.

52. Room for One More—We are happy to see such a large crowd. Frankly, we did not expect so many to attend, but we are glad you came. We can always find room for people we like. In this regard we have the same theory as the woman who arrived at a hotel late in the evening, tired and weary. She went to the hotel desk and the clerk told her that he was sorry, but he could not give her a room. The hotel was all filled up.

The woman kept asking for a room and was most insistent. "If the President of the United States should come here tonight, would you find a room for him?" she asked.

"Yes," replied the hotel clerk, "we would find a room for the President of the United States."

"Then," insisted this woman, "he is not coming. Give me his room."

As I said before, we find room for those we want, and we want all of you. We are happy you came.

INTRODUCTIONS

53. Lowdown—Our next speaker is a man who often has been praised as being just lower than the angels. Recently, he's been getting lower and lower.

54. Easygoing—Our next speaker is an easygoing sort of person who has never been known to take infinite pains with what he is doing—or to give them!

55. Repeater—Our next speaker is one of the world's greatest historians. They say that history repeats itself. Well, need I say more?

56. Quite a Feat—It is a pleasure to introduce a man who is known for his love of sports. He likes to bowl and claims that he has never lost a ball.

57. Kind Man—Here is a man who possesses the finest qualities of human kindness. He is the kind of man who, if he saw someone beating a donkey, would step up and order that man to stop. That is what I would call a demonstration of brotherly love on his part.

58. *Ready to Talk*—The experiences which our next speaker had left him speechless. Fortunately, he has now completely recovered from this condition.

59. *Two Sides*—We have heard so much about our next speaker—now we will have a chance to hear his side of the story.

60. *Loud and Clear*—The next person we call on is a very sound speaker. And boy, those sounds!

61. *Wordy*—I wouldn't say our next speaker isn't smart, but he never could win any of those contests which we hear about. He never was any good in saying something in fifty words or less.

62. *Definition of an Expert*—Our next speaker is an expert. You know what an expert is. Well, in spite of the general opinion to the contrary, an expert is not a person who can discuss something which everybody understands and make it sound confusing. He takes a subject which is confusing and makes it simple for others to understand.

63. *Needy*—Our next speaker is a man who needs all the introduction he can get.

64. *The Right Word*—I hope I use the right words or expressions in introducing our next speaker because he deserves the best. It is important what you say about people. Take, for instance, our relatives. If they are poor we call them relations, but if they are rich and important we refer to them as connections.

65. *Extra Push*—What I have to say about our speaker, I hope will be presented in well-chosen words which express our high respect and admiration for him. I've always been a little worried since the time at church when a preacher was leaving and a member of the congregation got up to present him with a farewell gift. He said something to the effect that, since the preacher had announced his departure, the congregation was anxious to give him a little momentum.

66. *Valuable Name*—Our next speaker has a very impressive name, and I do not mean this in the same way as the glamorous young blonde who was being introduced to a wealthy young fellow in a night club. The girl asked, "How much did you say your name was?"

67. *Witty Speaker*—Our next speaker is a man who has a reputation for being delightfully witty, and I don't mean it like the rich man who was asked by a friend if his newly acquired wealth had changed him any. "Yes," said the new-rich fellow, "now I am delightfully witty when I used to be disgustingly rude."

TIME FILLERS

68. *Silence*—The lull is something none of us appreciate. I can only compare this silence to that of the time a preacher was playing golf with a friend. The clergyman was having trouble with one shot. He missed the ball several times. Then he stopped, glared at the ball, while his face reddened. After watching him for a moment, his friend said, "Reverend, that was the most profane silence I have ever known."

69. *Reason for Delay*—While we are waiting, I wish to take up this time to explain how we select (SPEAKERS or WAITERS or whatever is causing a delay). We use a system devised by an expert at the race track. This expert went to the races one day and won most of his bets, while his friend who went with him lost every race he bet on.

The friend was downhearted and discouraged. "How do you do it?" he demanded of the expert. "I use a pin to pick my winners—punch the program with a pin and the horse I hit I bet on."

"It never works," replied the expert. "I have a better method. I always use a fork."

It looks like the expert who arranged this affair used a fork to pick his entries.

70.   Bad Manners—It looks like we've gotten ourselves into trouble and we don't know who is the responsible person—like the story about the girl who was sent to a finishing school by her crude and uneducated parents. They had accumulated money in spite of their lack of education and culture. However, they wanted their daughter to learn good manners and sent her to an expensive and fashionable finishing school. At the end of the year she returned home—pregnant. The parents were in great consternation over the situation and asked their daughter who was the man. The girl insisted that she didn't know the name of the man who was the father of the child to be born. The mother, at the end of her patience, screamed, "We've spent a young fortune to educate you and see that you have good manners. And now look! When you go out with a man you permit a thing like this to happen and don't even have the good manners to ask, 'With whom do I have the pleasure?' "

71.   Embarrassing Moment—I am as embarrassed as the woman who was eating at a swanky restaurant with her young son. The boy hardly touched his dinner and the mother called the waiter over and ordered, "Waiter, wrap up these roast beef leftovers for my dog, please." The little boy piped up in a loud voice and exclaimed, "Gee, Mom, are we going to get a dog?"

72. *Confusion*—Right now I am about as confused as the fellow who went to see a doctor and complained, "Doctor, can you do something about my snoring? I've started to snore so loud that I'm beginning to wake up myself."

"That's easily remedied," the doctor told him. "Just sleep in another room."

73. *The Cure*—Don't worry. Something will come along and change all this. Nothing is impossible. I understand that medical science is now working on snakebites to cure the liquor habit.

74. *Correcting a Mistake*—Someone has made a mistake. It may be me or it may be someone else, but it is obvious that a mistake has been made. In trying to determine who made the mistake, I cannot help but think of a little story.

The owner of a cheap watch brought it to a jeweler to see what could be done with it.

"The mistake I made," he admitted, "was dropping it."

"I don't suppose you could help that," replied the jeweler. "The mistake you made was picking it up."

Let us not argue to see who will get the blame for the mistake. Instead, let us try to determine who will receive the credit for correcting it.

75. *Not Worth It*—I hope you are not too concerned about what goes on here at this time. You should be like the woman who was looking for a winter coat. The saleswoman showed her two which looked about the same to her, except one was priced at $150 and the other had a tag on it for $175. The woman asked the saleslady what was the difference—why one coat sold for $150 and the other which looked the same sold for $175. The saleslady explained, "We charge more for one because it's virgin lamb."

The woman shopper shrugged her shoulders and replied, "For twenty-five dollars I should worry if the lamb was a virgin!"

76.   *Fill Time*—While we are waiting for the program to get going, I will deliver a speech.

77.   *Point of View*—There is always something that puts a question in our minds and gives us something to wonder about—like the fellow in the Army who received a picture which showed two couples on the beach and his best girl sitting with them, lonesome and neglected without an escort. The army man was delighted with his girl's faithfulness until the question popped into his mind, "I wonder who took that picture?"

78.   *Fast Watches*—I'm sorry we can't go right into our program, but things have been delayed. What we need around here are more people carrying those marvelous, new modern watches. They are wonderful. They run an hour in forty-five minutes.

79.   *Some Baby*—Something always seems to happen to disturb our enjoyment. Now we have this disturbance. It is hard to account for these things, like the case of the young married couple who were in the judge's private chambers airing their troubles, preliminary to seeking a divorce. The young wife sobbed, "We were so happy, Judge—then the baby came."

"Baby," inquired the judge, "boy or girl?"

"Girl, of course," the wife snapped back. "She moved in next door."

80. *An Early Start*—Evidently some people do not believe in getting started on time. They are like the draftee who was spending his first night in army camp. His sleep was disturbed when the platoon sergeant stuck his head in the barracks and shouted, "It's four-thirty!"

"Four-thirty!" gasped the rookie. "Man, you better go back to bed. We've got a big day tomorrow."

81. *Too Late*—If the person we are waiting for doesn't show up pretty soon, he may be like the newspaper reporter from the city. He was sent by his editor to a nearby town to get the facts on a murder which had just been committed there. The young reporter dashed up to the house where the crime had been committed and was stopped by a policeman on guard.

"You've got to let me in," the young reporter protested loudly. "I've been assigned to do the murder."

"Well," responded the policeman, "you're too late. Somebody's already done it."

82. *Long Wait*—Whenever I have a long wait I always think of the story about the actor who was telling a friend that he hadn't worked for five years and he was beginning to think maybe he should get out of the acting business.

83. *Mixed Values*—There is something wrong in our way of doing things when we have instant coffee and then waste an hour waiting for something to happen.

84. *Hard Waiting*—I know what they mean when they say that all the world loves a lover except the people waiting to use the phone. Waiting can be a tough job.

85. *Doubtful Prospect*—A good program is in store for you, but it begins to look like the store is going to be closed for the night.

86. *Almost Everything*—Don't get discouraged. Remember, everything comes to he who waits—except the time you have lost waiting!

87. *Patience*—I'm sorry, folks, for the delay, but I must ask you to have patience. Patience is described as the ability to idle your motor when you feel like stripping your gears.

88. *A Late Start*—I'm sure all of you are beginning to feel like the fellow who lived far out in the suburbs. He stayed late in town with a friend to do some drinking. Finally they decided to leave. They found the auto where it had been parked and started out—entering a one-way street against traffic. "Where are we heading for now?" asked the passenger. "I dunno," hiccuped the driver as he tried to maneuver his way down the one-way street, "but we're sure late. Everybody's coming back." In the words of this tipsy driver, I will say that we're sure late.

89. *Annoying Delay*—This delay is annoying to all of us, and now I know what they mean when they say that in the space age ahead man will be able to go around the world in two hours—one hour for flying and the other to get to the airport.

90. *Laughter*—I enjoy hearing laughter because it is an important symptom. Josh Billings explained that laughing is the sensation of feeling good all over, and showing it principally in one spot. That, of course, doesn't take into consideration the belly laugh.

91. *Missing Something*—At least when nothing happens we have one thing less to worry about. We don't have to worry that we are missing something. Just think of the poor, unfortunate fellow who read in a magazine advertisement about a

new strapless gown. The ad proclaimed, "This is a strapless
that stays up." The poor fellow moaned, "Apparently there
has been a lot going on lately that I have been missing." Well,
nothing has been going on here that you've been missing.

92. *Punctuality*—I am sorry about the delay, but some
people just don't understand the meaning of the word punctual. They evidently subscribe to the belief that punctuality
is a fine virtue, if you don't mind being lonely.

93. *Endless Voyage*—It seems like time is passing by end-
lessly without getting anywhere. Such things have happened
before to other people. For example, there was the pretty
young blonde who met a sailor at a bar in New York City
and confided she would like nothing better than an ocean
trip to Cuba. He told her he would fix it up for her and at
night smuggled her onto a ship and into a lifeboat, where
he covered her with a tarpaulin. Thereafter he brought her
food and managed to climb into the boat on occasions and
spend as much time with her as possible. This went on for
day after day until finally the girl could stand it no longer.
She jumped out of the lifeboat and ran up to the captain,
crying, "Captain, how soon do we get to Cuba?" "Cuba?"
repeated the skipper. "Young lady, you've been stowing away
on the Staten Island ferry."

94. *Lots of Time*—I hope none of you are becoming impatient. After all, we may be city folks but we're still very
much like the country fellow who named his daughter Annemariebelinda—one word! A tourist stopped, engaged the
farmer in conversation and asked the girl's name. When the
farmer told him it was Annemariebelinda, the tourist was
amazed and asked the farmer, "Isn't that a rather long
name?" The farmer shrugged his shoulders and replied,
"We're not city folks. We've got time."

95. Left Home—Right now we're waiting for the show to begin and can sympathize with the brother in the story about a young fellow who got in to see *My Fair Lady*. A friend of the family spotted him and asked how he managed to get to the show. The boy replied, "I came on my brother's ticket."

"And where is your brother?" asked the friend.

The boy shrugged his shoulders and replied, "I guess he's home looking for the ticket."

96. Wake Up—(For use if the audience seems to be day-dreaming.) The other day when I was driving my car I saw on the highway a golden chariot pulled by two white horses. The man in the chariot carried a sword and was dressed in a white tunic. All of a sudden the horses bolted upright and climbed through the air and disappeared into a cloud.

I can't understand it. A few minutes ago when I was telling you the truth, you were going to sleep. Now, when I tell you a big lie you are all wide awake!

4

Toasts and the Toastmaster

DRINKING a toast and appointing a toastmaster to conduct the ceremony are customs which have had a long history. It was considered a bit of special luxury, an Epicurean treat, to put a piece of spiced toast in an alcoholic beverage before drinking it.

This, evidently, was not sufficient to delight the senses of the person who was drinking the beverage. Therefore, someone thought up the idea of saying aloud the name of a beloved lady before drinking the liquid. The simple process of giving the name of a lovely lady was supposed to enhance, in some way, the pleasure derived from the drink and have the same effect as a piece of spiced toast in the drink. Usually the name of the lady mentioned was someone the drinker knew personally and admired very much. Later, as the custom developed, it was not necessary for the person making the toast to know the lady personally. She might be what was described in those days as the reigning belle.

The toast, in connection with drinking alcoholic beverages, is generally believed to have originated during the reign of Charles II, sometime between the years 1660 and 1684. The custom became more prevalent, and by 1746 it was the general practice to drink a toast to the good health of one's friends, male or female, or to some person well known in public life. A popular official of the government, or the king and queen, would frequently be named when drinking a toast. From this custom came much later the practice of giving a toast to the land or country in which a person lived or to some special and important event, as well as to an individual.

On occasions when a number of men would get together for the purpose of drinking and giving toasts, it became necessary to keep some sort of order and prevent matters from getting too noisy. For this purpose, a toastmaster was appointed who would keep everyone quiet long enough for the individual making the toast to have the name he mentioned heard by all. In Henry Fielding's book *Tom Jones*, published in 1749, there is reference to a toastmaster whose duties were to propose or announce the toasts.

The duties of the toastmaster were simple in those early days. He acted merely as a referee to give everyone a fair chance to propose a toast in turn and to be heard by his fellow drinkers. As time progressed and the evolution of the toastmaster brought about certain changes, his duties took on additional responsibility. He was expected to keep things lively throughout the evening and provide entertainment as well as call for toasts.

Gatherings such as these were held in public taverns, and the general atmosphere was one of uninhibited gaiety. The ribald and raucous humor of those days became even more exhilarating and vulgar as the evening progressed and more drinks were consumed. The insult, being the lowest and easiest form of humor, was frequently employed with the toastmaster depending heavily upon it to get laughs. As Oscar Wilde once said of a well-bred man, "He never unintentionally insults anybody." In the same way, the toastmaster would engage in insults with a premeditated intention of getting laughs. Those who were the objects of the insults were expected to take these as a matter of course. The toastmaster had to be a man of good humor, whose humor, even though mean and vicious, was accepted in the spirit in which it was given—all in good, though not so clean, fun.

To understand something about the level of humor which prevailed at these tavern gatherings presided over by a toastmaster and something about the kind of fellow generally selected for this role, we might very well study the character of Sir John Falstaff. This was a character created by William Shakespeare and generally represents the typical humorist and fun-loving joker who frequented the tavern of those times.

97.   Falstaff was a man who had nothing to recommend him except his good humor and his ability to create an atmosphere of good fellowshrip through the medium of laughter. He was the kind of man who would be described today by the terms of rat and louse. He was despised and feared by those who tolerated him because he provided entertainment. He flattered the wealthy and those of royal position because they could be helpful and of benefit to him, but behind their backs he ridiculed and made fun of them.

He was fat from overindulging in good food and abundance of drink. He lived to laugh and he laughed to live. He was a man without a sense of honor or a restraining conscience. He joked and laughed because he enjoyed laughter, and mirth was his stock in trade to provide for his very existence.

This huge fellow with a jovial spirit and a quick wit was a frequent visitor at taverns. He possessed all of the qualities and qualifications necessary for an exceptionally gifted toastmaster. The thing which was most remarkable about Falstaff was that his remarks were short and to the point. He never became so voluble in his discourses that he would bore his listeners. He was a good listener as well as a bright and clever conversationalist.

Falstaff enjoyed telling a joke, but he also enjoyed hearing one. He was a lovable old rogue who could set a fast pace at repartee. He not only was clever in his own remarks but he could inspire others to a smart response which would evoke laughter. Falstaff was not only a fictional character created by Shakespeare but he also may be regarded as the best representative of a perfect toastmaster.

The custom of the toast and toasting and the toastmaster was not a part of the general scene at the time that Shakespeare was living. Otherwise, there no doubt would be recorded for all time in the works of Shakespeare long and detailed accounts of Falstaff's activities in the tavern. No doubt his toasts would delight us even today, and he would have been in constant demand to serve as a toastmaster.

98.   George Jessel is a fine example of a modern toastmaster. He is so outstanding in this role that he has been given the honorary title of Toastmaster General of the United States.

This title is a distinctive one which carries with it a certain amount of honor. It was bestowed upon him by President Harry S. Truman, during the war years when Jessel was frequently called upon to serve as toastmaster at banquets and special affairs held, directly or indirectly, through the White House to promote various official and semiofficial military and business matters. George Jessel's outstanding work as toastmaster at these affairs resulted in numerous calls upon him for such service. In many cases, it was almost a government activity. President Truman, in appreciation for this work performed by George Jessel, gave him the honorary title of Toastmaster General of the United States. The title proved so appropriate that it was taken up by newspaper writers and has since always been associated with the name of the great entertainer who created a role of toastmaster in such a capable manner that others have not attempted to imitate him.

George Jessel is a modern version and a pocket-size reincarnation of that lovable and laugh-provoking old rogue, Sir John Falstaff. As toastmaster he not only takes charge and runs the show, but he is the show. He is full of surprises and no one can be sure whether his remarks concerning the honored guest will be flowery and saccharine, sweet with compliments, or bitter with sarcastic humor. He is a senti- mental man who knows show business and has an apprecia- tion for pageantry. He can move his listeners to billowing laughter or tears. He is, by profession, a monologist who, as a hobby, has taken over the duties of a master of ceremonies and thereby created a role for himself which is known as a toastmaster. Only he could fill that role. George Jessel is regarded as one of the finest humorists of our times, but he is more than that. Those who have heard him deliver a final eulogy at the funeral of a friend and joined in the weeping recognize in this man some very deep and sincere human quality which rises above mere laughter. This does not mean that he is any less of a humorist because he is more of a humanitarian than most comedians.

Along with his gift for comedy, he has a way of making friends with an audience instantly from his opening sentence. Right from the start there is a bond of understanding and good fellowship between Jessel and those who have gathered to hear him or to watch him preside at a dinner when he will serve as toastmaster.

He can think on his feet and has a quick wit to take advantage of every opening and opportunity to set a fast and lively pace. Sometimes those who have gathered to hear George Jessel perform and expect flowery exhortations are puzzled and disturbed when he starts a routine of sarcastic observations and insulting remarks. The speakers on the pro- gram and the honored guests at a testimonial dinner may be the object of his comedy line which he dispenses with perfect technique.

This bull thrower, like the skilled bull fighter, knows how

to hesitate, repeat and then thrust home for the kill with an absolutely true aim. As a toastmaster, he doesn't drool, he doesn't put on any airs of false joviality and above all he doesn't ever condescend. He strikes out straight from the shoulder with a spontaneous wit and a rare spark of comedy genius that keeps everyone laughing and makes the evening a success.

TOASTMASTER'S TIDBITS

99. Memorizing Jokes—Being a toastmaster is a tough job. I was up all last night memorizing a few spontaneous and extemporaneous jokes for this evening.

100. Brevity—I will try to avoid taking up too much of your time with my own part of the program. My presence here happens to be a necessity, but I realize a necessity is something most people do without in order to pay the installments on their luxuries. Therefore, we will try to cut down on the necessities of this program and bring you the luxuries.

101. Modesty—Our next speaker is a very modest man. He never brags about himself or his family. In fact, he has said that the only member of his family who ever made a brilliant marriage was his wife.

102. Welcome—Our speaker today is nothing like money. They say that money doesn't have to go far because it is welcome wherever it stops. We hope our speaker will go far in his remarks because he is welcome wherever he starts. Since you are all so anxious for him to begin, I'll call upon him to start.

103. Drinks—Take it easy on the drinks. It's not the ice that makes you slip, but what you mix with it.

104. Cosmetics—What a lovely audience of beautiful women! They must be using that new face cream that takes the wrinkles out of a woman's face and puts them where they won't be noticed. They say that cosmetics were used way back in the Middle Ages. Well, it seems like they are still being used in the middle ages.

105. Speeches—Banquet speakers may dish out speeches that deserve mention, but it's usually the meat and potatoes which get most of the attention.

106. Drowsy Audience—Maybe it was the food, but some of our guests seem to be a little bit drowsy. I think I'll have to call on the speakers to give me a hand, like the preacher who interrupted his sermon to direct his remarks to a small boy sitting beside his father who was nodding. The preacher said, "Billy, wake up your father."

Billy replied, "Wake him up yourself. You put him to sleep!"

107. Old Grads—Some people have been coming back to these meetings year after year. They are what we might call habituates of this gathering. I note that here also are a few sons of habituates.

108. Tragic Banquet—After listening to what has been going on here tonight, our friends will probably talk about this banquet which occurred tonight. They refer to weddings, receptions, dinners, banquets and the like as taking place. Calamities and tragedies occur. You can tell your friends that this banquet OCCURRED tonight.

109. Routine—Tonight things are going to be different. I know you are all tired of the same old routine, like the elevator operator who became so tired of having people ask him the same question over and over again—"What time is it?"—that he hung a clock in the elevator. Now, all day long people ask him, "Is that clock right?"

110. Speak for Your Supper—I suppose you wonder why most after dinner speakers are men. This is not necessarily true. I know one young lady who was a habitual after dinner speaker. Whenever she spoke to a man, she was after dinner.

111. Indigestion—Don't worry about the food tonight. We're using Unguentine for salad dressing, so you won't get heartburn.

112. Broad-mindedness—We've got a broad-minded crowd here tonight, so we ought to have a good time together. They say that after forty, a person's mind gets broader. That's not the half of it!

113. Nice Guy—It gives me a great deal of pleasure to introduce to you a real nice guy. I believe it is very nice to be important, but it is even more important to be nice.

114. Worried Speaker—As I look at our next speaker he reminds me of a girl who was wearing one of those French bathing suits. She had on two bandannas and a worried look.

115. Praise—We have so many wonderful speakers here tonight that I'm in the same situation as the publicity agent for an automobile manufacturer. He complained, "When better cars are built—where will words be found to describe them?" That's me! Where will I find the right kind of words to introduce these exceptionally fine speakers?

116. Snide Remarks—I'd answer those snide remarks, but I'm thinking over what to say. I believe it is best to think

twice before you speak, and then you may be able to say
something twice as insulting as if you spoke right out at once.

117.   Short Program—The way our speakers have been saying only a few words, without taking up all the time which
has been allotted to them, makes me begin to worry about
our program for the evening. It's like the rookie soldier who
got into the Army toward the end of the war. He was reading
in the newspaper about the big advances the Russians were
making against the Germans and he observed, "The way the
Russians are killing off Germans, I don't see how this war can
last for the duration."

118.   Just Talk—Unaccustomed as some people are to public
speaking, they still do!

119.   Flattery—I never flatter any of the speakers I introduce. They say that flattery is merely telling someone what
he already thinks of himself. I like to tell them something
different.

120.   Talkitis—You think our speaker is something now!
When he was a baby he used to run off the mouth so much
they had to diaper him at both ends.

121.   Lies—As toastmaster, my job is to introduce our
speakers and perhaps kid them a little bit. I hope they don't
mind if I exaggerate and tell a few lies about them. I'm like
the newspaper editor who printed some uncomplimentary
remarks about a politician running for office. The politician
stormed into the editor's office and demanded, "What's the
big idea printing lies about me in your paper!"
    The editor waved to the politician to calm down. "Take it
easy," he said. "Just suppose we had printed the truth about
you."

If some of my remarks sound like lies I'm sure the speakers will forgive me. It is the lesser of two evils.

122. *H-Bomb*—When I say that was a terrific speech, I'm like the fellow who was talking about the H-bomb and remarked, "Boy, that H-bomb is dynamite!"

123. *On the Town*—Well, I see everybody here is as dressed up and gay as the florist's daughter. She had two orchids in her hair and Four Roses on her breath.

124. *Treated Lightly*—Please forgive me if I treat this affair with humor. There is nothing wrong with a few laughs. Just remember that Benjamin Franklin may have discovered electricity but Thomas Edison became famous because he made light of it!

125. *Loquacious Wives*—The only reason this fellow ever attends a banquet is that it gives him a chance to talk. He's like all married men. A radio-television survey was made. When the question asked of men answering the phone, "To whom are you listening?" 95 per cent of the male answers were, "To my wife."

126. *Ladies' Man*—He's quite a ladies' man. I understand he made a perfect 36 on the golf course the other day, but she dropped him when she found out he was married.

127. *Golf*—I'd like to return those remarks but I'm in the same boat I was in playing golf with a fellow the other day. I wanted to kill him, but I didn't know which club to use.

128. *Insane Asylum*—This is just like having dinner in an insane asylum. That's where they serve soup to nuts.

129. Long Sessions—This has been a long session, and I am sure all of you are getting tired of sitting, even though you have given evidence of enjoying our program. It recalls to my mind the case of an English professor who visited a burlesque show in America. After he had seen the show he commented about the chorus girls, "I have never seen such sad faces and such gay behinds." About this time in our program I would like to comment, I have never seen so many gay faces and such sad behinds.

130. Happy Audience—I want all of you to be like the soldier who was asked what he was in civilian life. The answer, "Happy."

I hope all of you can be happy and enjoy yourselves. Look forward to our program with enthusiasm as you would a vacation trip. Don't be like a person coming back from a holiday but rather as one who is going into it. When I say this, I am thinking of the traveler who just returned from a tour of Europe. He was asked if he had seen much poverty in Europe.

"Not only did I see it," said the returned traveler, "I brought some of it back with me!"

131. Optimistic Family—Don't mind me, folks, or what I have to say. There must be some insanity in my family. Just to show how nuts some of them are, they keep writing and asking ME for money.

132. Shiny Headstone—He's a fine fellow. Did you ever notice that diamond ring he wears? A number of years ago an aunt left it to him when she died. Well, she didn't exactly leave it to him. She gave him five hundred dollars. Just before she died she called him to her bedside and gave him the money. She said "Here's my money. Buy the nicest stone you can find."

133. *Psychiatrists*—This job of being toastmaster—all evening I make flattering remarks concerning other people. Nobody says anything good about me. I'm beginning to feel like the psychiatrist who met another psychiatrist on the street one morning. He greeted him this way, "Good morning. You are very well. How am I?"

134. *Well-fed Group*—The turkey is luckier than we are. It isn't stuffed with chestnuts until it is dead.

135. *Cowboys*—A toastmaster knows about speakers like a Western girl knows about cowboys. An Eastern girl thinks a cowboy is part boy and part cow. A Western girl knows he's all bull.

136. *Lawyers*—If you want a good story to use in razzing a lawyer friend, here is a joke that is made to order:

It seems that the gate broke down between Heaven and Hell and St. Peter appeared at the broken part of the gate and called out to the Devil. "Hey, Satan, it's your turn to fix it this time."

"Sorry, sir," replied the boss of the land beyond the Styx. "My men are too busy to worry about a broken gate."

"Well, then," growled St. Peter, "I'll have to sue for breaking our agreement."

"Yeah, and where will you get a lawyer?" came the retort.

137. *Chin Up*—My advice to the next speaker—keep your chin up! One of the best things about keeping your chin up is that it also keeps your mouth shut.

138. *Male Speakers*—Maybe you wonder why after dinner speaking is an avocation monopolized by men. The reason is that women can't wait that long!

139. Time Limitations—I must inform the speakers that time limitation requires each one to keep his remarks brief. Be guided by a famous doctor's effective diet which he prescribes for his patients. The diet consists of just four words: "No more, thank you."

140. Humiliated—Every person who appears before an audience as an entertainer, speaker or toastmaster must learn about humility. Believe me, I certainly learned it tonight. I've never been so humiliated in all my life.

141. Starvation Diet—I have tried to make my introduction as complete as possible, but I know that no matter what you say about ——— there is always something more and something good that can be added, like the letter the parents received from their young son at camp. He wrote: "Please send food packages. All they serve here is breakfast, lunch and dinner."

142. Respectability—I want to warn our speakers that we have a strict rule here regarding time limits. It is like an advertisement which appeared in a New England paper at the beginning of summer: "Waitress needed in resort hotel. Must be respectable—until Labor Day only."

143. Watch Your Language—I would like to give this bit of advice to our speakers. It comes from the Talmud, the Jewish book of law. The Talmud points out that at funerals the orators who are to speak at the ceremony should bear in mind that there is a judgment day, not alone for the deceased, but also for the orators.

144. Cut the Speech—I must ask the speakers to limit themselves to the time we have allotted to them. I know this may be difficult, but I want to give them the same formula which golfers use to cut off four to eight strokes from their score.

It is not difficult to cut off four to eight strokes from your golf score—just leave out one hole. In this same way I would like to say to the speakers if you want to cut our four to eight minutes from your speech, just leave off some part of it as you go along.

145. *Bully*—Bullfighting may be a quaint old Spanish custom, but in my day as a toastmaster I've met more bulls than a matador.

146. *On Being Clever*—My observation for our speakers is to take this advice of Plato: "The Athenians do not mind a man being clever, as long as he keeps it to himself."

147. *Good Head*—Yes sir, he has a nice head on his shoulders. It would look better on his neck.

148. *Long-winded*—Boy, this fellow should have a beautiful girl standing next to him when he delivers his talk. She would look grand with the wind in her hair!

149. *Jerks*—I'm like the girl elevator operator. The ups and downs never bothered her. It was the jerks.

150. *Hard Decision*—I don't know what we would do without you—but we would rather!

151. *Sense of Humor*—Don't be afraid to laugh right out. The fellow who laughs last may laugh best, but he gets a reputation for being dumb.

152. *Loud Talk*—I should have told our speaker to speak a little lower. We could still hear him.

153.   Fathead—If you think you can get my goat, I want you to know that you've got a fat chance, and a head to match!

154.   Noisy—Well, I finally broke through the sound barrier and got a word in edgewise.

155.   Keep It Brief—A last word of advice to the speakers before we begin our program—it is shortsighted to be long-winded.

156.   More to Come—The police inform me that we have among our speakers this evening a second-story man. If you don't like his first he always tells a second story.

157.   Keep Laughing—Let's laugh and be happy. If a hyena can do it, you can too. Laughing hyenas eat only once a week and mate but once a year. What have they got to laugh about? Well, all of you have a lot to laugh about and I hope you do!

158.   Wide Awake—I read somewhere that the amount of sleep required by the average person is about an hour more than he gets. Please don't try to get it here. Let's make this a wide-awake audience tonight.

159.   S.O.B.—I am not making any personal references about anyone here tonight, but I would like to tell you about a bee that had a baby. He was the son of a bee.

160.   Watch That Cocktail—Before we go much further along I would like to offer this word of warning to some of our members who are imbibing freely. It isn't the ein or the zwei but the drei martini that gets you down!

161.   Nasty Remark—I want to say this about our speaker who had such nasty remarks to make about me. When he was a boy he used to like to play post office. Now he likes to play building and loan. He wants me to get out of the building and leave him alone!

PERSONAL REFERENCES

162.   Tongue Twister—Pardon my mistake. I just got my tongue twisted like the radio announcer who was broadcasting the arrival of the Governor of the Virgin Islands to Washington some few years back. The radio announcer who made the unfortunate error garbled his words and said into the microphone, "Today the White House is to have a special guest—the Virgin of Governor's Island."

163.   Mistaken Identity—I represent a big organization. It is so big and so important that I believe the remarks your chairman made about me personally are really out of place and he should have directed his compliments to the organization I represent.

My relationship to the organization and the compliments paid me rather than the organization reminds me of a story told about little Bobby who played daily in a park near his California home and grew very fond of a statue of General Grant on horseback.

One day, when Father announced that they were moving to New York City in a few days, Bobby begged his father to take him for a farewell visit to the statue. When they reached the park and stood before the statue, Bobby burst into tears.

"Good-by, Grant," he sobbed. "Good-by!"

Then, as he was led slowly away, he asked suddenly, "Daddy, who's that man on Grant?"

164.   Busy Man—I'm getting good at this job. I'm like the doctor who last year performed forty operations. If things keep up that way for him, he'll have to get a license.

165. Last One Out—Speaking to such a small gathering is always a disappointing experience. However, I have never had it as bad as the speaker who was faced with a small gathering and not long after he began to speak, those in the audience started to leave, one at a time. Finally, there was just a handful. An usher came to the platform, interrupted the speaker momentarily, to hand him a note which read: "When you are through, will you please turn off the lights, lock the doors and leave the key in the manager's office."

166. Hearing Aid—I'm sorry if I don't hear too well. That's my penalty like the woman who didn't stop when the cop on the corner whistled at her. When he finally caught up with the lady she explained that she was a little deaf. "Oh, that's all right," replied the cop. "You'll get your hearing in the morning."

167. Sleepwalker—It is quite embarrassing to me to see so many people leave the room. It is like the case of a minister who noticed that one of the members of the congregation got up during the middle of the sermon and walked out of church. After services, the minister sought out the wife of the man and apologized, "I hope I said nothing to offend your husband. I noticed that he walked right out in the middle of my sermon."

"Oh, don't pay any attention to Henry," the woman laughed. "He has been walking in his sleep for years."

168. Good Health—Everybody tells me I should change my mind and my way of thinking. I guess I'm like the fellow who thought he was a dog. He went to a psychiatrist and took the course of treatments. When it was all over a friend asked him how he felt, and he replied, "Fine, feel my nose."

169. Eyeglasses—I'm like Jack Benny. I really don't need glasses. I just wear them for seeing.

170.   *Undeserved Praise*—The congratulations which I have received are undeserved, like that of the doctor who had a man come into his office and shake him by the hand. "Doctor," this man said, "I just dropped in to tell you how much I benefited from your treatment."

The doctor looked over the man and protested, "You must be mistaken. You are not one of my patients."

"Oh, I know that," replied the stranger. "But my uncle was and I'm his heir."

171.   *Hush*—Every time I try to say something I get shushed, like at the wedding when the minister asked, "If there is anyone here who knows why these two should not be joined in wedlock let him speak now or forever hold his peace."

In a loud voice the words rang out, "I want to say something!"

"You keep out of this," snapped the minister. "You are the groom!"

172.   *Speech Refusal*—I regret I must pass up this invitation to say a few words. I'm like the North Woods hunters. They never open their traps more than three times a year.

173.   *In the Air*—Right now I'm like the fellow who had never been in a plane. One day he went to the airport, climbed into a plane, pulled on a few gadgets and before he knew it he was up in the air. I'm in the air, too, and don't know how to get back down.

174.   *Bumming Cigarettes*—I smoke "Impromptu cigarettes." I pick them up as I go along.

175.   *Speechless*—Well, those remarks certainly are a surprise. I don't know what to say, except I'll be like the cow that turned to the farmer while he was milking her and asked, "What do you think you are pulling?"

176.   *Smart*—I'm not really very smart, although sometimes I have been given credit for intelligence. It makes me wonder whether I'm a budding genius or a blooming idiot.

177.   *Forced Lesson*—I learned to jitterbug in thirty seconds. It was at one of those gay parties. A fellow thought my hip pocket was an ash tray.

178.   *Inexperienced Opinion*—I have been asked to give my opinion on a difficult subject. Frankly, I hesitate to speak with my authority because I feel that in this case I am in somewhat the same position as a young doctor.

Fresh out of medical school, the young doctor opened his office in a small town out West and waited all the first day for his first patient. The person who finally walked in was a man covered all over with a purple rash.

The young practitioner riffled through the pages of his medical books, but could find nothing even remotely resembling the disease.

"Did you ever have anything like this before?" he eventually asked the patient.

"Shore thing, Doc. It plumb had me down six times last year."

"Well," diagnosed the young doctor, "you've plumb got it again."

Any opinion which I might give would carry about as much knowledge and experience as the diagnosis of this young doctor so I will ask to be excused.

179.   *Lucky*—I feel lucky tonight—like the millionaire Texas oil man who went to see his dentist. The dentist told him his teeth were in perfect condition. The Texan pleaded with the dentist, "Drill anyway. Today I feel lucky!"

180.   Win a Prize—I am overwhelmed by all of the flattering remarks which have been made concerning me, but I still have a sneaking suspicion that the situation is like that of a department head who was about to retire from his position. One of the employees started selling tickets for a farewell dinner for the departing boss. One co-worker balked at buying a ticket, and the fellow getting up the dinner pleaded with him, "Look, there'll be good food and fun and prizes. You might even win a prize!"

The other fellow wasn't impressed. "I'd rather give the old geezer a good swift kick in the pants," he observed, concerning the retiring department head.

"You're psychic!" exclaimed the employee getting up the dinner. "That's the first prize!"

181.   Buckeye—A native of Ohio is called a buckeye. Even though I am not a native of Ohio, I still believe I am entitled to be known as a buckeye. A buckeye is a hairless nut of no practical value.

182.   Thank You—My good friends, I have often wished there were some truly clever way to say, "I thank you." If you try to be witty, you often find your thoughts rolling in on some very flat verbal tires. As a wit—I feel I am only a half-wit. Poetry might be a good bet. But I live such a glorified rat-race of a busy life, hoping to get enough laid away to bury me, that I never look inside a public library and all the books I have are either on my trade or who-dun-its that help to get me to sleep. So poetry is out. And I'm no orator. So oratory is out. And maybe after all it will be nearer the right thing for me to say, and, with all my heart, thank you!

183.   *Old*—I'm so old that I count my birthdays in Roman numerals.

184.   *Not Drunk*—I never get drunk. I get inebriated. I'm a college man.

185.   *Bookworm*—When I was a kid I always had my nose in a book. I couldn't afford a handkerchief.

186.   *Old-Fashioned*—I guess you would call me old-fashioned. I understand that they have created an electronic device to make children. I still like the old ways much better.

187.   *Enjoying Flattery*—Without silly flattering, I want to say that I am truly honored to receive this recognition from our chairman. To my children I'm plain Daddy—without any honors of any kind whatsoever. To the lady who took a wild chance and married me I'm—in her own words—"a big but very precious lug." Yet after all, my friends, a lug is nothing more than a lug. Even a lug you can hug. In my own work, I fear I'm just the "old man." Once I was called "Boss"—and I walked on air for a week. But right here before all these nice people the chairman has gone out on a limb—and, to say the least, exaggerated my very few and limited achievements. Maybe he expects me to pick up the check, when we next have luncheon together. And just maybe he is about to run for office and expects both monetary and political support. Anyway, it was very gracious. And for me—I'm glad I'm here and heard it!

188.   *Special Request*—I was born in MY CITY at the request of YOUR CITY.

189.   *Baldy*—My wife is always going to the beauty shop to get a permanent wave. I'd be satisfied just to have permanent hair.

190.   *Don't Judge by Appearances*—I am the speaker who was advertised to appear here today. I hope you do not judge me by appearances and jump to a quick conclusion. I'm going to start right on my speech because I'm in the same situation as the opera singer who married a handsome playboy. This handsome playboy was going out with two girls—the opera singer and a beautiful but dumb chorus girl. He didn't know which one to marry but decided on intellect and talent, so he married the opera singer. They spent their wedding night at a swanky hotel. In the morning, as the dawn's light began to shine through the window, the groom looked at his waking bride, shuddered and cried out, "For heaven's sake, sing something!"

191.   *No Comb Necessary*—I'm not really bald-headed. I just have a tall face. It doesn't bother me because there is one good thing you can say for baldness—it's neat.

192.   *Comeback*—I haven't got any more comeback than the fellow who was up before the judge and the judge asked him, "Are you the defendant in this case?" This fellow didn't know what to answer so he said, "No, sir. I'm the guy who stole the automobile tires."

193.   *Go Together*—One thing about me, I always have a clear conscience. Fortunately, also, I have a very poor memory.

194.   *Consolation*—When I was younger I used to give free rein to my imagination. In my later years I have tried to develop my sense of humor. We all come to realize that imagination is given a man to compensate him for what he is not. A sense of humor consoles him for what he is.

195.   *Out for No Good*—Frankly, I am here for only one reason. They say that the natural man has only two primary passions—to get and beget. Since my wife is at home, it shouldn't be hard for you to figure out the reason why I am here.

196. *Hard Work*—This is more work than I've done in years. As they say, when you start to push (GIVE APPROXIMATE AGE), that's all the exercise you need.

197. *Average*—I'm just an average person. The average is the poorest of the best and the best of the poorest.

198. *Self-Made*—I wish to say that I am a self-made man. I say it because it relieves God Almighty of a big responsibility.

199. *Stupid*—I've never been accused of being scatter-brained. Perhaps it is because I haven't any brains to scatter.

200. *Expensive*—This ring I wear once belonged to a millionaire—Woolworth.

201. *Reserved*—They call me Calvert—I'm so reserved!

202. *Appearances*—They tell me I look like a million and they mean every year of it.

203. *Not Enough*—They tell me that I've got more talent in my little fiinger than Marilyn Monroe has in her whole body. But who wants to look at fingers?

204. *Outnumbered*—I'm not really bald. It's just that other guys are hairy.

205. *It's the Color*—I'm not really bald-headed. I just have flesh-colored hair.

206. Cheating—I have a million-dollar figure but the middle part is counterfeit.

207. Hooky—I played hooky so much when I was a kid that I was the only youngster ever to be thrown IN to school rather than out of it.

208. Grade Repeater—I have fond memories of my childhood and my many years in school. I recall how one day when I was promoted from the sixth to the seventh grade I was so excited I could hardly shave without cutting myself.

209. Buddy—Many a young girl has admired my complexion. I have cheeks like roses and a nose to match.

210. Income—I never brag about my income, but I will say my earnings run to four figures—my wife and three daughters.

211. Beautiful—You may not believe it, but I used to be a very beautiful baby. In fact, my parents used to have me kidnaped just so they could see my picture in the papers.

212. Knows the Way—I'm as sure about where I'm going as the fellow who took castor oil.

213. Looks—I never did have much looks, but that's because of what happened before I was born. My mother was frightened by my father.

214. Hurdle—The only thing that ever kept me from going to college was high school.

215. Only Human—I am only human, which is more than some people here can say for themselves.

216. *Afterthought*—I excuse my own shortcomings with the thought that man was made at the end of a hard week's work when God was tired.

217. *Always Something*—I never get a break in life. When I have less hair to comb, I have more face to wash.

218. *Ninety Plus*—I am not an old person. I am only twenty-one years of age and some months—to be exact 212 months.

219. *Repeat Purchase*—I am indebted to all of you for your congratulations and good wishes. However, I don't feel too happy about it all. In fact, I feel very much like the man who went to buy a tombstone for his wife. The man who sold tombstones said to the customer, "Why do you want a tombstone for your wife? I sold you a tombstone for your wife three years ago."

"Yes," replied the poor fellow, "but I married again."

"Oh," blurted out the tombstone dealer, "congratulations!"

220. *Sure of His Facts*—I never take the responsibility of passing along information unless I myself have had a chance to check and make sure it is correct. In this respect I am like the old Shakespearean actor who was once asked if—as an expert on Shakespeare—he would know if there actually was an affair between Romeo and Juliet. The old actor thought for a while before committing himself and then replied, "Well, I can say for sure that there was in our road company."

221. *Tribute*—That is a nice tribute you have given me, but somehow I keep thinking of a tribute paid to the honored guest at a testimonial dinner. One of the speakers got up and, intending to deliver a tribute, got mixed up and made this statement which might equally well apply to me, "Our honored guest has been named the man of the year. Our organization couldn't have made a better selection UNLESS it had tried."

222. *Poor Voice*—I'm not going to say anything about my voice but I'm like the opera star who had her voice insured for $25,000. When she told this to a friend the friend asked, "What did you do with the money?"

223. *High Living*—Prosperity goes to some people's heads. It goes to my stomach.

224. *Bewildered*—I won't say that I am lost in all of this discussion, but I'm like the famous Indian scout who was asked if he had ever been lost in the woods. He replied, "I've never been lost, but once in the mountains I was bewildered for three days."

225. *Once Is Enough*—I've never been regarded as the best looking man in a crowd, but I will say that when my wife first saw me it was love at first sight. She couldn't bear to take another look.

226. *Poker*—When I was a kid, I lived in a tough neighborhood. After school we used to play jacks—jacks or better to open.

227. *Turnabout*—When my son went to college I gave him a pair of loaded dice. I was the only father with a boy in college who wrote his son for money.

228. *Shorty*—I am so short my feet hardly touch the ground.

229. *Skinny*—I am so anemic that I have to get a transfusion to bleed.

230.   *Famous*—Benjamin Franklin flew a kite and became famous. I should have listened to what people have told me for years. For years people have been telling me to go fly a kite!

231.   *The End*—I always felt that I was a natural football player in my youth. I understand when I was born my father looked at me and exclaimed, "That's the end!"

232.   *Speech Defect*—I hope you will overlook my poor delivery. I have a speech impediment. I have to stop to breathe once in a while.

233.   *Twin*—I used to be a twin. The family album has a picture of me when I was two.

234.   *Bald*—You can see that I am a man of polish—mostly around my head.

235.   *New Look*—The new look isn't going to do me much good, because they can't give you the new look if you only have old parts.

236.   *Philosophy*—Early in life I came to appreciate the value of philosophy. Philosophy makes it possible for a person to be unhappy in an intelligent manner.

237.   *Talking Picture*—I was unfortunate in my inheritance. I turned out to be the picture of my father and the sound track of my mother.

238.   *Growing Old*—I'm at that time in life when my thoughts begin to turn from passion to pension.

239.   *Severe Critic*—I believe that this is a critical audience. There is one fellow here tonight who I know is exacting in his demands. Why, he told me that only last week he went to a movie and the performance was so poor he had to sit through it three times to get his money's worth.

240. Incomplete—I'm a self-made man. Only thing is I got tired and quit the job before I was finished.

241. Fair Warning—My mother always told me that if I made an ugly face it would stay that way. So I can't say that I wasn't warned.

242. Speaking Frankly—I have a few words to say on this subject and I intend to say them—even if it doesn't please some of my friends here. I may disturb you but it's like they say about married couples. Married couples can have pleasant conversations—if the husband doesn't start talking back.

243. Bushed—I'm sorry if I do not seem to be up to par, but I must admit I'm bushed. My wife and I have been giving a great deal of time to this activity. My wife was so tired last night that she did the dishes in bed.

244. Vague—I am going to make my remarks very brief because I do not want you to say of me what some poet wrote about another speaker:

> He never knows a thing to say
> Or what to talk about;
> But you must listen long before
> You ever find that out.

245. Old Age—Being old has its advantages. You can take a nap when you feel like it without being called lazy.

246. Wanted—I do not like to brag about myself, but I will say that I started out in life as an unwanted child, and by the time I was twenty-four years of age I was wanted in eighteen states.

247.   Mustache—I'll tell you this confidentially. I have a mustache, but I keep it shaved off.

248.   Dull Talk—When people want to kill time, they always call on me to speak. That is, if they are the kind of people who like it dead.

249.   Waistline—My doctor told me that I should watch my waistline. It's lucky that I have it right out in front where I can.

250.   Think Before You Speak—I wish to apologize for saying the wrong thing. I know how important it is to express yourself correctly, like the young fellow who intended to tell the girl he adored that when he looked into her eyes time stood still. In his embarrassment he forgot the words he was going to use and instead told her that her face would stop a clock!

251.   Taking off Years—I try to keep up a youthful viewpoint. I have always had great admiration for H. L. Mencken's observation that thirty is a nice, comforting age for a woman —especially if she happens to be forty. Men, too, can come in on that.

252.   Large Family—I am what is known as an old-timer. I can remember back to the time when a child had more brothers and sisters than he had fathers.

253.   Wrong Message—This is the time of the year when all the muscles in my body cry out for exercise and send a message to my brain to run and dance and turn somersaults across the lawns. And my brain sends back a message to my body, "Who? Me!"

254. Fuss—Please don't make any fuss over me. Treat me as you would any other great orator.

255. Competition—I am a modest fellow who never likes to brag about himself, but I believe you should know that two big business firms are fighting over my services. The loser gets me.

256. Uncomfortable Surroundings—If I seem a bit upset, it's because these strange surroundings affect me like an altar affects a bachelor. They say that an altar is a place where a bachelor loses control of himself.

257. Forgotten—I'm sorry that I haven't with me the information which I should have brought along. I feel like the fellow who arrived at the railroad station with his wife, loaded down with luggage for a trip. The train was due to leave shortly. The man turned to his wife and said, "Gee, dear, I wish I had brought along the piano."

"The piano!" the wife exclaimed.

"Yes," replied the poor fellow. "Our train tickets are on it!"

258. Small Talk—I have very little to say. I believe in brevity, and the shortest distance between two points is fewer words.

259. Enemies—I try to make as few enemies as possible, but unfortunately I cannot be like the dying dictator who called for a confessor as the end approached. The confessor asked, "Do you forgive your enemies?"

"I have no enemies," the dying dictator replied.

The confessor was somewhat puzzled by this and asked the dictator if he were sure. "Yes, I'm sure," the dictator replied. "I have had all of them shot." Unlike this dictator, my enemies bear with me.

260. *Middle Age*—I've reached that time in years which they describe as middle age and explain as the period of a man's life when his daydreams center around a banker saying yes, instead of a girl.

TOASTS

261. *Toast to Wife on Wedding Anniversary*—On this occasion when we celebrate our wedding anniversary, I wish to offer a toast to my beautiful and beloved wife. All through our married life I have tried to do what I could to bring her happiness. I knew that she always enjoyed the little attentions of a bouquet of flowers or a box of candy. Therefore, I always made a point of speaking about these things occasionally. As a general rule, though, I have never expressed my sentiments or the deep love which I have felt for her, and it is only on an occasion such as that that I can get sentimental and tell my wife that the love which was ours when we were married has grown stronger and held us together with a bond which has made my life a happy one filled with joy and satisfaction. To my wife, whom I love and adore, I offer this toast to her good health and long life.

262. *Toast to Bride*—We are fortunate to share with this lovely bride an event which is perhaps the most important ceremony of her entire life. Her happiness has made this a festive occasion for all of us, and we gather in some of the sunshine which she radiates in the warmth and pleasure of the wedding ceremony. We want to wish her and the groom the very best of everything and a life filled with joys and contentment. May God watch over her and the household which she is now establishing.

263. *Tribute to a Career Woman*—We have gathered here to pay tribute to a woman who has distinguished herself in her chosen vocation. We know it is not easy for a woman to compete in a man's world and reach a position of influence and importance. A woman has many handicaps, and a man has many advantages in this competition. For one thing, a man who is married has behind him all the help and inspiration, encouragement and drive of a woman who is his wife. Someone has said that women are at a disadvantage because of the biological nature which makes it impossible for her to have a wife who will serve as a helpmate and push her along the road to success and fame. That is why we are more amazed when a woman will make a success in her work, competing with men. She deserves our highest praise and admiration. I am happy to join with others in paying tribute to this distinguished and most successful career woman.

264. *Toast to the Ladies*—We are delighted to have the ladies as our special guests at this meeting. According to the Bible, woman was made while man was asleep. She has kept him awake and alert ever since. The presence of the ladies at this meeting will make all of us more alert, and I am sure we will enjoy the program better because of our feminine guests. To them we want to offer our best wishes and our thanks for being with us.

265. *Toast to Feminine Guests*—It is my privilege and pleasure to deliver this toast to our special feminine guests. On behalf of my fellow members, I wish to tell you how happy we are to have you here and how delighted we are with this opportunity to be surrounded by so much feminine charm. Making a toast to the ladies is an easy task for any married man. Most men have had considerable experience making toast for their wives every morning at breakfast. This toast which I am offering is a little different, although I want it to be rich, golden brown, delightful and appealing in every way. For this reason, I will not leave it on too long as it might get burned and ruined. So I'll make it short and to the point when I say here's to our feminine guests who have brought with them so much loveliness and charm.

266. Toast to a Worthy Woman—The sweet charity of her works and the generosity of her spirit are not matched by a desire for attention and praise. She is a worthy woman and an honest one. I am sure she is blushing and feels self-conscious to be the center of all this attention and hear so many flattering remarks. We could not spare her this embarrassment because it is the only way we can show our love and affection. Thus, I join with others to express my own sentiments as I say we have been blessed by having in our midst this worthy woman.

267. Toast to a Successful Candidate—The people have spoken and their words have been recorded in the annals of the history of government. Our candidate has won the support and approval of the voters. They say that there are two sides to every question, and a good many politicians often take both. Our friend, whom we are honoring today, had the wisdom of getting on the right side early in the campaign. I don't know whether the people voted for him because they thought he was on their side, or because they wanted to get on his side. Nevertheless, he got the most votes and deserves all the honors which we can bestow upon him. I wish to add my voice to the shouts of victory and good luck which have been ringing in his ears.

268. Toast to a Teacher—Here is a toast to a friend we hold dear. Her life has been devoted to the task of helping to educate and train our children. Parents will be indebted to her throughout their lives, and our nation will benefit from the good work which she has done. Children were indeed fortunate who had our honored guest as one of their teachers and will never forget her kindness, loyalty and sympathy. She has been a person of noble character and wise counsel. She is a woman who deserves well the tribute which we seek to pay her on this happy occasion.

269. *Toast to a Man of Service*—Here is a man who gave liberally of his time and talent to the cause of service for his fellowmen. The story of his life presents us with an inspiration that is noble, uplifting and humanitarian. His life has been dedicated to the service of others. We can never repay him, but on this occasion we can tell him that we appreciate everything he has done and honor him for the many contributions he has made to humanity. He is a great man because he is a good man, and goodness is greatness.

270. *Tribute to a Humanitarian*—The man we are honoring is known as a humanitarian. He regards his fellowmen as members of society and we spell that with a small "s." Not every person who is regarded as human may have the distinction of being called a humanitarian. There is a distinction between a human being and being human. Our honored guest is a man who throughout his life has devoted himself to being human. I would like to speak for all of the hundreds of people he has helped and given aid and who are unable to be present here themselves to join in this tribute to a most deserving and worthy member of the society of mankind.

271. *Toast to Charter Member*—A charter member is one who was there at the very beginning when our organization was born. Like most organizations, it started on a shoestring and our honored guest was one of those who furnished that shoestring. He took a chance while others wanted to take only the rewards of the efforts of others. He was willing to get in and do the hard work necessary to get our organization started. He had faith in this organization and confidence in its future. That faith and confidence have been vindicated, and now, as a strong and well-established organization, we gather to pay tribute to one of our founders, this charter member. I say thanks to you. We appreciate so very much what you helped start for us to carry on and enjoy.

272. **Toast to a Gracious Gentleman**—Here's a toast to a man of gracious manner and the character and breeding of a gentleman. He has endeared himself to all who know him by his tolerance, sympathy and understanding. He has successfully combined charm with intellectual capacity, and his life is an example of the finest traditions of good manners and good cheer. We want to wish him well.

273. **To Woman**—Here is to woman, and other expenses. She is first in our hearts and first in our pocketbooks. By now we are all ready to agree that it is the woman who pays and pays. The man merely deposits.

274. **To Our Country**—I offer a toast to our beloved country. We delight in the beauty of its grandeur. We take pride in its power and strength. We find joy in its tremendous capacity for producing in abundance everything we need for a comfortable life filled with enjoyment. Above all else, we sing the praises of our country because of the liberty, the freedom and the independence which it permits all people. Here's to the greatest and most noble country that ever existed on the face of this tired old world.

275. **To Our Church**—Let us pay tribute to our church. It is the place where we go for worship and for spiritual guidance and inspiration. It is here that we join with other God-fearing people and find good companionship with them. Our church makes our life better and brighter and more worthwhile. We are blessed by our church and we want to return this blessing to it.

276. *To Friendship*—We love our friends because they love us not for our virtues but in spite of our faults. The Lord provides us with relatives when we arrive on this earth, but we must find our own friends. Friendship can be the greatest thing in this world, but we must make it so. Thus, to friendship, our most treasured possession, I offer this toast.

277. *To Our Host*—A person is judged by the company he keeps. We think that the company gathered here is the best. This makes our host tops. There is none better!

278. *To Our Guests*—Tennyson once wrote that knowledge comes, but wisdom lingers. That is a most appropriate thought as I offer this toast to our guests. Our guests come to this meeting, and the pleasure they bring us with them lingers on. Thank you for making us so happy by joining with us at this gathering.

279. *To a Special Guest*—This dear guest who means so much to us has brought us pleasure and happiness by his presence here. May he take away our best wishes for his good health, prosperity and the best of everything in his life.

280. *To a Champion*—Here's to a champion because he's the best. He has won a victory because being good is not good enough. Nothing less than the very best was necessary for him to earn his crown and title. For this champion, who is the best in his sport, we want to wish him also the best in everything else.

281.   *To a Sportsman*—Here's to a sportsman who loves good sports. The highest praise we can give him is to call him by the name of a good sportsman. We offer a toast to a really good sport.

282.   *To a Team*—A team begins by being a group of people who play a game together. If it is a good team, it plays the game well. If it is a perfect team, it does more than play a game. It brings people together in a close bond of friendship and understanding which enables them to execute an activity as a single unit. Thus, we have a team—from many into one— and one toast for all.

283.   *To Our City*—A city is like a river. It goes on and on forever, but it can do something a river can't. It grows in size and becomes more beautiful through the years. I offer this toast to our city: May it grow and become more prosperous and more beautiful through the years.

284.   *To a Graduate*—Here's to our young graduate. We give him the three R's. Rah, rah, rah!

285.   *Birthday Toast*—Birthday comes but once a year, so we give a birthday cheer: Rah, rah, rah (John Smith)!

286.   *Anniversary Toast*—Good friends have gathered to celebrate this anniversary. An anniversary marks time which has passed. This gathering marks a celebration held in the present. Our thoughts mark our good wishes and best hopes for the future. Thus, on this anniversary the past, the present and the future all come together at one time, and it is a good time for all of us.

287.   *Testimonial Dinner Toast*—Here's to our honored guest at this testimonial dinner. We have gathered here as a testament of our affection, admiration, respect and love for our honored guest. When we think of testaments, we think of the Old Testament and the New Testament. At this testimonial dinner we also have old testaments from old friends and new testaments from new friends, but whether his friends are old or new, they all join in this toast to his good health and future success.

288.   *To a Bachelor*—Here's to a man who knows what he wants, but doesn't always get it. He likes love better than home cooking. He's not sure whether marriage offers bliss or blisters, but he doesn't want to find out. In the land of the free and the home of the brave he prefers to be free rather than brave.

289.   *To a Beauty Contest Winner*—Here's to a beautiful young lady. She has what it takes and what it takes she took. She took the beauty crown and we are all delighted to watch her wear it with such a regal manner. Long live the queen of beauty!

290.   *Toast to a Retiring Officer*—Here's a good word for our retiring officer who has had so many good words for all of us. He has served our organization well and faithfully. We were happy in his coming and we applaud to show our appreciation at his going. Let's show him how much we appreciate him with our applause.

291.   *Toast to Retiring Employee*—To retire from a job, you must first be on a job. Here's a toast to a man who has always been on the job! He takes with him our best wishes and leaves behind a good record. He should be happy to have so many friends and well-wishers and proud to leave behind a record which will long be remembered favorably.

May the years ahead be filled with joy and satisfaction for him.

VOCATIONS

292. *Actor*—All of the world is a stage and many of us are bad actors. Here's to a man who is always a good actor, whether he is behind the footlights or just another good fellow playing a good role for his many good friends.

293. *Air Force*—They fly high so when we offer a toast to the Air Force there is nothing we can do except praise them to the sky.

294. *Army*—Here's to the warriors in our Army. Because they are ready to die for liberty, the rest of us can live and enjoy it.

295. *Athlete*—An amateur doesn't amount to very much except in the world of sports, and then he is the very best. I offer a toast to an amateur who is one of the best. We love him because he is a good guy, a good sport and an outstanding athlete.

296. *Auto Dealer*—The automobile started out as a luxury and has ended up as a necessity. Many families have two necessities and one swell auto dealer, like the fellow we are honoring here tonight. May he live long to enjoy many new models.

297. *Baker*—Here's to a fellow who made loafing a career. The rest of us must be content to follow the advice of an old proverb that half a loaf is better than none.

298. *Banker*—Bankers and undertakers have long been regarded as men of frigid austerity, cold reserve and aloofness. Today this is no longer the case. The undertaker has become a funeral director, and the banker has become a human being. I propose a toast to a modern banker who is a good example of a sweet, lovable and kindly human being.

299. *Barber*

> He cuts our hair
> And shaves our face,
> And talks and talks
> With ease and grace.

300. *Book Dealer*—Education comes to college people by degrees, to chorus girls by stages and to all the rest of us by books. A book dealer leads a useful life and we hope a happy one. At least, we feel sure that tonight is a happy time for our honored guest.

301. *Broker*—Most of us hate the thought of going broke, but here's to a man who is always broker and makes a career out of it.

302. *Chief*—Hail the chief! He is often called the brass, but to us he is solid gold.

303. *Dentist*—Here's to a man who spares no pains to do a good job. He will bore you to tears, but we love him still—and he prefers us that way.

304. *Doctor*—I offer one little toast to the good health of a man who offers his entire life to the good health of others. It is so little that we do for someone who does so much.

305. *Druggist*—I offer two toasts to our favorite druggist because he is a man who has two careers—a profession and a

business. He must be twice as good as anyone else, so I feel
he deserves two toasts from me.

306.   Editor—We have with us tonight a man who deals in
headlines and by-lines. For him I have just an ordinary line:
Mr. Editor, you are the most!

307.   Entertainers—Here's to the men and women, girls and
boys, who have entertained us this evening. They have shown
us a good time, and now is a good time to show them our
appreciation. Many thanks to all of you.

308.   Executive—Here's to a man who knows how to get a
job done—he hires someone to do it!

309.   Funeral Director—Two men whose words are law are
the elevator operator and the funeral director. When the
elevator operator says, "Going up," you go up, and when the
funeral director says, "Going down," you go down.

310.   Grocer—Our honored guest lives so we may eat, and
because we eat what he sells, he lives. Long may he live and
keep our tables well filled.

311.   Hardware Dealer—Here's to a fellow who can stand
on his own two feet and face the world squarely without
blinking an eye. He calls a spade a spade!

312.   Insurance Agent—I offer this toast to our popular
insurance agent. He keeps us poor all of our lives so we can
die rich.

313.   Jeweler—What is more precious than rubies and
diamonds? I'll tell you what! It's our friendship for the man
who sells them.

314. *Judge*—Here's a toast to a man of great trials and many convictions!

315. *Lawyer*—The way to win a lawsuit is to have a good case, a good lawyer and good luck. To a good lawyer I wish good luck and I hope you will always have good cases.

316. *Manufacturer*—Manufacturing is the greatest contribution to modern civilization. Without men such as our honored guest, we would probably be spending our days hunting and fishing instead of toiling over some big machine. I don't know whether to be happy or sad about this; all I know is that our honored guest, a manufacturer, is one of those who helped to do it.

317. *Merchant*—He keeps a store because a store keeps him. I hope he will always be a well-kept man.

318. *Musicians*—Here's a toast to our musicians who provided such delightful music for our program this evening. Many fine words and poetic expressions have been used to praise music and musicians, but all I want to say is that the music was swell and we sure enjoyed it a lot.

319. *Navy*—Here's to the men of the Navy who sail the ocean blue. They man our ships, guard our land and to our flag are true.

320. *Nurse*—The spirit of Florence Nightingale lives on in the work performed by nurses today. No one could be better employed than doing the work of a nurse. To our guest of honor we say bravo and many thanks for the good work that you are doing.

321. *Politician*—Here's to a politician, who has the most promising of all careers. He spends half his time running for office and the other half trying to elude those who would catch up with him.

322.   Preacher—Here's to a man who never expects to go to Hell, but spends much of his time talking about it so some of us may not go there either.

323.   Public Official—Here's to a man who works for the public when he can get the public to work for him.

324.   Railroad Man—The story of civilization is a story of transportation, which began with the wheel. One of the most important chapters in that story has been the development and work of the railroads. It is fitting that we pay tribute to a man engaged in the important work of railroading.

325.   Real Estate—Actions speak louder than words. Therefore, I have no words which are loud enough for our honored guest to hear because he puts his trust in deeds.

326.   Restaurant Owner—There are all kinds of restaurants, but we can say for purposes of definition that a restaurant is an eating place that doesn't sell drugs. It is the only business that doesn't have to create a demand for its product. For our honored guest I give this word of cheer—you may never grow rich, but you need not fear starving to death.

327.   Salesman—Selling is an art and a science, and a good salesman must understand human nature. Therefore, I propose three toasts—to an artist, a scientist and a psychologist—who earns his money as a salesman.

328.   Scientist—In the good old days idealists told us to hitch our wagon to a star, but they didn't really believe we could do it. Now comes the scientist who makes it possible for us to hitch a rocket to the star so that the dreams of the idealist may some day come true.

329. *Shoe Dealer*—Here's to a man who puts us on our feet. You can't expect to win the race of life unless you are well shod.

330. *Teacher*—Here's to the teacher, the noblest work of all. He would rather starve than give up his career, and often he almost does. He doesn't get much reward in life so let's at least be generous in our praise.

FAMILY

331. *To Mother*—Here's to Mother and mother love, which cannot be borrowed nor can it be bought. Mother love is given free and it is the greatest and most enduring gift in the world.

332. *To Father*—Here's to Father, a kindly and lovable chap. We call him the head of the family, but this designation is used only to make sure who is to get the family headaches.

333. *To My Wife*—Here's to my wife, a beautiful and charming lady. She swept me off my feet before marriage and has kept me on them ever since we were hitched.

334. *To My Husband*—Here's to the most important man in my life. He can always be a Mr., but without him I could never be a Mrs.

335. *To a Sister*—Here's to my sister, the greatest blessing of mankind. She provided me with companionship, someone to play with and someone to fight with. Now I find in her someone to love and admire.

336. ***To My Brother***—Here's to my brother who—when he was young—was the sap of the family tree. Now he is a peach!

HOLIDAYS

337. ***New Year***—New Year is a time of joy when we forget the past and look forward to the future. May the New Year fill your life with gladness and every day be bright and cheerful.

338. ***Abraham Lincoln***—We honor Abraham Lincoln on his birthday for many things. However, one thing always stands out above all others and that was his example of living life according to the best policy. What is the best policy? Everybody knows that honesty is the best policy.

339. ***St. Valentine***—St. Valentine's Day is a day for romance and sweethearts. There is a difference between love and sentiment, but St. Valentine made it possible for everyone to be sentimental.

340. ***George Washington***—George Washington's birthday is a time to remember this great man for his many accomplishments and invaluable service to our republic when it was founded. He died as a hero and lived on as a legend.

341. ***St. Patrick***—Here's to St. Patrick, who brought Christianity to the Emerald Isle. He drove out the snakes. He created a glorious past for Ireland and he promises a marvelous future for the Irish.

342. ***Flag Day***—Here's to the flag of the United States and the fifty stars of the states. Old Glory has been tested in the fire of many battles since Valley Forge and Yorktown. It remains today, as it was at its first creation, a symbol of everything that people of the world want but few have the opportunity to enjoy—freedom, democracy and the pursuit of happiness.

343. *Independence Day*—I offer this Fourth of July toast to our nation in the words of Thomas Jefferson: "Freedom of religion, freedom of the press and freedom of person under the protection of the habeas corpus, these are the principles that have guided our steps through an age of revolution and reformation."

344. *Labor Day*—Here's a toast to the men and women who keep the wheels of industry humming in our nation. Our slaves are the machines which we have created to do our work, and the men and women who operate those machines are the masters.

345. *Thanksgiving*—We toast our country on this typical American holiday of Thanksgiving. How times have changed in a few hundred years. This country which once had the least to offer its inhabitants now has the most. To the Pilgrims, America was a land of freedom and little else. To our people today, America is a land of freedom and everything else.

346. *Christmas*—A toast to Christmas—the happiest and most cheerful season of the year. Christmas is a season rather than a day. It has become a spirit which touches all people. Christmas is different from all other religious, patriotic or social holidays because it reflects a spirit of fellowship and generosity which gives mankind a new outlook on life and a keener appreciation of his family, friends and just anybody he happens to meet at this time. Merry Christmas to any and all who may be listening!

5
The Emcee

THE master of ceremonies or, as he is generally called, the emcee, is a comparatively recent development in our social entertaining ways. The emcee as we know him today is in reality a combination of the toastmaster and the program chairman. The term "emcee" comes from an abbreviation of M.C. for master of ceremonies.

The toastmaster is a humorous and a very talented entertainer, who not only has the duty of introducing the speakers on the program but also contributes a major share to the evening's fun. The program chairman is the fellow completely lacking in any of these qualities. He is not an entertainer and has no special gift or qualifications for humor. He has done all the work of arranging the program and getting it together in proper form. He has had the responsibility of making sure that the speakers or other persons who will be on the program will make an appearance and understand what they are supposed to do and how much time they have been allotted. Because he knows better than anyone else how the program should go and also as a reward for all of his hard work and unpaid efforts, he is asked to play an important part at the banquets or dinner meetings and announce those who are to appear on the program. The program chairman who has a glib tongue and a gracious manner, with some command of humor and the ability to tell a joke well, is elevated one step higher than program chairman and is given the title of emcee. Thus we see the emcee ranks one step above the program chairman and one step below the toastmaster. He is a combination of the two, and may possess in unequal measure some of the traits of both.

The emcee plays a role in the field of entertainment which is contrary to all the old, established rules of comedy. Action was always regarded as the fundamental ingredient for a good comic. A person should wear a costume, jump around or do something perfectly ridiculous in order to add to the humorous effect. Old-time stage comedians were amazed to discover that Groucho Marx could sit on a stool and be funny, that Jack Benny could just stand there and look at the audience and get laughs, and that Perry Como could take charge of an entire entertainment as master of ceremonies while in an apparent state of suspended animation.

The responsibilities and tasks of the emcee are relatively simple as compared with that of the toastmaster. He can be funny if he has a nature and personality which lends itself to humor, or he can be the quiet, gracious and courteous type. If he is funny, he can get by almost entirely with the gag, which is regarded by some as the lowest form of humor with the possible exception of the pun. He can even use the pun and get away with it.

The main thing for a good emcee is to keep the program moving at a fairly good pace and show consideration for those who are to appear on the program and for the others who have gathered to be entertained. If someone gets mixed up, makes a mistake or a wrong move, it should be corrected discreetly so that no one is ever humiliated or offended. The emcee should be liberal in his praise and not attach to his compliments the same value that Walter Winchell gives to his famous orchids. Walter Winchell can hand out an orchid to some young performer or an unappreciated old-timer and cause a miracle to happen. An orchid from him is frequently regarded as a ticket to fame and fortune. Winchell doesn't give these orchids out easily or very often. The orchids tossed about by the emcee are like valueless confetti thrown into the wind to provide color and gaiety but have little meaning beyond this.

One of the most difficult jobs that the emcee is required to do is to keep the speakers and others on the program within the limit of their allotted time. This is a problem which goes back to ancient history. As long as there have been orators and speakers, mankind has always been presented with the problem of getting them to shut up. The ancient Greeks and Romans used a clepsydra to limit speeches. This device measured time by the flow of water much like an hourglass operates with sand. Other methods have been tried. One of these has been to require that the speaker stand on one foot all of the time that he is talking, and the second that the other foot should touch the ground he would be through.

Somewhat similar to this was a method for placing a limit on the length of speeches by taxing the endurance of the speaker by means of ice. The speaker would be required to hold in his hand a large piece of ice while he was talking, and the second that he dropped the ice he was forced to halt his remarks. The modern emcee does not resort to such methods and devices, but he must use a great deal of tact and depend upon diplomatic suggestion and courteous action to keep the program within the bounds of the prescribed time limit.

347.   Ed Wynn has the distinction of being the first emcee in the United States. It all began back in the year 1913 when Ed Wynn was playing the Palace Theater in New York City. The part of the stage in front of the curtain is a decorative arch called the proscenium. At one side of the proscenium arch, it was the custom in vaudeville days to have a sign which would announce the next act. The Palace had a newly installed electric board that would be illuminated with lights.

On the opening bill, the lights for the electric sign failed to work, and Ed Wynn, being the only American on the opening bill, was asked to announce the acts in the order of their appearance. The idea went over so well that he was requested to continue with this job after the lights were fixed. At that time he was called a co-ordinator of acts. He developed the technique used today by the average emcee of preparing a little joke suitable to introduce each act. Later, he would not only introduce each act, but on occasions he would take a part in each act that was presented and held the center of interest throughout the entire show. He created the role of the modern emcee which is the glue that holds all the parts together.

THE EMCEE AND AFTER DINNER SPEAKING

348. *Tact*—It is an art to say the right thing graciously at the right time, like the young man who was telling his dancing partner at the night club, "Waltz a little faster, dear. This is a rhumba."

349. *Pioneer*—Our entertainer was a pioneer on TV. He was one of the first to be turned off.

350. *Money Doesn't Count*—It's not his money. People just hate him for himself alone.

351. *Loose Tongues*—The difference between our program for this evening and a cocktail party is that here everybody speaks too much BEFORE they have had anything to drink.

352. *Rundown Places*—This isn't much of a place. In fact, the fellow who runs it, whenever he doesn't feel well he dashes outside. He wouldn't want to be caught dead in here.

353. *Mansion*—What a place this is. On a clear day you can see the ceiling!

354. *Having Fun*—Let's be like the monkeys. Monkeys have a wonderful spirit of fun. Monkeys have such a good time because there are so many of them, and there's so many of them because they have such a good time.

355. *Unimportant Position*—I am your Chairman of the Entertainment Committee. Actually, this isn't much of a job. I realized this when I heard a noted authority on marriage give this advice to women: "A smart wife is one who makes her husband feel as though he's head of the house, when actually he's ONLY chairman of the entertainment committee."

356. *Singing Practice*—You wouldn't believe it, but I have a beautiful voice. But it always comes out ugly. I developed my voice singing in the bathtub. Maybe I should take more baths.

357. *Singer*—That was a beautiful song, but—eh!—what of it! If I had his voice I could sing just as good as he does.

358. *Prayer*—Inasmuch as our time for speeches is very limited, we can be guided by the prayer uttered by George Eliot, "Blessed is the man who, having nothing to say, abstains from giving us wordy evidence of the fact."

359. *Favorite Audience*—Among our favorite folks are those who forget the jokes. They laugh when first the joke is told, and laugh again when it is old.

360. *Cold Audience*—When I look over all the long faces in our audience and the coldness which seems to prevail I can say that we belong up with the Eskimos, about whom one youngster wrote in school, "The Eskimos are God's frozen people."

361. *Windbag*—Almost every day we see some evidence of great advances made in our country. For instance, even at this meeting tonight we have such evidence.

Let us go back to the day when Cornell University was founded. One of its founders and its first president was Andrew D. White. Those were the days when football was played as a student activity rather than a college spectacular. The story is told that President White was asked to give his permission to send the Cornell football squad to Ann Arbor for a game. The university president resented this request very much and replied in anger, "I will not permit thirty men to travel four hundred miles to agitate a bag of wind." Now we can see how times have changed. The bag of wind has traveled here to agitate us. Of course, I refer to our speaker for this evening.

362. *Silence Is Golden*—Before we begin our program for this evening, I would like to relate a little story especially for the benefit of our speakers.

The story concerns a lion which was making his way through the jungle, when suddenly it came upon a herd of bulls. The lion sprang upon one of the bulls and killed it while the others ran away. He ate the beast at his leisure. After the lion had finished his feast, he felt so good that he roared and roared. The noise of the lion's roar was eventually heard by a hunter who approached with his gun. He came into view of the roaring lion, raised his gun and shot the lion dead. The moral of this little story is: When you are full of bull, keep your mouth shut.

363. *A Wonderful Time*—Let's be happy—like the young fellow who was beginning a career as a clergyman. After he served sufficient time he was permitted time off for a Sabbatical year. His little brother was telling some friends about it and said that the preacher was off to enjoy his Bacchanalian year.

364.   Faint Praise—I don't want to hear any complaints tonight. Regarding the food, I'll say to you the same as the youngster who was sent away to camp. The parents finally received a note from their nine-year-old camper which read: "Dear Mom and Pop: The food here is wonderful, and they don't make you eat it. Love, Mike."

365.   Bore—I want to warn the speakers that we treat all men alike. They say that a clever man keeps his mouth shut and listens intently when a bore is speaking, especially if the bore is rich. We're not so clever or courteous . . . so don't be a bore!

366.   Unprofitable—This may not be a very profitable evening for all of you, but then you can be like the farmer who paid three dollars for a pig and spent five dollars more on feed for it until it became a hog and sold it for eight dollars. He didn't make any money, but he had the company of the pig all summer.

367.   Humorous Entertainment—For the benefit of our speakers, I wish to say that we have a very good audience for them here tonight. This is the kind of audience that had gathered in a college auditorium filled with students and a few faculty members. There was a well-known entertainer supposed to be present and deliver a humorous address. However, it was getting late, long past the time when the entertainer should be there, and he was not yet present.

The chairman of the meeting noticed that the audience was getting restless and some were starting to leave. In an effort to hold them he called upon one of the professors to come forward and start the entertainment. The professor got up on the stage and began his remarks with this statement, "Your chairman has asked me to come up here and say something funny."

From the rear of the auditorium a loud voice piped up, "You will tell us when you say it, won't you?"

The professor looked in the direction from which came the heckler's voice and answered back, "I will tell you! The rest will know."

I am sure everyone here will know when any of the speakers says something funny, and I am sure they will show their appreciation in the usual way in which we respond to humor and good entertainment.

368. Conversation—Television hasn't done much for speakers, but it has improved conversation. There is much less of it.

369. Cold Audience—(When seeking applause.) Thank you for that wonderful burst of silence.

370. Miracle—In the old Biblical days it was regarded as a miracle if an ass spoke. Times sure have changed!

371. Uninspired—After listening to what is being said around here, I am forced to conclude even though Samson once finished a whole war with the jawbone of an ass, that weapon is no longer as potent as it was in Biblical times.

372. Popular Songs—The most popular thing about most popular songs is that they can't last too long.

373. Foolish—Anatole France said that if fifty million people say a foolish thing, it is still a foolish thing. In this case, only one person is saying a foolish thing so it is a very, very foolish thing.

374.   *Laughter*—Enjoy yourself. Remember, he who laughs—lasts!

375.   *Not Appreciated*—That speaker sure has a good line. Too bad he didn't hang himself with it!

376.   *Happy Ending*—Well, our program is all over for the evening. I won't ask you whether you enjoyed it—like the mother who asked her young daughter when she returned from the movies whether the picture had a happy ending. "It did for me," responded the girl. "I was glad it was over."

377.   *Advice to Speakers*—Before we begin our program I would like to give this brief advice to our speakers. In making your speech, when you are finished it is a good idea to stop talking.

378.   *Unsuccessful*—That went over like a pregnant woman on a pole vault.

379.   *Mixed Audience*—Ladies and gentlemen, and those in between . . .

380.   *Single-Track Mind*—I want to thank our speaker for his talk and for proving to us once and for all that there is nothing wrong with having a one-track mind—provided you are on the right track.

381.   *Hot Speech*—Our speaker certainly is hot on his subject. However, we must remember we can't have light without heat, and if our speaker seemed to grow overheated somewhat during his talk we must remember he was furnishing us a great deal of light.

SPEECH STARTERS

382. *Apology*—Unaccustomed as I am to public speaking, I still do it.

383. *Build-up*—After such a terrific build-up by the chairman, I can hardly wait to hear what I have to say.

384. *Shortest Introduction*—The most complimentary introduction ever given anyone is accorded the President of our country. When he is introduced it is with these words: "Ladies and gentlemen, the President of the United States." Lesser lights take longer to introduce. You can tell how far down I rate by how long it took the chairman to introduce me.

385. *Humility*—I wish my wife and family were here to listen to the glowing words of flattery bestowed upon me. They are not equally well impressed. In fact, their attitude toward me reminds me of the anecdote told by Senator Frank Lausche about himself when he was Governor of Ohio. As he was crossing a park in front of the State House, he noticed a mother with a camera and a little boy. He stopped to talk to them and then suggested, "Would you like to take a picture of me with your son?"

The mother replied, "I am sorry, sir. I have only one film left and I want to take a picture of the squirrels."

386. *No Improvement*—That beautiful introduction was really a capital joke. Did you ever hear the story about the little boy who came up to a visitor in the house and told her, "My, how ugly you are!" When his horrified mother scolded him the boy said, "I only meant it as a joke." The mother tried to smooth over matters before the visitor and told the boy, "How much better the joke would have been if you had told Mrs. Smith how pretty she is." That is why I say it was really a good joke when the chairman told all of those nice things about me.

387.   Unusual Woman—I always enjoy very much the remarks of the program chairman when I am introduced. It is like the case of the henpecked husband who always went to a woman dentist. It made him happy to have a woman tell him to open his mouth instead of shut it.

388.   Captive Audience—One reason I like public speaking is because of the advantage you have over your listeners. It's like the case of the pretty young girl who wanted to get a job as a stewardess on a plane so she could meet lots of men. A friend told her, "There are lots of jobs besides stewardess where you get a chance to meet men."

"Yeah," replied this girl, "but not where the men are strapped down."

389.   Stage Fright—Have you ever stopped to think what a wonderful thing the human brain is? It never ceases working for you from the time you are born until the moment you stand up to make a speech.

390.   Unexpected Speech—I don't know what I'm doing up here, since I came to this gathering as spectator and not a speaker. I'm like the little boy who fell into the lake during a picnic. As he was being pulled out of the water he was asked, "How in the world did you happen to fall into the lake?"

The explanation was simple enough. The boy said, "I was looking in the water, when all of a sudden I heard a kerplunk —and it was me!"

The same goes for me. I was just watching and all of a

sudden here I am up to my neck in the lake and expected to make a speech.

391. *Liar*—I wish I could say the same kind of praise and tribute to our chairman as he has said about me. Unfortunately, I can't. I'm not as big a liar as he is!

392. *Unfamiliar Species*—I don't know whether to take the remarks of the chairman as a compliment or an insult. They sound to me like the note written by a school boy to a government extension worker, who visited the school and spoke to the students at great length about the dangers of rats and rat infestation. This particular youngster was so impressed that he wrote the lecturer a note and said, "We never even knew what a rat looked like until you came here."

393. *Good Script*—What I need to make a successful speech is the kind of help that is given a noted wild West hero who is seen regularly on television. He exists for weeks in the wild woods with only a knife as a weapon; he fights almost bare-handed against wild animals; and escapes from Indians. He always outshoots and outfights his enemy. One day he was asked what was his secret of success. How did he manage at the last minute in every dangerous situation to escape with his life.

The hero of television thought it over for a minute and replied, "Good writers."

394. *Too Flowery*—I feel like a pancake that has just had sirup poured on it.

395. *Before and After*—Those were very complimentary remarks I heard about myself before I started this speech. I wonder what they will be saying after I am through. It may be like the husband who comes home late at night. First his wife asks him where he's been, and then she tells him where to go.

396. Flattery—That was a very beautiful and flattering introduction which I received. It's like the thousand dollars a man paid for a very rare dog which was part schnauzer and part bull. A friend asked him what part was bull and he answered, "The part about the thousand dollars."

397. Vital Subject—This is one speaking assignment I have looked forward to for a long time because I feel sure all of you are interested in what I have to say. I'm not repressed and discouraged like the millionaire inventor of rat poison. He and his wife had just come into their fortune as a result of his new rat poison invention and were undertaking to break into society. They gave an elaborate dinner party. All through the dinner, the husband was silent and completely reserved. As they were leaving the table, the wife found an opportunity to snarl at him, "What's the matter with you tonight? Why don't you talk?"

The millionaire husband shrugged his shoulders in disgust and snapped back, "Aw, what's the use of talking? Nobody here knows anything about rats!"

Well, there is a use of me talking because all of you are familiar with the subject and I hope you will enjoy hearing me talk about it.

398. Small Town—In our town we are all good friends, have known each other for a long time and often things are pretty well set and settled for us. Changes don't come about as often as in a little West Virginia town. A stranger happened to be in this little town and he was asking a native about it. During the conversation, the stranger remarked, "Nice little town you've got here. How big is your town?"

The native replied, "Oh, the population never changes

much. Every time a new baby is born, one of the men leaves town."

399. *Nonplused*—That was a most delightful introduction. Certainly it was nothing like the remark made by a young bride to her husband when they started for a party to meet some of their friends. "Henry," she said, "if anybody asks me what I see in you, what shall I say?"

400. **Too Much Praise**—I haven't had so much praise since I could remember. In fact, the compliments of the chairman reminds me of the interview of a young reporter with the widow of a man who had just died. The grieving widow called the newspaper and asked them to send out a reporter to get the details about her husband for an obituary. When the reporter arrived the widow told him all about her husband's charity, his love for and devotion to his family, his varied services for the community, his support of the church and the like.

Finally the reporter broke away and returned to the newspaper office. His editor asked him, "What mortuary will conduct the funeral?"

"I don't know," the reporter admitted, "but I think he will probably go direct."

401. **Taken with Salt**—I certainly feel greatly inspired by the words of praise which I have just heard. With all due respect to the sincerity of those who have uttered them, I cannot help but recall a little story I heard not so long ago which makes me take with a grain of salt any flattery or compliments which may come my way. The story concerns a man who went to Arizona from Los Angeles for his health.

They brought his corpse back to Los Angeles and his wife and her brothers were viewing the remains. She said, "Oh,

Joe, doesn't he look nice?" And Joe replied, "He sure does. Those two months in Arizona did him a lot of good."

402.   Not Serious—I love flattering introductions. Flattering introductions are like smoking. They don't hurt you if you don't inhale.

403.   Help from Above—I am very happy to have this opportunity to speak to you. While I can't promise too much as your speaker, at least I can begin my remarks with a clear conscience, like the young fellow who was taking an examination at a school where they had the honor system. When they had finished with their work, each student was asked to sign a statement that he had neither given nor received any help during the examination. This particular student was troubled and did not know whether to sign or not. He took his paper up to his teacher and explained that during the course of the examination he had prayed for help, but he was not sure whether he had received it or not. The teacher took his paper, looked it over briefly, handed it back and said, "I think you can sign."

I, too, have prayed for help in meeting this speech assignment, but I am not sure whether I got it or not.

404.   Build-up Through Bribery—There is a lot of cherry-tree honesty in me. I wish I could take that nice parade of kind words seriously. But the truth is this: The truth is that the tuxedo suit the chairman is wearing is actually mine. And when the chairman offered to rent it from me, I said, "My friend, I do not need your filthy lucre! Instead of money give me a neat little build-up. You see, my wife will be there and I'd like her to hear it."

I admit that is a pretty sneaky way to get a verbal bouquet. But I'm just low-down enough to think up just such schemes, for often a fellow gets starved for praise. You know that. I've even tipped a newsboy a nickel so I could feel a very filmy halo arise from my noble head—for a brief but glorious moment. So don't let that build-up frighten you. The chairman and I understand each other. And sometime when I'm not present he'll confess our scheme about the tux—and the big bouquet. And meantime I thank him for a very neat job indeed.

405. Fed Up—I am glad that you are so anxious to hear my remarks. I appreciate the introduction of your chairman and your enthusiastic response. Nevertheless, I shall be careful not to take advantage of your interest and good nature.

I think every speaker should take heed from a situation similar to that described by a school child when he was asked to write an essay on why he liked TV. The young man wrote his essay as follows: "I like TV because I do not have one. When you have one, you get fed up with it."

In the same way, an audience gets fed up with a speaker very soon, and it is wise not to overstay the limits which mark the end of enjoyment and the beginning of boredom.

406. Home Run—After listening to that flattering introduction I realize how lucky I am. Everybody notices the good things about me. Just think how terrible it would be if my errors were tabulated and published like a ballplayer!

407. Main Event—I am always a little bit wary about being introduced as the main speaker of the evening. It makes me think of a boxing match or a wedding, where the preliminaries are often more entertaining than the main event.

408. Too Good to Be True—I want to thank the chairman for his flattering introduction. I admit that I like flattery.

Flattery, you know, is something nice someone says about you and you wish it were true.

409.   Tender Words—I always start a speech with a prayer, "Oh, Lord, let my words be tender and sweet, for tomorrow I may have to eat them."

410.   End of the Talk—It is certainly nice to hear those flattering remarks. At least, it is better than what happened to one speaker after he finished his talk. A woman came up to him and asked, "Did anyone ever tell you what a great speaker you are?"

"No," this fellow replied.

"Then," said the woman, "what ever gave you the idea?"

411.   Good Shot—Those were very flattering remarks concerning me made by your chairman, but I am an old skeptic who feels the audience usually thinks differently. The audience's viewpoint is generally more like that of a sign which was displayed near the speakers' platform at a convention.

The sign was placed near the speakers' platform for the benefit of the newspaper photographers. The sign read: "Do not photograph the speakers while they are addressing the audience. Shoot them as they approach the platform."

412.   Nothing to Say—I appreciate being called upon and the opportunity given to me to speak, but I admit that I am like the fourth student. It was Monday morning and the professor was calling upon the students to see how many had completed the assignment over the weekend.

The professor called on the first student and the first student said, "I didn't know what the assignment was for our lesson, so I did not read it."

The professor called on the second student who said, "I

misunderstood the assignment and read what I thought was the assignment, but it was incorrect."

The professor then called upon a third student to answer a question taken from the assignment, but this student replied, "I read the assignment, but this particular question is one that I just couldn't find an answer to."

Finally, the professor called on the fourth student and this student said, "I don't believe I can add to anything that has already been said."

413. *Silence*—I wish to warn you at the beginning that I am not much of a speaker. For one thing, I never know what to do with my hands when I am up here giving a talk. I mentioned this problem of my hands to a friend who had heard me give a number of talks, and he suggested, "Why don't you just hold them over your mouth?"

414. *Psychiatrist*—It is nice to be able to stand up and be here for this speech. The last time I was called upon to speak it was before a group of psychiatrists. The chairman asked me to lie down and say a few words.

415. *Borrowed*—What I have to say, I will say in a few APPROPRIATED words.

416. *Stump Speaker*—I don't know where they got the expression about a stump speaker. All I know is that every time I get up to speak I find myself out on a limb.

417. *Brief Talk*—I'm sorry but my remarks must be especially brief. You see, my wife has me on an allowance—five hundred words a day.

418. *Compulsive Speaker*—With me, speaking is like marriage to a beautiful, young girl. These girls usually marry at an early urge.

419.   *Intelligent Luggage*—That was a wonderful introduction which I received and I am almost tempted to believe what has been said. Somehow I look upon chairmen who must introduce speakers and drugstore scales which give you a fortune with your weight as on the same par. I feel that way ever since a friend of mine who was going on an airplane flight wanted to know how much luggage he was going to carry, so he took his packed suitcase down to the corner drugstore and put it on the scale. He put the suitcase on the scale and dropped a penny in the slot. Out came a card which read: "You weigh seventy pounds. You possess a keen mind, and your good judgment often helps you in solving problems of others."

420.   *Open Mind*—I don't have too much to say because I have always believed that what this world needs are more open minds and fewer open mouths.

421.   *Empty*—I came here tonight empty-handed with a head to match.

422.   *Great Expectations*—I do not like introductions such as I have just received. It puts me in the same position as the big, fat fellow at the banquet. After all the courses had been eaten the big fellow seemed to be in discomfort and suddenly he belched. The woman sitting next to him gave him a horrified look. The man looked back at her just as disdainfully and exclaimed, "What did you expect—chimes?"

423.   *Who's He*—I wonder if the chairman was talking about me. Sounds like he's been playing that new contest they have on TV. They give the contestant a bottle of whiskey. After he drinks the whiskey the contest starts. He has to guess who he is. The chairman's flattering remarks make me wonder if it is really me he is talking about.

424. *Same Country*—I feel that I am in strange surroundings here, but I am as hopeful for your kind reception as the young fellow from Georgia who joined the Army. At camp he was sent through the routine and found himself in the office of a dentist. He had never before been to a modern dentist's office and was terrified by the instruments and equipment he saw there.

"Wheah you all from?" the young recruit asked the dentist, trying to delay the start of operations.

"I'm from Massachusetts," the dentist replied with a friendly smile.

The young recruit from Georgia was able to hide his dismay and replied cheerfully, "Ah'm a Yankee, too."

425. *Full Up*—That reminds me of an introduction a chairman once gave for a speaker who was connected with the Soils and Fertilizer Department. The chairman said, "Our next speaker is connected with the Soils and Fertilizer Department. His talk should convince all of you that he is just full of his subject."

426. *Mutual Pleasure*—This opportunity to come before you and deliver a talk is a pleasure that is mine. However, I hope it will not be my pleasure entirely.

427. *Big Wheel*—That very flattering introduction makes me feel like a big wheel. It is nice for a man to be someplace where he can feel like a big wheel. Most men who think they are big wheels when they are out are just flat tires at home.

428. *Condensed*—My remarks will be like the milk you get in cans—condensed.

SPEECH STOPPERS

429.   Sound Advice—I had prepared a great deal more material for my speech and have much more I can talk about, but I feel the time has arrived for me to conclude my remarks and follow the old advice often given speakers—to avoid trouble and insure safety, breathe through your nose. It keeps the mouth shut.

430.   Traps—This is a good time for me to recall a story that happened on a golf course and follow the advice given. One golfer said to the other, "The traps on this course are very annoying, aren't they?"

The other golfer, who was trying to putt, replied, "Yes, they are. Would you mind closing yours?"

431.   Too Much of a Good Thing—Speeches and money are different in many ways. For instance, most people make good money but not enough of it. The average speaker makes a good speech but too much of it, so I think this is a good place to stop.

432.   Enough Said—I had a lot more to say but I keep thinking of a silent prayer which an elderly preacher always used to say before he began a sermon. "Lord, fill my mouth with worthwhile stuff and nudge me when I've said enough."

433.   Safety Play. I hope you forgive me if I cut my remarks short. I believe in the advice which a mama whale gave to her baby whale. Mama whale said, "Only when you're spouting are you likely to be harpooned."

434.   Anesthetic—I hope my speech hasn't seemed as endless as that of the politician who was orating like this, "I want land reform; I want housing reform; I want educational reform; I want political reform; I want—"

"Chloroform," came a loud voice from the audience.

435. When to Stop—I may not be the best speaker but I get along all right because I know one thing—the same as John Smith who walked into a bar with a friend for a drink. This John Smith took four straight shots of whiskey and promptly fell flat on his face on the floor. The friend looked over at the bartender and remarked, "That's what I like about John. He knows when to stop!" That's me, too. I know when to stop.

436. Only Speaker—It is always a special privilege to be the only speaker at a meeting. I can leave my audience with this happy thought: It's never so bleak that it can't be bleaker. There might have been a second speaker.

437. Coming Back—Now the complete truth is this, my gracious audience: Few of us have enough forensic terminal facilities to come to the very end—to arrive—to get through, if you want it in blunt American speech.

Yet in my heart there is a real desire to make you know and feel that I have appreciated your attention. For it is not easy to listen for any length of time to an ordinary sort of guy like me. But, say, weren't you the polite bunch, though! You made me feel the little time I was before you that I was worth listening to. That flattered my ego. And I'll leave this room feeling rather inflated.

One great newscaster leaves his radio audience with the very familiar, "so long!" Well, I'll punish you not with "So Long" but with the hope that it will not be so long before I get the chance to say all I know before you again!

438. Sure-fire Bet—Nobody has yet devised a perfect system for stopping speakers on time—at least, not as workable as the sure-fire method one fellow discovered to stop a runaway horse. Put two dollars on it!

439. *A Hit*—I am sure that my speech has made a tremendous hit with you, and this is a good place for me to stop while I'm ahead. You see, speeches these days are like phonograph records. It is no longer possible to make a hit record just by being different or singing badly. These days you have to be awful! On the same basis of judging speeches, I think my speech should be a hit so I'll end it now.

440. *Overtime*—I see I have been speaking much longer than I expected—or you expected. Taking up this extra time puts me in the same class as the product which was being advertised on the radio and the announcer shouted, "This product sells not for seventy-five cents, not for fifty cents, not for twenty-five cents . . . but for one dollar!"

441. *Speed-up*—I see the chairman is giving me the yellow light and I know exactly what it means. I'm like the young fellow who was learning to drive an automobile and his instructor asked him if he knew what it meant when the traffic light showed yellow. The young fellow answered, "The green light means go. The red light means stop and the yellow light means go like hell."

I've got the yellow light and I will try to go like hell and finish up my remarks.

442. *Optimist*—I'm going to let all of you be optimists. An optimist is described as a fellow who puts his shoes back on when the speaker says, "And, now, in conclusion."

443. *Short and to the Point*—I am not a bit frightened about getting up before an audience and making a speech, but often I wish I could be like the soldier when the enemy charged.

He was telling his family about it later when he got out of service. "I wasn't frightened," he said, "but I passed a lot of guys who were." If you fear a long speech, I'll reassure you now.

444. *Couldn't Last*—I think I had better end my speech. For me to be with you and meet you has been a wonderful experience and a great pleasure, but then you may be like the fellow who was telling about his marriage. He said, "For twenty years my wife and I were indescribably happy—and then we met!"

445. *Another Channel*—It is nice to go somewhere and be appreciated. I can't help thinking of the time I was asked to deliver a speech broadcast by TV. The next day a neighbor asked my young son, "Did you listen to your father on TV?" My boy replied truthfully, "Naw, I don't even listen to him at home."

446. *Finished*—Well, I am frankly exhausted after delivering this speech. I am now what you can call a finished speaker.

6
Humor for Toastmasters

ONE of the most difficult things to do is try to analyze a joke and determine why it gets a laugh. We know that different people will laugh at different things, but we do not know why laughter itself became a human trait and what accounts for it.

Trying to analyze a joke or a laugh is like trying to analyze the Stock Market. Suddenly, prices will go up, or there will be a big crash on the Stock Market. Immediately, all the experts offer intelligent and logical reasons to explain the sudden and unexpected action of the stocks. While these explanations seem logical, it is strange that nobody could think of them in advance and anticipate what course the Stock Market would take in the immediate future. In the same way, experts can explain why a certain joke got a big laugh, but they cannot always predict how well any bit of original humor may go over with an audience. Audiences will differ and their reactions are not always the same.

Many professional gag and joke writers follow the technique of the detective story writer who starts with a solution to a crime, and then works backwards till the very beginning when the crime itself is committed. These professional humorists are always keeping themselves under observation. Every time they laugh, they try to think back and analyze all the circumstances leading up to the laugh, in order to determine what caused it and how it might be repeated. Gags and jokes are created through hard work rather than inspiration. A person must be an expert in the use of words to find the exact word to convey the meaning desired. These should be words that may be spoken or read aloud without creating any confusion or misunderstanding. They should be words that are easy to pronounce and could not create the difficulties of a tongue-twister. The gag must come directly to the point and be centered around one idea only, eliminating all elements or distractions which would use unnecessary words and confuse the issue. The laugh itself has been described as an emotion that was carefully built up to a certain pitch and then released suddenly to create surprise. Certain subjects lend themselves easily to jokes and gags, such as the mother-in-law joke and the precocious child. Gag writers say that one sure-fire subject for their brand of humor is lampooning dignitaries. When you make fun of somebody really important, particularly if he is dignified and somewhat pompous, it is sure to get the nod of approval from most audiences. Almost as dependable for the humor writer is any joke in which wives get the worst of it.

Every experienced comedian knows that there is a difference between funny acting and acting funny. There are many types of comedy which begin with the physical comedy or action. These are body and face comics who must be seen to be appreciated. They use their bodies and faces in strange contortions and wear outlandish clothes and costumes to amuse those who observe them. The lowest form of this type of humor is the fellow who gets it in the face with a custard pie or does a pratt fall to get a laugh. A good example of physical comedy would be the burlesques of Al Schacht and Nick Altrock when they cut comic capers on the baseball field to amuse the fans. The highest form of physical comedy is the pantomime, such as presented by one of the most talented performers in this field—Jimmy Savo. His presentation is that of a silent comedian who by his action alone could convulse any audience.

Physical comedy represents the beginning of humor. When certain familiar objects or gadgets are added, then we have another type of humor that strives for a laugh through the means of physical comedy and a ridiculous device. Ed Wynn, carrying a telephone in his pocket, is a good example of this. A development or refinement of the gadget comedy is the situation humor. In a situation comedy, the comedian becomes involved in some situation which makes him look ridiculous and has the audience laughing at him as a result of an imaginative condition, just as they would laugh if he should trip on the stage and fall flat on his face.

When comedy begins to get out of the realm of the physical and into the realm of the imaginative or intellectual, we have the pun and the gag. Both of these are considered low forms of intellectual humor. The pun has a bad reputation and is usually greeted with a groan by those who hear it rather than a laugh. The gag is the sharp and pointed one-line condensation of a humorous observation, an expression of a personal viewpoint, wit, wisdom or philosophy used effectively by humorists such as Bob Hope, George Jessel and Milton Berle. Gags are usually supplied by writers working from a comprehensive card index of jokes. A joke can be distilled down to get the essence and this is the gag. A gag is a joke in a nutshell. Usually, the most effective gags are those which ridicule well-known people or fellow performers on the same program. Since gags are generally ironic and sardonic by nature, they create no real affection for the humorist who depends chiefly upon them. Comedians like Bob Hope win the affection of the audience not by their gag routines, but through the characterizations they play in the skits and sketches which are part of the entertainment.

One of the highest forms of comedy is the creation of a humorous character, such as Jimmy Durante, W. C. Fields or

Bert Lahr. Jack Benny's perennial popularity has been possible because he built for himself a humorous character exemplified in the role of a miserly individual who always comes out second best in everything he undertakes. Jack Benny can build a routine around something that in itself is funny, such as his violin, his vault where he keeps his money and an old auto.

The most successful comedians have always been the common man's common man. The fellow who tells jokes well and can entertain others is usually a man of the streets. Most successful stage comedians have been fellows who had a tough time in their early years. As children they were born into poverty and had little opportunity for education and culture. People of good breeding are supposed to learn how to subdue their emotions and humors. A polished gentleman will smile but not laugh loudly. For this reason, the common man is more easily given to humor, and low characters on the stage—those which appear in tattered clothes and speak in slang and uncultured tones and dialect—usually excite more laughter than the fellow in a business suit. The person who wants to entertain by means of humor in speaking should never lose the common touch.

Professional comedians have many advantages over the amateur humorist and parlor wit. For one thing, they have an established reputation as a comic, and people go to some trouble and pay money to watch their performance. For this reason, the audience is prepared to laugh and is in a suitable, receptive mood for the offering of the humorist. The professional, to make sure that the audience is in a susceptible mood, will often plant in the audience shills or stooges to lead the laughter.

A funny man like Dick Collier could assure the success of any humorous entertainment. Laughs are infectious and contagious. Dick Collier makes his living just by laughing. He has a repertoire of some two hundred varieties of laughs.

Another advantage of the professional humorist is that he need not say things which are in themselves funny. He can depend upon his talents for mimicry and his reputation for being funny to get by. For instance, Al Kelly never says anything which in itself is funny, but he creates howls of laughter with his double talk. Al Kelly begins to rattle off his strange sounds, which seem as though they should mean something interesting and worthwhile. The mumbo jumbo of gibberish is completely unintelligible, but somehow it strikes one as being funny. The professional humorist has another decided advantage over the amateur entertainer and parlor wit. The professional can heckle the audience and challenge them to laugh. Furthermore, the professional is at liberty to turn the tables and get the audience to laugh at him for being such a fool and trying to palm off such bad jokes.

When telling a joke, make it as short as possible and try to remember the exact words and the continuity of the story. Every word counts, and the sequence of narration must follow in proper order to lead up to the punch line. Don't talk too fast. When telling a story, it is best to go slowly so that everyone catches each word and inflection. Make good use of the pause while speaking. Experienced humorists frequently pause, look around the room, take a breath and then begin to speak once more. Do not be afraid of the pause. It is not necessary to keep speaking continuously. There are times when a short silence can be more eloquent than words. Listen to the other speakers so that you will not use a joke which they may have included in their talk. Never read a speech, especially a joke, from a manuscript. Never—but never—introduce a funny story by saying, "This reminds me of a joke I once heard—" Never use a dirty story or say anything, even to get a laugh, that will offend anyone present in the audience.

Experienced humorists and all professional comedians understand the meaning of timing when telling a joke. Timing is the rate of delivery and determines when a person should speak a line or merely pause and say nothing at all. The comedian who understands the use of timing knows exactly when to say a line, or when to pause and how long to wait between lines. This will make the difference between a big laugh and a dud. A boff is a professional term which means a good response of laughter to a joke. A belly laugh is a loud, unrestrained laugh which convulses the individual. Impromptu or extemporaneous means remarks which are delivered without preparation or advance notice. Extemporaneous remarks are usually suggested by the occasion and are believed to have been planned while the speaker is sitting at the table or on the platform, waiting for his turn. Impromptu or extemporaneous remarks are frequently carefully prepared in advance so the speaker will know exactly what he is going to say. For this reason, we regard today as extemporaneous remarks the talk delivered without notes or not read from a manuscript. Ad libitum, or as the popular term is ad lib, refers to a remark the person may make during his talk or in conversation with another person while speaking before an audience. Such remarks are definitely not prepared in advance and are entirely spontaneous. The person who can ad lib must have a quick wit or a good memory for old jokes so that he can bring forth an appropriate humorous remark.

The development of a distinctive personality has always been the stock in trade of successful humorists. The following thumbnail sketches show how famous humorists of the past and present generally build up their individual types of humor around a central theme and then stick to it. These sketches also reveal practical know-how on the timing and delivery of stories—know-how that will be of value to any person who is called upon to make a speech.

447. *Joe Miller*—A stale joke, something so old that it has whiskers on it, is usually called a Joe Miller. This refers to the fact that the original joke was probably included in the famous *Joe Miller Joke Book.* The correct title of this volume which originally consisted of 247 alleged humorous stories was *Joe Miller's Jests.* Joe Miller himself had nothing to do with the collection of humor brought out under his name or its publication. It was after he died that a friend by the name of John Mottley decided to bring together some jokes which he thought Joe Miller might have used or enjoyed and published them in a volume with the idea, no doubt, of turning to his own personal profit Joe Miller's reputation as a comedian. Joe, or more correctly Joseph or Josias, was an English comic actor who appeared at the Drury Lane Theatre in London between 1709 and 1714. He was not a very important actor in the company, but he gained considerable popularity because he always played comic roles. Joe Miller himself was supposed to be a rather ignorant and uneducated fellow, who could not read his lines and had to learn them by having them read to him. He never had anything whatsoever to do with the joke book which came out in the year 1739, after his death. As the years went by, the book was reissued and revised many times, being enlarged with the addition of new jokes. By the year 1865, a *Joe Miller Joke Book* was published with more than 1,200 humorous stories, which was quite an enlargement on the original 247.

448.   *François Rabelais*—This French author, whose books were filled with humor and buffoonery, is pointed out as the originator of the so-called dirty or risqué story which has gained such favor in the quiet corners of social gathering places. These are the stories which are not considered suitable for mixed groups but gain widespread circulation at all levels of polite society. Actually, Rabelais is not deserving of the somewhat shady and disreputable reputation he has achieved through these years. It should be remembered that during the Middle Ages, when François Rabelais lived and wrote his

could not stoop to the common level and permit a joke to enter into their most serious discussions. Lincoln mingled his serious oratory with ever-ready humor that was the despair of his political opponents. With a few pointed remarks and an appropriate story he could shatter in small pieces the most elaborate argument of those who might oppose him.

The solemn and dignified Abraham Lincoln was not the dead-pan humorist you would expect. He laughed heartily at his own jokes, and his ringing laughter induced others to join in the merriment. His jokes were really illustrative anecdotes or modern-day parables. He told a story not to entertain or to arouse laughter but to illustrate a point and clinch an argument. His stories were always short and to the point. The point was so clear that most people could recognize what he was trying to prove. The stories were all centered around the life with which he was familiar, particularly the early days of his youth on the farm and in small towns.

Because Lincoln's stories were concerned chiefly with the rough life of the rural, frontier land, there were many critics who called them coarse and vulgar and condemned Lincoln for indulging in this type of humor. There were others who criticized him severely for indulging in humor during the seriousness and tragedy of the Civil War. They did not understand his use of humor to help him get his message to the people and felt that it detracted from the purposes of the war and the dignity of the President's high position as national leader. However, it is interesting to note that some of the most effective support he received during the trying years of the war came from a humorist who used his talents to influence popular opinion in support of the Lincoln administration. This was David Ross Locke, who wrote under the pen name of Petroleum V. Nasby. The Nasby letters were supposedly written by an ignorant and rowdy Copperhead and gained considerable circulation. It is said that President Lincoln enjoyed the humor and frequently read the Nasby letters to some of his closest advisers. The humorous letters, together with President Lincoln's own ability to tell a story well, endeared him to the people and gained their sympathy and support during the most critical time of his life.

450. Bill Arp—This humorist of the South, who gave his people encouragement as well as many laughs during the difficult years following the Civil War, had a talent for saying the things that the average person would like to say himself or hear. Charles Henry Smith began his career by writing humorous letters to amuse the Confederate soldiers, but it was not until after the war ended that he became popular and was called upon to lecture and express his homely philosophy through his writings. He endeared himself to his audiences as a kindly, well-meaning, warmhearted human being. He brought cheer to the sadness of the people of the South, and his rich and mellow humor, based on a knowledge of human nature and conditions of the section where he lived, gave the people the laughs they needed so badly at that time.

451. Major Jack Downing—This was the name of a fictitious character created by the author and editor Seba Smith. Mr. Smith conceived the idea of having a young, uneducated and unsophisticated youngster come into town with some farm products and homemade articles for sale. This required several days of his time, and while waiting for the buyers to take up his offering he spent some of his time wandering around town and visiting the halls of the legislature. The doings were all strange and unintelligible to him. He further passed his time by writing letters about his experiences to friends at home, and these letters were so humorous and contained such apt comments upon the doings of the politicians from an uninformed person's point of view that they quickly gained attention throughout the country and brought considerable reputation to Seba Smith as an outstanding political critic. President Andrew Jackson, along with the mass of the people, was greatly impressed by the humor of the letters and helped to increased their popularity.

452.   *Finley Peter Dunne*—This humorist was not known so much for himself or under his own name but rather as the creator of Mr. Dooley. Mr. Dooley was supposedly an Irish-American with some good opinions regarding politics and politicians and some very poor spelling and grammatical expressions. Mr. Hennessy was the stooge for Mr. Dooley. Mr. Hennessy was a gullible individual who believed every-thing he read in the newspapers and took up every printed and well-publicized solution to all national and international problems. Mr. Dooley with his wit and satire, writing with what would be regarded as the spoken Irish brogue, analyzed the political issues and social problems of the day and deliv-ered his opinions with wit and homely good sense. Finley Peter Dunne wrote these amusing sketches which earned for him the reputation of an outstanding humorist of his time. The dialect often proved difficult for the reader and should serve as a warning to those who would essay humor to avoid dialect unless it can be expertly done and easily understood by others.

453.   *Popular Humorists*—Among the humorists and come-dians of the stage who also gained distinction as speakers and banquet entertainers was Chauncey Olcott. On the stage he gained great popularity in Irish character roles, and he as-sumed the part of an Irish entertainer when he appeared as a speaker at banquets.

George M. Cohan was an actor, song writer, playwright and producer who also did well as a humorous speaker and fre-quently was called upon to act as toastmaster or special guest as an after dinner speaker. He had a sophisticated manner and a natural bent for eloquence which added to his popularity.

William Collier was an actor and also wrote plays. His specialty was that of a comedian, and he was called upon frequently to attend banquets where he entertained and his sharp wit brought him into constant oratorical crossfire throughout the evening with the other speakers and the toastmaster.

DeWolf Hopper was a stage comedian who possessed what is described as a dry sense of humor and a genius for the preposterous. Those who could understand and appreciate his special brand of humor enjoyed his efforts very much.

George Bernard Shaw has said that all genuinely intellectual work is humorous, and he never believed that there would be any loss of dignity if he employed satire and comedy to stress his point. In fact, there were times when he paid public tribute to the jester's cap which he voluntarily wore in order to amuse people. His theory was that if you can amuse people or arouse their anger and make them furious at you, you will gain their attention. Shaw used these devices of humor and wit to amuse or arouse the emotions of anger and resentment in people and became known as one of the greatest playwrights, as well as humorists, of his time.

William Sydney Porter, who wrote under the name of O. Henry, made one of the greatest contributions to story-telling. O. Henry's writings have been described as urbane humor. The characteristic thing about his story was the unexpected "reverse twist" ending. The surprise ending always delivers a punch in a humorous story, but O. Henry added to this what is described as the reverse twist, which completely changed the order of things and altered the viewpoint, making the unexpected conclusion explosive.

Ring Lardner was a literary humorist who has been described as America's most notable pessimist. Ring Lardner used humor merely to attract and hold the interest of listeners. He had no desire to be funny or to entertain. He was the first outstanding writer to knock the sports hero off his pedestal and picture him to the public as a not-so-bright and not especially worthy idol of public adulation, which popular sports figures were accustomed to receive. Ring Lardner was a master of satire and a melancholy man with a gift of humor, which he used to destroy those who were living on unearned glory and undeserved power.

Ogden Nash is America's leading writer of humorous verse. As a humorist and a poet, he is in great demand for lecture appearances and uses his own material to entertain the audience with his sparkling wit and poetic genius. He is particularly effective when reading his own comic verses.

Dorothy Parker possesses a sparkling wit, which she can use with devastating effect. She is regarded as a serious person who makes use of humor in a sophisticated manner as an adjunct to her literary career and not as its main purpose. Her natural talent could very well make possible for her a successful career based on her ability to deliver sardonic, humorous bons mots in an ironic manner.

James Thurber is another of the humorists with a hidden motive. He uses humor generally to sugar-coat the bitter pill of some serious thought he is trying to express. If one would try to judge Thurber by his zany drawings and often equally fanciful writings, one might not be aware of the profound thought that goes into them and the deep philosophical thinking of the creator.

Three different types of humor are best illustrated by such comedians as Bob Burns, Mischa Auer and George Burns. Bob Burns came to radio and made a tremendous impact. He never had a chance to show his talents in television. He was what might be called a personality humorist, but he was more than that. He was a master of the tall or fantastic tale. He told stories about his kinfolk in Van Buren and exaggerated all of their weaknesses and ignorance. The stories were based upon an exaggeration of the elements of human nature, and they gave the listener not only a good laugh but a feeling of superiority and sophistication.

Mischa Auer is a humorist who got laughs through his peculiar antics. He started out acting in serious roles. In one picture he was required to give an imitation of a monkey. It got a laugh that established a record in the movie industry, and this imitation and the response it created is still regarded as the longest sustained laugh ever recorded for a movie. It was what Mischa Auer did, rather than what he said, that struck the audience as being especially humorous.

George Burns gained the title of comedian by acting as a stooge or straight man for that delightful, mixed-up, blundering Gracie Allen. Nevertheless, George, since Gracie retired, steps out of character as a straight man and gets laughs on his own with a few fast quips. His type of humor is characteristically the applied or apt gag. It is not a gag for the single purpose of getting a laugh. It is a gag that fits into the situation and turns the situation itself into something humorous.

Victor Borge has the unique talent for waving his magic wand and making from a cultured and polished gentleman a monkey. He makes monkeys out of the revered composers, and he destroys pomposity wherever he finds it. Borge sits down to the piano to play the classics and he plays the clown. He does it so well and with such art and finesse that he completes with success something no other single performer would dare to do. He will undertake to hold the attention of an audience as the single star performer for an hour, or even as much as two hours at a time. His unusual brand of humor combines an appeal to the finer sensibilities as well as frenetic clowning.

Sid Caesar is a comedian who found in television a suitable medium for his talents. Basically, his humor is derived from his imitations, but also there is a fine intellectual quality, especially when he starts to mumble nothings and they come out sounding like something funny.

Henry Morgan is unusual among humorists because the audience seems to enjoy itself watching him having a good time. Henry Morgan seldom smiles and practically never laughs. He never seems to bother about trying to amuse or entertain anyone else. Instead, his personality is that of a quiet and gay individual who chuckles to himself and seems to be greatly amused by what is going on, while completely ignoring those about him. Somehow, this seems funny to others and proves entertaining.

Art Baker has a cheerful disposition which puts others in a pleasant mood. He is noted for his perpetual smile, a voice which inspires good humor and his friendly manner.

Frank Sinatra was able to extend his success as a singer into more dramatic roles and television appearances, because he has a pleasing way of expressing himself. He talks to the audience in an intimate manner that is warm and friendly. He has a great deal of self-confidence and stage presence, which is a big help to any person who must appear before an audience, especially a speaker. The audience can sense whether a person is nervous and afraid or whether he has control over himself and the situation well in hand.

Bert Lahr is a comedian who appeals to the public because he makes the average person look ridiculous and demonstrates that no one should feel ridiculous because we humans are all in the same boat. Bert Lahr's spaniel face and mushmouth way of talking are perfect for his part of the incompetent buffoon who wants to do everything right and never seems quite able.

Wally Cox is another comedian who arouses the sympathy of those who watch his work because he is a lovable fellow who never seems to get along too well. Here is the little, undersized fellow with glasses, who is the butt of every joke and the fall guy for his friends. However, he makes people feel sorry for him without arousing an emotion of sorrow. Because Wally Cox himself overcame his natural shyness and learned to laugh at himself and his own troubles, others laughed at him also in the spirit of fun.

Victor Moore established a reputation as a humorist with a specialty. His specialty was the bewildered, crackly voice and the befuddled and agonized manner of a timid soul.

Dick Shawn possesses a humor technique of building up to an explosive climax. He begins his comedy routine in a quiet and mild manner, gradually increasing the tempo and pitch until he reaches the high point of action and wild shouting.

Joe E. Lewis is a modern version of what people imagine to be the original Rabelais. This comedian goes in for what are described as smoking-room stories and the uninhibited gaiety of the cabaret. Joe E. Lewis enjoys the liquor he drinks and the stories he tells in his ribald, thick-voiced manner.

Jimmy Durante is a comedian who gets laughs because he is so human. His nose is part of his comedy routine, but it is merely something which helps him to be one of the boys— one of that large group of all of us who has something wrong with him but who refuse to permit it to give us an inferiority complex. Jimmy Durante destroys the English language, takes pride in his own physical shortcomings, such as his nose and bald head, and makes merry in spite of these handicaps so that he wins the approval and admiration of others and creates a friendly atmosphere where his jests and jokes are enthusiastically received.

Ernie Kovacs is the bull in the china shop. His mustache fairly bristles and he bangs his way around in a blustering, heavy-handed manner. His comedy may be best described as brash humor.

Herb Shriner is the sophisticated country boy. This Hoosier humorist has been away from the farm long enough to see the humor in small town life and tells others about it. Naturally he exaggerates the peculiarities of the small-town individual and does so in a certain manner which would be best described as a small-town big-city man. He is the fellow who escaped from the small town to the big city and now glories in his thin veneer of city sophistication. Herb Shriner does not himself impersonate the country yokel and does not get his laughs through his own character, such as Maurice Gosfield when he plays the role of Private Doberman on the Phil Silvers Show. Private Doberman tries to look dumb and act dumb and gets laughs by creating a ludicrous and laughable character.

Tom Poston has achieved a measure of success with an unusual style of humor. He has an absent-minded manner and seems to gaze off vaguely into space, then comes down to earth with some very original and humorous observation.

Don Knotts is best known for his nervous mannerisms, a voice that breaks under every emotion and a puckish look. He is what is known as a body and face comic and gets his laughs through physical actions.

454. Mark Twain—Few people today know that Mark Twain was primarily a humorist of the lecture platform and secondly a comic writer. Furthermore, Mark Twain made his first success as a humorist on the lecture platform and later turned to writing humor, which was accepted because he had already established himself as a humorist in his public speaking appearances. It was as a humorous speaker that Samuel Clemens, who wrote under the name of Mark Twain, was supreme and in a class by himself. He was essentially a showman all his life, and even tried to put on a show in his writings. What he wrote was always better if read aloud. It would seem that when he wrote he imagined he was talking to an audience so that everything had a personal touch. Mark Twain began his career as a humorist when he returned from a newspaper assignment in Hawaii. His newspaper articles on the conditions he found in Hawaii, or what were then called the Sandwich Islands, were read by few and with little interest. However, he took to the lecture platform to describe his experiences in the Sandwich Islands, and these reports were so hilarious that he quickly achieved fame as a humorist. After establishing himself as a humorist of the lecture program, he took to writing and his books were equally well received by the public. However, it was as a lecturer that he excelled.

When Bret Harte attempted a lecture tour in New York, he was a complete failure. At this time, Bret Harte was a well-known writer of Western stories, while Mark Twain was comparatively unknown. Bret Harte made the mistake of going to New York and trying to impress New Yorkers with his sophistication. He dressed in the most stylish clothes of the day and assumed the air of a polished gentleman who would be at ease in the drawing room of any New York social leader. The people of New York were not looking for this type of individual from out of the West. Mark Twain, the natural-born showman, gave them what they wanted. He also was from the West, but unknown as a writer. However, he had a flair for the melodramatic and dressed as New Yorkers expected a Westerner to dress. In later years, he adopted a theatrical white costume. His heavy mane of hair followed the Buffalo Bill hair style, and he spoke in a slow and carefully cultivated drawl, typical of the West. His mannerisms and way of telling a story were in the Mississippi River tradition, delivered in a slow drawl with the solemn gravity associated with Western characters. As a speaker, he was irresistible. His humor concerned personal accounts of what he had seen, what he had done and his views on things in general. His river stories and tales of the West captivated his audience. While Bret Harte was a failure on the platform because he did not look the part expected of a Western writer, Mark Twain was a success because he put on a good show.

It is unfortunate that there was no television in his day to preserve for posterity the Mark Twain of the lecture program, which would be recalled long after his writings may be forgotten. He was, perhaps, the only writer of all time who gained fame as a lecturer before he achieved recognition for his writings. Usually, it is the other way around. When a person becomes successful as a writer, he is asked to appear as a speaker.

455. *Chauncey Depew*—The honor of being the champion in his field and America's outstanding and most distinguished after dinner speaker goes to Chauncey Depew. There have been many famous entertainers who have been regarded highly as after dinner speakers, but it should be remembered that they first got and also maintained their reputations as humorists through their stage activity. Chauncey Depew was different. He gained his reputation as an entertainer because of his after dinner speaking. In this one field alone, he achieved lasting fame as a humorist and an outstanding citizen of our country. In fact, his popularity was as great, if not greater, in foreign countries than in the United States. The people of London and Paris looked upon Chauncey Depew as a typical and representative citizen of the United States. This distinction came to him chiefly through his efforts as an after dinner speaker and was a tribute to his wit and genius for humor. His services were constantly sought for dinners and banquets. He was a raconteur without equal. In the field of entertainment, Chauncey Depew was an amateur who took up after dinner speaking as a hobby and to provide relaxation for himself. He kept it that way all his life and never did any professional entertaining. His professional career was that of lawyer and politician. His material could be regarded as high level, but presented in a popular manner. He was a student of the classics and used illustrations and examples from them frequently in his talks. His name will be long remembered as one of the greatest of all humorists and speakers in the category of banquet entertainment.

456. Joseph Choate—His brilliance as an after dinner speaker will be an example for all time of a polished and eloquent gentleman who can be funny. For some reason, it seems that a person cannot make a success as a humorist or comedian unless he was born into comedy, suffered hardship as a youth, never had much opportunity for education and came up the hard way through life. This has been the background of practically all our popular and successful humorists and comedians. Choate was a remarkable exception. His father, a graduate of Harvard, and his mother came from distinguished Colonial families. He was related to some of the most notable individuals in New England history. He possessed the gift of eloquence and a ready wit which could find something humorous in ordinary situations. However, he was always an aristocrat with his dignified manner and bearing. As an after dinner speaker, he avoided the role of the clown who would destroy himself to get a laugh. Joseph Choate came to the banquet table with the primary idea of maintaining his personal dignity and gaining the respect of those present. His second and less important purpose was to entertain in a bright and intellectual manner on the level of those who had gathered to hear him. In these endeavors he was most successful and was greatly sought after as a banquet speaker, proving that a dignified gentleman can, if he possesses wit and eloquence, be entertaining when he so desires.

457. Artemus Ward—This successful humorist of the lecture platform never laughed or permitted a smile to form on his lips. Charles Farrar Browne, which was Artemus Ward's real name, presented a sad and most solemn expression as he delivered his talk in a soft and mournful voice. He seemed to be completely unconscious of the humor of his remarks, and never at any time showed any appreciation or enjoyment of them himself. He spoke slowly and would employ long pauses, giving his audience a chance to laugh or to regain their composure between hilarious outbursts. He was a practical joker at heart and a lover of burlesque. He carried these qualities with him to the speaking platform and was forever playing little jokes on his audience. For instance, he might pause during the middle of his talk and announce that he did not feel well and, therefore, would like an intermission of fifteen minutes. He would give the audience a little while to think this over and then quickly announce that during the intermission he would continue to speak.

A story is told about a time that Artemus Ward was to lecture in a small, inland town where he was not known. He was purposely late for the appearance, and the impatient audience began to make loud noises with their hands and feet and to whistle. About this time, Artemus Ward walked onto the platform with a dust cloth and began to move the chairs about and dust the desk and chairs. The people thought this was a stage assistant and became even more impatient. In the midst of the turmoil, the humorist dropped the dust cloth and held up his hand before the audience, announcing that since he had completed his task of dusting the furniture he would now begin his lecture. In the matter of titles for his lectures, Artemus Ward also liked to play jokes on the audience. One of his most popular lectures was entitled "Babes in the Woods." It was his custom to begin talking about more or less irrelevant matters until he reached the end of his lecture, when he would announce the title and then say that due to the lateness of the hour he could not discuss it. He had another lecture which he called "Sixty Minutes in Africa." In this case the first thing he would announce to his audience was that he was there for the purpose of raising money in order to pay his expenses to visit Africa, and then he would not mention Africa again the rest of the evening.

His humorous lectures consisted of jokes and satire on many timely subjects, especially well-known Western customs. His droll observations were strung together without any central idea or theme to hold them together. Much of his material consisted of burlesques of people and conditions delivered in his customary funereal manner.

458. Josh Billings—Henry Wheeler Shaw, who was known as Josh Billings, made a career out of spelling words wrong and pronouncing them in an odd and peculiar manner. He wanted to be a writer, but could make no success in this field until he took an old article which failed to get any attention and rewrote it in a phonetic style with the title "An Essa on the Muel." This style of spelling gained favorable attention for him, and soon his writings became popular. This led to the lecture platform, where he gained even greater success. Many people found Josh Billings' spelling difficult but enjoyed his peculiar use of language in his humorous talks. He had a melancholy appearance that made him look particularly rustic and uncouth. He made a point of wearing ill-fitting and simple clothes which added to his peculiar backwoods manner. He had a Western type of country humor which he delivered in an awkward manner as though he were a clumsy lout unfamiliar with the speaking platform. His remarks, while humorous, usually had a moral or a point based upon some platitude or homely philosophy. His lectures consisted of detached bits of humorous observation and pithy sayings, strung together without much connection or general theme.

459. Bill Nye—This humorist, Edgar Wilson Nye, was best known for his writings and for his entertaining lectures. He and James Whitcomb Riley, the poet, made a most successful team. The poet and humorist drew large audiences wherever they went. However, Riley later gave up his lecture work because it interfered with his time for writing poetry. Bill Nye continued on the lecture platform with the support of a musical program. He had a rustic style and adopted quaint and homely expressions to create a homespun type of character. His humor was basically satiric, and he was constantly trying to expose false notions based on superstitions and misconceptions arrived at by lack of proper investigation or through pretense. His opinions on the proper use of humor represent a different viewpoint from those of Samuel Goldwyn, as represented in this story about the motion picture producer. According to the story, Samuel Goldwyn was seeking a film story for Bob Hope. He received a phone call from a Hollywood writer. "I have a wonderful comedy," the writer told him with great excitement. "It's ideal for Bob Hope."

"Fine, fine," Goldwyn responded enthusiastically.

The writer went on excitedly, "Not only is it a great comedy, but it also has a message."

"A message?" Goldwyn shouted in disgust. "Just write me a comedy. Messages are for Western Union."

Bill Nye was a humorist who would not agree with this viewpoint. He considered a message important, and his humorous lectures usually contained ideas and worthwhile thoughts, so that a person who came to hear him would leave with something in addition to the memory of a few good laughs.

460.   *Will Rogers*—This poet lariat of the lecture platform was a true democrat in every meaning of the term. He made the common man feel that he was as good as a person in the highest office of the land by bringing down the notables to the level of the mass or majority of the people. He is best remembered with a wad of gum in his mouth and a grin on his face, twirling a rope and making sarcastic remarks about politicians and comments on the political issues of the day. Will Rogers always made fun of those in high office when they were on top and riding the crest of the wave of popularity. When they were down and out of favor, he never made them a target of his biting remarks.

A typical story concerning Will Rogers and his method of humor relates the time that someone made a bet that even Will could not get sour-faced Calvin Coolidge to laugh. Will offered to try, and he was taken to the White House to meet the President. When Will was introduced to President Coolidge, instead of extending his hand to shake hands, he cupped his hand to his ear and said in his delightful drawl, "Beg pardon, but I didn't catch the name." History records that Calvin Coolidge laughed heartily on this occasion. Nobody seemed to mind having Will Rogers poke fun at him. He was a humorist who made himself loved by all. His memory is still venerated by great numbers of Americans who enjoyed him during the years of his life. As an example of the great respect paid to his memory, a public speaker tells the story of the time he was to deliver a talk in Will Rogers' home town of Claremore, Oklahoma. As the speaker sat on the platform waiting to be introduced, the chairman of the meeting leaned over and whispered to him, "I don't know what you are going to talk about, but if you don't spend the first ten minutes talking about Will Rogers, you are a dead duck."

Will Rogers was known to most people through his writings in newspapers and magazines, because not everyone could see him on the stage or attend one of his popular lectures. However, it is interesting to know that he became a newspaper writer as a result of the reputation he attained as a speaker. At the time that Will Rogers was known only for his theatrical efforts on the New York stage, he was asked to attend a political campaign meeting and say something in favor of the candidate. He attended the meeting, and his remarks were so hilarious and original that the newspapers gave them a great deal of attention and he was asked to write humorous newspaper articles.

Will Rogers was in great demand as an after dinner speaker, where his intimate style of discussion was a tremendous success. On the lecture platform he was a non-conformist. He did everything wrong and contrary to the accepted rules of public speaking. He began in the wrong way by trying to avoid the customary introduction. When he visited a town, it was the general rule that some locally important individual or dignitary of the city or state would be given the honor of introducing him. Will Rogers would endeavor to come to the meeting at the very last minute and go directly to the stage and begin talking without any introduction whatso- ever. A story is told about the time that Governor Ross S. Sterling of Texas was to introduce the humorist. Will Rogers was late as usual, and then dashed out on the stage and intro- duced the Governor before Governor Sterling had a chance to say anything about Will. While delivering a talk on the platform, Will Rogers was restless and informal. He seldom stood still very long, but would walk about, lean on a desk or piano, sit on a piano stool or chair, and he might even come to the edge of the stage and sit down, letting his legs dangle about. As the final or concluding part of the lecture, he would bring out his ropes and twirl them while he continued his comments.

The lecture itself consisted of epigrams and observations which exaggerated the truth and deflated the pompous. His greatest sources of material were newspaper headlines and the information he could get about local politics and issues when he came into a town. He would find out something about local conditions, the political situation and also if there was an outstanding rich man in the town. All these things were good targets for his humor. He would go over them carefully and make suitable, humorous comments before going into the really big stuff. The big stuff consisted of his views and observations on important national and interna- tional events reported in the newspapers and subtle criticism aimed at those in high political office. Will Rogers never told a joke or funny story in the conventional meaning of the word. Instead, his humor consisted of comments which represented his own opinion, which in turn were the things that the common people would like to say themselves, if they were clever enough to think of them and had the nerve to express their opinion in public. No wonder Will Rogers became the idol of millions and was greeted enthusiastically wherever he went.

7
Speech Brighteners

THERE is such a thing as a "quick laugh." This is a passing humorous reference or extraneous observation interpolated into the main body of a speech or toastmaster's remark in such a way that it does not interrupt the continuity of thought. It may be called a speech brightener.

A speech brightener differs from a joke in many respects. For one thing, a speaker who relates a joke often has to prepare the audience for the fact that he is going to interject a joke, tell the joke, then pick up his speech again at the point where it was interrupted. If a speech may be compared to a speeding train, one could use the illustration of a train being brought to a stop on a side track to permit a fast express—the joke—to pass through. Then the train gets back on the track and resumes its progress toward its destination.

A speech brightener does not interrupt. It merely emphasizes a point a speaker is seeking to make and offers a quick laugh for a change in pace to provide freshness and variety in the talk. If a speaker says that in his opinion something is foolish, he might add that it is as foolish as ——— and select a suitable analogy to emphasize his point while introducing some welcome humor into his remarks.

Occasional use of an appropriate and carefully selected speech brightener has many advantages for the speaker. In the first place, it is fast. The audience is not prepared for a joke, and the unexpected humorous reference catches the members off guard and heightens the effect. It is well known that surprise is one of the most important elements of humor. The speaker regains the attention of those whose minds may have wandered afar. There is no interruption in the continuity of the thought. The speech brightener helps to advance the ideas or message of the speaker. Furthermore, the speaker who uses brighteners is looked upon as a wit, original, charming and entertaining. Humor of this type brings more credit and praise to the toastmaster and speaker than conventional-type jokes which may be related during the course of the remarks.

I'M THE KIND OF PERSON WHO . . .

461. Is very punctual. In fact, I buy everything on time.

462. Believes in keeping everything clean and sanitary. Even with my own kids, I teach them to use a straw when sucking their thumbs!

463. Likes books. I like *Little Women*. In fact, I like them better than books.

464. Insists on the best—no matter where I go. When I broke my arm and went to a hospital I wouldn't let them bandage it. I had it gift wrapped.

465. Believes in good manners. Sometimes I don't exactly understand what they are, like the little girl who returned home from school and her mother asked her what she had learned. The little girl told her mother that the class had spent the day studying good manners and then she added proudly, "When you are seduced, you shake hands."

466. Is often called a cynic. I think other people are as bad as I am.

I'M THE KIND OF PERSON WHO . . .

467. Knows where he is going. That's why I never carry life insurance. I carry fire insurance.

468. Tells you one thing and does another. For example, I'm against gambling, and I'll bet you 10 to 1 that the state will never legalize it.

469. Believes that things should be done in a tactful manner. Diplomacy is the art of letting someone else have your way, and we should be diplomatic.

470. May not always be right, but I am never wrong.

471. Goes all out and ends up all in.

472. Doesn't believe it would do us any good to see ourselves as others see us. We wouldn't believe it, anyway.

473. Always tries to do the right thing. I even put my gloves in the glove compartment of my car.

474. Believes you should love your enemy. It will drive him crazy!

475. Feels you should always put off until tomorrow the things you shouldn't be doing at all!

476. Believes that life is just what you make it—until somebody comes along and makes it worse.

477. Trusts everybody, but I always cut the cards.

478. Doesn't mind suffering. It's the pain that gets me.

I'M THE KIND OF PERSON WHO . . .

479. Is always suspicious of anyone who hits me in the head with a blackjack.

480. Has things happen to him that happen to nobody else. When I went to see my dentist he checked my mouth carefully and then told me, "Your teeth are in good shape, but your gums will have to come out."

481. Believes in making things clear in advance to avoid trouble and misunderstandings later like the father who took his son aside on his first day at school and told him, "Son, you are going forth into the world to meet other little boys. Let's get one thing straight. Your dad is not going to lick their dads!"

482. Believes nothing is impossible—if I don't have to do it myself.

483. Believes that the so-called upper crust is just a bunch of crumbs stuck together by their own dough.

484. Follows the advice given by a Texan who lived to the age of 105. When asked to what he attributed his long life, he gave this good rule, "I never stole a horse and I never called a man a liar to his face."

485. Expects nothing. Therefore, I'm never disappointed.

486. Is like the boy who wanted to grow up so he could wear long pants. Now he wears them longer than he ever dreamed he would.

487. Can't take surprises. Why, when I was born I was so surprised I couldn't talk for a year and a half.

I'M THE KIND OF PERSON WHO . . .

488.   Believes that many a person who boasts he has an open mind should have it closed for repairs.

489.   Always has trouble with my glasses. I can never find a place to put down the empties.

490.   Has trouble getting names straight. I'm like the student who didn't know what a cannibal was. The teacher asked, "What would you call a fellow who ate his mother and father?"
     The boy replied, "An orphan."

491.   Judges whether or not I had a good time at a party by how I feel the following morning.

492.   Might be described as a man of few words—or less. I believe that it sometimes calls for a perfect command of the English language to say nothing.

493.   Believes in being cautious, but at the same time we must take some risks. We can't be as careful as the fellow who went to the dog races and bet on the rabbits—to show!

494.   Believes it is better to remain silent and appear a fool than to speak and remove all doubt.

495.   Doesn't mix in with things that don't concern me. I believe that plastic surgery can do anything with the human nose except keep it out of the other fellow's business.

496.   Is never upset or perturbed by things which go on around him. I believe that if you can keep your head when all about you are losing theirs—you just don't understand the situation.

I'M THE KIND OF PERSON WHO . . .

497.   Complains about the money I can't get. Only the rich complain about the money they can't keep.

498.   Believes that a kick in the pants does some people more good than a pat on the back.

499.   Believes in being polite. I agree with one famous French ambassador's explanation of the requirements for a successful diplomat. He said that it is not sufficient merely to be stupid. A diplomat must also be polite.

500.   Could go out with a bubble dancer and find out it is no soap.

501.   Doesn't believe a person should make his bed and then try to lie out of it.

502.   Possesses talents. Have you ever heard of speakers getting lost in a fog? Well, I create my own fog!

503.   Believes in getting things done, even if I have to do them myself. I'm like the woman who had two children by her first husband, two by her second husband and one by herself.

504.   Is known as a careful driver. I drive on the sidewalks to avoid traffic.

505.   Gets to the point quickly, like the new income tax short return form. This short return has only questions. 1. What is your income? 2. How soon can you return it?

I'M THE KIND OF PERSON WHO . . .

506. Believes in being generous around home. Last Christmas I gave my wife a check for two thousand dollars for a fur coat. Next Christmas I may sign it.

507. Keeps up with the times. When I travel I take one of the new jet planes. I can have breakfast in Los Angeles and bicarbonate of soda in New York City.

508. Believes a speaker can never deliver a good will talk unless he has good will in his heart.

509. Believes in following the rules of etiquette. A person should know which finger to put in his mouth when he whistles for the waiter.

510. Tells the truth. Then you don't have to remember what you say.

511. Knows the score. In fact, I invented the game!

512. Is one of those rugged, nature-built men. I grew up without being petted and pampered. Even today I am no sissy. When I go to bed at night I turn the electric blanket down to medium.

513. Can always spot a well-informed man. His views are the same as mine.

HE'S THE KIND OF A PERSON WHO . . .

514. Uses a Marilyn Monroe calendar to tell what day it is.

515. Has no ambition. When he was a kid he wanted to be Vice-president, that was all.

HE'S THE KIND OF A PERSON WHO . . .

516. Thinks twice before he says nothing.

517. Believes in law and order, as long as he can lay down the law and give the order.

518. Thinks he's a gentleman because he prefers blondes.

519. Always goes out with the upper set. He leaves the lower set at home.

520. Was a premature baby. He was born before his father and mother were married.

521. Is so well known that if he walks down the street with a mayor in any town he happens to visit, people stop and ask each other, "Who is that fellow walking down the street with (NAME OF PERSON)?"

522. Is a regular freight train of wordage with no terminal facilities.

523. Always dresses perfectly. He could drop dead and they wouldn't have to do a thing to him at the funeral parlor.

524. Is a real pessimist. He is always building dungeons in the air.

525. Can trace his family tree back to the time when his family lived in it.

526. Some day is going to go too far, and I hope he stays there!

HE'S THE KIND OF A PERSON WHO . . .

527. Will spare no expense to save a penny.

528. Knows all the answers. Too bad he doesn't know a few of the questions.

529. Is like a button—always popping off at the wrong time.

530. Is a pain in the neck. In fact, some people even have a much lower opinion of him.

531. Doesn't hesitate to bawl out the President of the United States but is always polite to policemen.

532. Thinks his inferiority complex is bigger and better than anyone else's.

533. A man wouldn't trust too far and a girl wouldn't trust too near.

534. Is a true friend. He stabs you in the front.

535. Has such a low opinion of himself, he wouldn't want to belong to any organization which would take him in as a member.

536. Is very responsible. No matter what goes wrong, he is always responsible.

537. Worries more about a big waist than a thick head.

538. Has lots of brains but not enough sense to use them.

539. Must have been born in a revolving door. He's been pushed around ever since.

HE'S THE KIND OF A PERSON WHO . . .

540. If he ever makes an ocean voyage, he would have to be lashed to the bar.

541. Has a soft heart and a head to match.

542. Comes right out and says what his wife tells him to think!

543. Believes talk is cheap, except when you hire a lawyer.

544. Doesn't know the meaning of the word fear. And there are lots of other words he doesn't know the meaning of.

545. Can take it or leave it. Usually he takes it!

546. Hasn't any use for ambition. It gets a person into a lot of work.

547. Dreams that he is delivering a speech and wakes up suddenly to discover it is actually happening.

548. Is such a bore he can trace his ancestors back to the Wallflower.

549. Is so determined to have his way that a friend said to him last Friday, "Tomorow will be Saturday, if it is all right with you."

550. Should be named Serutan—he's so backward.

551. Has more than meets the I.Q.

552. Displays a lot of unexpected talent when it comes to acting a fool.

HE'S THE KIND OF A PERSON WHO . . .

553.   Has had a lifelong romance. At an early age he fell in love with himself.

554.   Feels cheated out of pleasure when he gets up to speak because he can't sit in the audience and listen.

555.   Never condemns inferiority in his friends. In fact, he enjoys it!

556.   Proves to all of us that a man with both feet on the ground can't fall far.

557.   Will sympathize with you in trouble—and if you haven't any trouble he'll hunt some up for you.

558.   Is so mercenary he was born under the sign—no money refunded!

559.   Never forgets a favor—especially if he did it.

560.   Used to be terribly conceited but he went to a psychiatrist who straightened him out. He tells everybody he now has the most wonderful personality in the world.

COMPARISONS

561.   *Not Involved*—It is easy enough to take this matter calmly when it doesn't concern you personally. In such a case, you can be like the fellow who always called a spade a spade until he stumbled over one in the dark.

562.   *Earning a Living*—Variety gives life its spice, but the dreary fact remains that monotony provides the groceries.

COMPARISONS

563. Something Cheaper—These plans are very nice and expensive. However, I think we had better be a little more practical. When we look the hard-boiled facts in the face we have to admit that roses are red and violets are blue, but they don't get around like the dandelions do.

564. Another Way Out—Nothing is absolutely hopeless. Usually Jack Benny gives his old friend, Phil Harris, a bottle of whiskey for Christmas. Last year, Phil's doctor absolutely forbade him to have any liquor, so Jack gave him something else which thrilled Phil just as much—the name of a new doctor.

565. Reversed Living—Things sure change these days. The fellow who was brought up on a farm, where they ate in the house and had a toilet outside, now lives in a suburban home with a barbecue pit. They eat outside and have the toilet in the house.

566. Conservative Estimate—This is a conservative estimate, like the case of the New Yorker who was talking to a booster from California. "Do you mean to tell me," the New Yorker demanded, "that in California you have 365 days of sunshine a year?"

The Californian answered, "Exactly, my friend, and that's a mighty conservative estimate."

567. Benefits of Automobile—About the only advantage I can see is what one student decided was the chief contribution of the automobile to modern civilization: "It has practically stopped horse stealing."

568. More Than Friendly—I have traveled a great deal throughout the country and I find America filled with

COMPARISONS

friendly people. It is not at all like the case of the distinguished foreign nobleman who was making his first visit to America right after World War II. When he was asked what he thought would interest him most he replied, "I theenk I wish most of all to meet zat famous and prolific Mrs. Beech, who had so many sons in ze last war."

569.   Mistake—Even the best of us can be wrong. After all these years, we find that Columbus was wrong. The world is FLAT.

570.   The Real Thing—We'll try to do our best to make this look like the real thing. If appearances mean anything, it'll be as true to what we want as the old saying, "Stone walls do not a prison make, nor iron bars a cage—but they certainly help a lot!"

571.   The Dressed-up Truth—You have to be diplomatic in your use of words and observations, and not like the husband whose wife came down dressed in a daring evening gown. The husband looked her over and said grimly, "I hate to tell you this, but you're getting fat."

The wife was naturally insulted and shot back at him, "In the best places, they say 'plump.'"

"So, all right," said the husband. "In the best places, you are getting plump."

572.   Fast—We're living in an age of speed. They've even got Minit-Rub down to thirty-five seconds!

573.   Be Original—We've got to do things our own way. You can't go around borrowing ideas from others all the time. If we do we're liable to end up like the young fellow who

COMPARISONS

took the motor from a Cadillac, the fenders from a Buick and the chassis from a Ford. What do you think that got him? Two years!

574. *Installment Buying*—It changes our way of life—like installment buying. Installment buying makes the days longer and the months shorter.

575. *Well Covered*—That fellow thinks of everything. I understand he even took out blanket insurance. He smokes in bed.

576. *Not His Problem*—You've got to look out for yourself like the young girl whose twin sister got married. They didn't have enough money to get their own home so they went to live with her parents. A friend asked the husband how he could tell one twin from the other and whether he might be making love to the wrong girl. "That doesn't bother me," replied the young husband. "When I feel like making love I grab one of the girls, and if she's not the right twin she starts defending herself."

577. *Spoken For*—As confused as the young girl who went to a strange church for the first time. The youthful pastor, noticing a stranger in his group, sought her out and tried to be friendly. "Where do you live?" he asked. The confused young maiden replied, "I already got a fellow."

578. *Big Ideas*—I guess it's a nice thing to have big ideas, but I'm a practical sort of person. I'm not like the farmer. Every time he took the hired girl to the barn he got lofty ideas.

COMPARISONS

579. *Modern*—This is really modern. It is as modern as the furniture in an apartment my cousin has in (NEARBY BIG CITY). I slept there in a bookcase one night because I thought it was the bed.

580. *Let the Matter Drop*—Maybe we had better not prolong this matter. Otherwise, we might be like the fire department. If it weren't for the fire department the place would have burned down in an hour. They kept it going all afternoon.

581. *Positive Failure*—The other side is as positive as the doctor who insisted that his diagnosis was correct, although the patient said ten other doctors disagreed with him. "I still believe I'm right," the doctor insisted, "and the post-mortem will prove it." Perhaps they are counting on a failure to show up the facts in the case.

582. *Fine Start*—We've made a fine start but somewhere along the line we slowed up. We're like the woman who bought a mud pack. Later the druggist who sold her the preparation asked her husband if the mud improved his wife's appearance. He replied, "It did for a couple of days, but then it wore off."

583. *Baffled*—This is as puzzling to figure out as the time a man asked his doctor how serious was his wife's illness. The doctor told him to prepare for the worst, and that really had him guessing.

584. *Vacation*—It's like going on a seashore vacation. Two weeks on the sands and then fifty weeks on the rocks.

COMPARISONS

585. *Wealthy*—He's so rich, when he sees Santa Claus he asks him, "What can I do for you?"

586. *Poor at Figures*—He's such a poor manager that he thinks that marriage is the cheapest way to get your laundry done free.

587. *No Choice*—Sometimes we do things out of necessity rather than desire. It's like the case of the young fellow who always went out with good girls because he couldn't afford the other kind.

588. *Big Mouth*—A person who tells everything he knows is like the man who was walking along a dark street when he was set upon by two rough characters who started to beat him and demanded his money. The man put up a terrific battle until he was finally brought under control by the thugs, who searched him and found only a few cents in his pocket. They were amazed and said, "How come you put up such a big fight for less than a dollar that you had on you?"

"Well," admitted the fellow who had received such a bad beating, "to tell you the truth I thought you were after the hundred dollars I have hidden in my shoe."

589. *Pun*—As Mama Gnu said to Papa Gnu—I've got good gnus for you!

590. *Know What You Want*—I think we should be as easily satisfied as the teen-age girl who wanted to be married—and quickly. She said she would be satisfied with a man who was simple and understanding, and then added, "There must be some millionaire who fits that description."

COMPARISONS

591.   *Always Problems*—You just can't win. No matter how you go about it you've got your problems. Life is like the warning which was posted in a machine shop. It was a notice to girls who might wander into the shop from the office and read, "If your sweater is too large for you, look out for the machines. If you are too large for the sweater, look out for the machinists."

592.   *Bragging*—I think we are bragging again, like the big firecracker said to the little firecracker, "My pop's bigger than your pop."

593.   *Skipping the Main Problem*—The way some of our members are trying to eliminate this nuisance is like one state eliminated all of its bad roads. Whenever a road got bad, they didn't call it a road—they put a detour sign on it!

594.   *Unhappy with Duties*—The tough thing about this job I have been assigned to do is pretending that I am happy with it. It's like the work of the ballerina who found that standing on her toes so long at a time wasn't as tough as having to smile while she was doing it.

595.   *Giving In*—I would say about our efforts the same thing that the late Secretary of State John Foster Dulles said about his efforts to reach an agreement with the Russians. He said that it is perfectly easy to reach an agreement with the Russians if you don't care what is in the agreement.

596.   *Changing Circumstances*—Our attitude toward people usually changes with circumstances. For instance, there is the story of the mountaineer who drove over to get a doctor. "I

COMPARISONS

want you to see what you can do for my son-in-law. He's in bad shape," the mountaineer explained.

The doctor climbed into the wagon and accompanied the fellow to his home and found that it was no exaggeration that the son-in-law was in bad shape. He was really beaten up but good. The mountaineer explained that they had been in a fight and he had worked over the youth.

"Aren't you ashamed," exclaimed the doctor, "to beat your own son-in-law like that?"

"Wall," drawled the mountaineer. "He waren't my son-in-law then."

597.   Commuting—As the commuter said, the long tiresome ride to work didn't bother him. It was the getting there that he didn't like.

598.   Misunderstood Motives—Our motives are good, but some people may think they are selfish and mercenary like the man who found two small birds which had fallen out of their nest and were killed. He proceeded to give them a decent burial for the benefit of his five-year-old son, who was watching the proceedings carefully. The boy evidently misunderstood his motives because he ridiculed, "What a crazy thing to do. They won't grow!"

599.   The Sunny Side—There is always a bright side in life. Consider the consolation that comes to the aging man who is finally able to whistle while he brushes his teeth.

600.   Real Reason—You've got to find the real reason behind things. For instance, everyone thinks that women's clothes are designed to make a girl look slim, but really they are designed to make a man look round.

COMPARISONS

601. *Wonderful Improvement*—There are always ways to make improvements. For instance, a local bartender has improved upon the drink known as Bloody Mary. He mixes vodka, tomato juice and Geritol, and calls it Tired Bloody Mary.

602. *Contribution*—We hear a lot of talk about giving financial support to this or to that worthy cause. When I hear this expression I think of the father of the bride who finally reached that hectic point where the daughter walked down the church aisle in her costly wedding gown. The father groaned and was heard to say, "I don't mind giving my daughter in marriage, but what gets me down is having her gift wrapped."

603. *Cutting Corners*—Trying to do this on a small, inexpensive scale is like the little girls playing weddings. They had a couple of bridesmaids, a bride and a maid of honor. The mother of one of the girls asked, "What about the groom?" One child quickly replied, "We don't need a groom. This is just a small wedding."

604. *Backwards*—This is doing things backwards, like out in Hollywood where the brides keep the bouquet and throw the groom away.

605. *Lack of Originality*—That's about as new as the idea of pay TV. I've had pay TV for years. I still owe $150 on my set.

606. *Anatomy*—It's like anatomy—something everybody has but on some people it looks better, particularly a girl.

COMPARISONS

607. *Inevitable*—It's like a young fellow getting a girl to marry him. If she doesn't want to, it can't be done. If she wants to, there ain't hardly any way to prevent it.

608. *Generous Judge*—Some people are as generous as the fellow who was hailed into court for failing to support his wife. "You've been a drunkard, a careless and negligent husband," announced the judge. "I'm going to give your wife one hundred dollars a month from now on."

"That's wonderful," replied the husband, "and, Judge, I'll try to slip her a buck or two myself from time to time."

609. *Unworkable Divorce*—That's like the case of the Hollywood couple who were getting remarried. It was just another one of those divorces which didn't pan out.

610. *Do It Now*—We should be like Gypsy Rose Lee—never put off until tomorrow what you can take off today.

611. *Penalty of Being Different*—Every time a person wants to do something different his friends think he's like Whistler's mother when the artist came home and found her scrubbing the floor. She was off her rocker.

612. *Gold Digger*—Like the girl who could take men or leave them. After she takes them she leaves them!

613. *Losing*—As good, but in the wong way as the cellar baseball team. The team were not only good losers—they were perfect.

614. *Contributing Circumstances*—Everything is relative. For instance, there was the case of two children who were

COMPARISONS

playing make-believe one day and were imagining different situations. "What would you do," asked one of the other, "if you found a million dollars?"

The other thought over the problem and then replied, "Well, if whoever lost it was real poor, I'd give it back."

615. *Principle*—He has no more principle than the guy who would steal the teeth out of your head and then come back for your gums.

616. *Peculiar Case*—This is a very peculiar circumstance and deserves careful investigation, like the case out in the mountains of Kentucky. A young girl came into the office of a doctor in a mountain town and told him, "I want you to do something about Grandma's smoking. She inhales."

The doctor tried to rest her fears. "That is nothing to worry about. Plenty of women who smoke, inhale today."

"Yep, but with Grandma it's different," the girl explained. "Grandma doesn't exhale!"

617. *Make Your Own Luck*—What happens to you isn't as important as what you happen to be. A black cat crossing your path may or may not be bad luck, depending upon whether you are a man or a mouse.

618. *Opinionated*—If you stick to your opinion, you possess the admirable quality of firmness. If someone else does it, then it is detestable stubbornness.

619. *New Gadget*—Science is always bringing out some new gadget or invention to delight us. It's like the dog that found his way to a parking meter and said enthusiastically, "Oh boy, pay toilets!"

COMPARISONS

620.   Wrong Track—Sometimes we look for the most obvious solution or answer to a problem and get off on the wrong track, like the woman visiting the prison to cheer up the inmates. She stopped to talk to one particularly pathetic-looking case and said to the man, "I feel sure, my poor man, that it was poverty which brought you to this."

"No, ma'am," answered the prison inmate politely. "As a matter of fact, I happened at the time to be coining money."

MISCELLANEOUS VARIETY

621.   Friendship—The small boy who defined a friend as someone who likes you, even though he knows you had something there.

622.   Golf Bug—They say golf is like a disease—the hoof and mouth disease. You hoof all day and mouth all night.

623.   Running Away—Often we are wrong to call a person a coward when actually it's just that his feet refuse to stand around and see his body abused.

624.   Compensation—There is always some compensation to everything. A fool and his money may soon be parted, but they are always in circulation.

625.   Literal Reading—You can't believe everything you read. I saw a sign to do your Christmas shopping early. I got up at five o'clock in the morning, and all the stores were closed.

626.   Who Needs Who—A friend is someone to have in time of need, and when you are prosperous he needs you.

MISCELLANEOUS VARIETY

627. Serious Error—I wish to apologize for my mistake. I realize that a serious error has been made and I am responsible. I hope it will not be as tragic as the case of the man who died and arrived at the gates of Heaven. A messenger of St. Peter took his name and disappeared. Later, the messenger came back and told the newly arrived applicant to Heaven that he was very sorry but his name was not on the books. He was not registered to be received in Heaven. The messenger suggested that he try Hell. The poor fellow made his way to the gates of Hell and was promptly interviewed by a representative of Satan. Here again he was informed that he was not on the books and not registered to be admitted to Hell. It was suggested that he return to Heaven once more.

The fellow, now thoroughly confused, returned to the gates of Heaven and announced that his name had not been found on the register in Hell and Satan had suggested that he try Heaven again. The fellow was taken to the office outside the gates and St. Peter himself carefully checked every name again. Suddenly, the name was discovered far down the list. St. Peter turned to him and said, "There seems to have been a mistake here. Someone made an error. You are not due to arrive in Heaven for six more years. Who is your doctor?"

628. Blaming Others—Why is it in spring when an old man becomes gay we say he has young ideas, but when a young man does the same thing we say he has the same old idea?

629. Unplanned—Sometimes things just happen instead of being planned. For instance, take the case of the young man who told the father of the girl he loved, "I feel sure that your daughter and I were made for each other."

The father was not so sure and replied, "Young man, you are wrong. At no time did her mother and I have such a thought in our minds."

MISCELLANEOUS VARIETY

630. Envy—People have never been known to love a winner —a successful person. Their attitude of envy and dislike explains why a wise man once said, "When you are getting kicked from the rear it means you're in front."

631. Beautiful Arrangement—This is a beautiful setting we have here. I've always had a fondness for beautiful settings. I'm not like the marriage counselor who told the young man that when proposing to a girl the setting isn't very important. What really counts is the diamond.

632. Human Nature—The trouble with our country today is that all the stupid people are cocksure of everything, and all the intelligent people are full of doubt.

633. Cold Cure—You never can be sure what miracle science and medicine will be able to perform next. Doctors have just come up with the answer to the common cold—*Gesundheit!*

634. A Man's Age—You can't tell a woman's age, but you can always tell a man's age by what he takes two at a time— stairs or pills.

635. Taking No Chances—We should be farsighted and look ahead, like the case of the psychiatrist who told a new patient, "You suffer from loss of memory. My fee is fifty dollars—in advance."

636. Modern Living—We should all recognize the fact that we are living in a new age—an era of science and invention. The woman of today no longer suffers from dishpan hands. Now she complains about push-button fingers.

MISCELLANEOUS VARIETY

637. *Modesty*—I know exactly what Mark Twain meant when he was told that man is the only animal that can blush. Mark Twain observed that man is the only animal that needs to blush.

638. *Accident Ahead*—The way traffic conditions are today, the best way to get your name in the paper is to walk across a street reading one.

639. *Almost Enthusiastic*—Enthusiasm is a great thing. A person should never get over being enthusiastic even if it means being like the young married fellow who was asked what he thought of wedded life. He replied with enthusiasm, "It's wonderful. It's almost like being in love!"

AS BAD AS . . .

640. The father who was bragging about his boy. It seems the boy said "Dada" three times that day—and he's only twelve years old!

641. The inventor who thought his ideas were sure to be honeys because he had bees in his bonnet.

642. The motorist who drove through a stop sign. When the officer stopped him and roared, "Didn't you see that stop sign?" the motorist replied, "Yes, I saw the sign, but I didn't see you!"

643. The report that 10 per cent of the normal-appearing people in our cities are mentally deficient. The only thing a person can do is to stay away from normal-appearing people.

AS BAD AS . . .

644. Your conscience. It doesn't keep you from doing anything wrong. It just keeps you from enjoying it.

645. The dentist who told a patient in his office he couldn't take care of her that afternoon as he had eighteen cavities to fill. When she left, he picked up his golf bag and cap and left the office.

646. The man who hadn't worked in thirty years. He had been off his feet so long they had to teach him to walk again.

647. The girl who had long black hair and wore long black gloves to cover it.

648. Income taxes. They are taxing us right and left. If you make out your tax report right, you won't have anything left.

649. The woman who spent ten dollars to get a finger wave. Isn't that the most ridiculous thing! Who wants wavy fingers?

650. The dog with a split personality. He's a regular Jekyll and Hydrant.

651. Some crazy guy who kept calling my brother up every night. Just to show you how crazy this fellow was—my brother doesn't have a phone!

652. The fellow who showed the poor taste of walking into an antique shop and asking, "What's new?"

653. The jerk who saw a bucket on which were painted the words "For Fire Only." He put water in it!

AS BAD AS . . .

654.   The time I picked up a baby and they told me to watch its head. It wasn't its head that needed watching.

655.   The fellows playing in a dishonest game. Nobody played the cards that the dealer dealt them.

656.   The hotel where a bell rang at four o'clock in the morning, and everybody would have to get out of bed and go back to his own room.

657.   The food I ate at a restaurant last night. I wouldn't say they served horsemeat, but I do know that the chef didn't use a cookbook to prepare it. He used a racing form.

658.   The fellow who drinks so much that when snakes get drunk they see him.

659.   The woman who called the Fidelity Insurance Company and wanted to have her husband's fidelity insured.

660.   The couple on the dance floor. When they played the mambo, everybody stopped to watch them. They were doing the minuet.

661.   The watchdog that one night watched a burglar steal half the house.

662.   The fellow who offered to get his friend a brand-new Cadillac for five hundred dollars. All he had to do was file a few numbers off the engine.

663.   The farmer who had land two thousand acres long and one inch wide. All he could raise was spaghetti.

AS BAD AS . . .

664. The old, retired sailor who paid a boy a dime to knock on his door early each morning and shout, "The skipper wants to see you immediately!" The boy would then leave and be on his way while the loud voice of the sailor roared out, "Tell the skipper to go to hell!"

665. The backward pupil who held up his hand to answer when the teacher asked the class, "Can anyone tell me where St. Louis is?" The surprised teacher nodded to the boy to answer and he replied, "Playing in New York."

666. The case of the fellow who had an atomic cold. He sneezed and a whole city block was wiped out.

667. The boy who was asked by his sisters to play school and he agreed. "O.K.," he said, "play that I am absent."

668. The woman who has been married so many times they won't give her a license any more. They just punch the old one.

669. The schoolteacher who didn't have any principal.

670. The street cleaner who was fired for daydreaming. He couldn't keep his mind in the gutter.

671. The fellow who said he could speak French like a native. He meant a native of Turkey.

672. A sewing circle—a place where women go to needle each other.

673. The story in the magazine that was discontinued on page 2.

AS BAD AS . . .

674. The announcer who was giving a commercial on a TV show. He took a deep puff on a cigarette, blew out the smoke and with great satisfaction exclaimed, "Man, that is real coffee!"

675. A wedding—a ceremony at which a man loses complete control of himself.

676. The library located in a tough neighborhood. It was so tough they took down the sign reading "Silence" and put up one "Shad up!"

677. The automobile described by its owner when a friend asked him what model it was. He replied that it wasn't a model. It was a horrible example.

678. The woman motorist who jumped out of her car after a collision with another auto and shouted at the driver, "Great guns, why don't people watch where they are driving? You're the fourth car I've hit this morning!"

679. The chorus girl who was showing her friend her new diamond necklace and mink coat. She said, "I may be good for nothing, but I'm not the kind who is going to be bad for nothing."

680. The bird which built a nest with a hole in the bottom. The bird loved to lay eggs but hated to bring up children.

681. The fellow in the Army who made such a good record he was told he would be recommended for officer's training and replied, "I've been in the Army long enough to know I gotta salute officers, but damned if I want to associate with them as equals."

AS BAD AS . . .

682. The fellow who was walking past a restaurant with his girl and she commented, "That tray of pastries in the window makes my mouth water," and he replied, "So, spit!"

683. The speaker who used material so dull and uninteresting in his talk that his tongue fell asleep.

684. The new cars with knee action. This new car not only hits a pedestrian but kicks him when he tries to get up.

685. The modern boss who wants men under thirty with forty years' experience.

686. The fellow who believed in taking a drink of whiskey when he was tired. It made a new man out of him. Then he had to take a drink for the new man.

687. The girl who not only kept her girlish figure, but she doubled it!

688. The man who donated a loud-speaker system to a church—in memory of his late wife.

689. The doctor who could take a small operation and make it into a big undertaking.

690. The fellow who left by plane from New York at nine in the morning and arrived in Paris twelve hours later. And boy, was he mad! He wanted to go to San Francisco.

691. The girl who was one of three things—either hungry, thirsty or both.

AS BAD AS . . .

692. The fellow who was married for two years before his wife told him how much money he was earning.

693. The fellow who was insulted when a friend offered him a drink. However, he swallowed the insult.

694. The operation performed on a young lady by an avaricious doctor. This doctor told his wife later that night, "I certainly performed that operation in the nick of time. Another few hours and the patient would have recovered without it!"

695. The fellow who crossed wires on his electric blanket and the electric toaster. It was terrible. All night long he kept popping out of bed.

696. The woman who called the Community Chest offices and wanted to make an appointment to have her chest examined.

697. A hospital. They won't let you alone. They wake you up at three o'clock in the morning to give you a sleeping pill.

698. The boss who gave the office boy a one hundred dollar bill and told him to go out and buy some cigars and get something for himself. The boy got himself a new suit.

699. The speaker who continues his remarks by saying, "In other words." He should have used the right ones the first time.

700. The fellow who gave his girl friend a diamond ring and told her, "If you like the ring, all you have to do is just keep on going with me and keep up the payments."

AS BAD AS . . .

701. The swanky hotel in Florida which even charged the tide to come in. In every room there are three water faucets—hot, cold and Chanel No. 5.

702. The house for sale at the seashore which was advertised with these words: "Where the Turf Meets the Surf." They should have said: "Where the Debris Meets the Sea."

703. The maiden lady who loved goldfish and had her bathtub filled with them. When asked what she did with them when she took a bath, the maiden lady answered with a blush, "Blindfold them, of course."

AS CONVINCING AS . . .

704. The teacher who told her class that the examination would be conducted on the honor system and then had them take seats three spaces apart in alternate rows.

705. The girl who, whenever she kissed a fellow, he knew he had been kissed. She left a note.

706. The movie cowboy who was such a tough, bad man that he carried two guitars.

707. The wife who insists she is an angel because she is always harping on something.

708. The wife who, in great annoyance with her husband, shouted at him, "That's the end! I'm going to get a divorce." The husband smiled and answered, "There you go trying to make up by saying something to make me feel good."

AS CONVINCING AS . . .

709. The woman who celebrated her twenty-ninth birthday, figuring it's better late than never.

710. The survey which shows that nine out of every ten people who inhale smoke.

711. The man who starts economizing when he runs out of money.

712. The fellow who insisted that in summer the hours are longer—sixty-five minutes!

713. The bride who had just been carried over the threshold. From then on, she put her foot down.

714. The country fellow who visited a city and was taken to view a beautiful, well-landscaped cemetery. He looked over the well-kept lawn, trees and flowers and then remarked, "These city folks—they sure know how to live!"

715. The young medical student who announced that if you could take all the blood vessels in a man's body—the veins, the arteries and the capillaries—and lay them end to end, that man would probably die.

716. The answer of a pregnant woman who was asked by a woman to whom she had just been introduced, "Are you going to have a baby?" She responded, "No, I'm just carrying this for a friend."

717. The lawyer who told his wealthy client, "Your troubles are my troubles." He forgot to mention the fee.

AS CONVINCING AS . . .

718. The little boy who insisted he wasn't pulling the cat's tail. He was just holding it and the cat was pulling.

719. A young man's vocational aptitude test rating which indicated his best opportunity lay in a field where his father holds an influential position.

720. The movie starlet who insisted that love was more important to her than money and she intended to wait for marriage until the right millionaire came along.

721. The boy who said he got a quarter from a friend for doing him a favor. It seems he was hitting the friend on the head, and the friend asked him to please stop.

722. The father who said what he wanted most out of his new auto was his teen-age son.

723. The wife whose husband accused her of infidelity. "That's an insult," she shouted. "I've been faithful to him dozens of times!"

724. A young girl who told the man to whom she was engaged, "When we get married I'm going to cook, sew, darn your socks and lay out your pipe and slippers. What more can any man ask than that?" To which the fellow replied, "Nothing! Unless he is evil-minded."

725. The youngster who came home from school and proudly announced that he learned to say "Yes, sir" and "No, sir."

"Did you really?" asked a friend of the family who was there.

"Yep," the boy replied.

AS CONVINCING AS . . .

726. Giving up smoking. I've done it dozens of times.

727. Learning to ski. There are only three steps to skiing: How to put the skis on, how to jump and how to walk again.

728. The person on a diet who lost seven pounds in a week by setting the scale back a pound each day.

729. Making one of those French bathing suits. Just take two handkerchiefs and throw one away.

730. Sending an S.O.S. signal backwards.

AS FOOLISH AS . . .

731. The complaint of the woman who lived in a bad neighborhood where dirty words were always being chalked on the sidewalks and sides of buildings. She complained that outsiders would get a bad impression of the people because the words weren't spelled right.

732. The fellow who walked the floor all night because he had a note coming due at the bank next day. He should have stayed in bed and let the banker walk the floor!

733. The fellow who regrets those follies of youth he didn't commit when he had the opportunity.

734. The fellow who would sooner die than think—and usually does.

735. The person who wants to live to be one hundred and doesn't know what to do with himself when he has one day off work.

AS FOOLISH AS . . .

736. The fellow who believes that if at first you don't succeed, try, try, try again. There's no use being pigheaded about it! He should have quit in the first place.

737. The fellow who married the girl for money and her father went bankrupt the next year.

738. A person who doesn't like to grow old. Many are denied this opportunity.

739. The fellow who bought a dictionary at a bargain price. There was only one little thing wrong with the dictionary— it wasn't in alphabetical order.

740. The fellow stopped by a cop for going through a thirty-mile zone at fifty miles an hour. "What of it?" he snapped back at the cop. "The dealer who sold me this car said I could go as fast as I liked the first one thousand miles."

741. The fellow who read his name in the obituary column of a newspaper, so he went out and shot himself. Don't believe everything you read.

742. The idealist who wanted to keep politics out of politics.

743. The fellow who thought he figured out a way to avoid a summer cold—get it in December.

744. A fellow who bought a truck farm because he heard that there is a lot of money in selling trucks.

745. The motorist driving through New England during the maple sirup time when shiny tin buckets were hung low

AS FOOLISH AS . . .

on the trunks of trees. "My," he commented, "they certainly have a sanitary bunch of dogs around here."

746. The young bride who was telling her friend about her new electric kitchen. "But, my dear," she said, "it isn't automatic. You have to turn on a switch."

AS GOOD AS . . .

747. The fellow who did a juggling act with twenty plates, a glass pitcher and a half dozen Indian clubs. He gave it up because he couldn't figure out what to do with the other hand.

748. A cigarette which is so mild that you have to stand before a mirror to see if you are smoking it.

749. A new fan dancer's insurance policy. If she loses her fans, she is still covered.

750. The fellow who got a dog for his wife. A good trade, eh?

751. A girdle for keeping a bad situation from spreading.

752. The fellow who played golf in a nudist colony. It was the first time he went around nine holes in nothing.

AS HAPPY AS . . .

753. The fellow who put tranquilizer drugs in his cigarettes. It won't stop lung cancer, but he just doesn't give a damn!

AS HAPPY AS . . .

754. The bride who had a perfect understanding with her new husband. One night a week he was allowed to go out with the boys, and the other nights she goes out with them.

755. The fellow who was old enough to know better—but kept on doing it anyway!

756. The man whose wife stopped him from reading his paper and exclaimed, "I've got a lot of things I want to talk to you about." He thought she wanted to talk about a lot of things she hadn't got.

757. The fellow who had some work done on his nose. He had it put between his eyes.

758. The fellow who offers this prescription for happy living—if you must live, be happy.

759. A woman who sees a double chin—on her husband's old girl friend.

760. A woman who shed herself of two hundred pounds of ugly fat. She divorced her husband.

761. A fellow who bought some real estate in the country sight unseen and found land on his property.

762. The girl who flashed a diamond ring on her finger and announced, "It's a boy—six feet tall and 190 pounds!"

763. The bride whose just-wed husband whispered to her, "Someday we will be rich." She answered joyously, "Honey, we are rich. Someday we will have money."

AS HAPPY AS . . .

764.   The man who came off the farm to the city and got a job as janitor in a girls' dormitory. When the house mother handed him the pass key to every room in the dormitory she asked, "Would twenty-five dollars a week be all right?" "Gosh," said this happy transplanted farmer, taken aback, "I don't know if I can pay that much or not, lady."

765.   The alcoholic sent to a special institution where the whole staff drinks—the doctors, nurses and patients. They don't cure alcoholics, but—boy!—does everyone have a good time!

766.   The man who was so rich he didn't know his son was in college.

AS IGNORANT AS . . .

767.   The famous old lady who lived in a shoe. She wouldn't have had so many kids if she'd known what to do.

768.   The hypochondriac who was on a vacation and mailed a card to his psychiatrist saying: "Am having a swell time. Why?"

769.   The woman who visited George Washington's house on the Potomac, Mount Vernon, and was amazed to discover that everything was furnished in Early American.

770.   The fellow who thinks he knows it all and keeps proving that he doesn't.

771.   The receptionist who was told to keep everyone out of the president's office during a conference. If anyone insisted he had an appointment, she should tell him, "That's what they all say." During the conference, the president's

AS IGNORANT AS . . .

wife showed up and demanded entrance. The receptionist refused, and the wife drew herself up stiffly and said, "You do not understand. I am his wife." The receptionist shrugged her shoulders and replied, "That's what they all say."

772. The fellow whose barber sold him a special non-caloric hair oil for fatheads.

773. The kid in the fifth grade who could beat up all the kids of his same age. He never had any fights because all of the kids his age were in high school.

774. The people in this town. I stood on a street corner all morning asking people for the time, and everybody gave me a different answer.

775. The fellow who was told not to spit on the floor and asked, "Why, does it leak?"

776. The highbrow who has been educated beyond his intelligence.

777. The boy who was in the same class so long all the other pupils would bring him an apple every day. They thought he was the teacher.

778. A young fellow in Paris who could speak only enough French to get his face slapped.

AS LOGICAL AS . . .

779. The idiot who won a lottery. He was asked by a friend how he happened to pick the lucky number, and he explained

AS LOGICAL AS . . .

that he used logic. For three nights he dreamed of the number seven. "So," explained the idiot, "three times seven is twenty-four. I bought a ticket with the number twenty-four and it won the first prize."

780. The fellow who was told by his doctor to give up drinking. He thought it over and told the doctor he would keep on drinking because he noticed that there are a lot more old drunks around than old doctors.

781. The American traveling in Europe who continued to speak to everyone in English—only louder!

782. The reasoning of the college student who said that going around with women keeps a person young. To prove it, he said he started to go around with women when he was a freshman four years ago and he is still a freshman.

783. The man who told his wife that if nature had intended for her to have a fur coat it would have given her one.

784. The booster who claimed the heavy wind storms were very unusual for that part of the country and pointed out the wind blew down trees that had never been blown down before.

785. The note which a man found in a Chinese fortune cookie. The fortune read: "You will be hungry again in two hours."

786. The observation made by a student at school that, if it were not for Thomas Edison, we would all be watching television by candlelight.

AS MUCH CHANCE AS . . .

787. The father who asked the nurse when she came out of the delivery room, "Is it a boy?" and the nurse answered, "The one in the middle is!"

788. The fellow who didn't know the difference between temptation and opportunity.

789. The bachelor who once tried his hand at cooking. He bought a cookbook but he was stopped because each recipe began the same way—"Take a clean dish."

790. Getting warm money. No one keeps it long enough to warm it up. That's why it is called cold cash.

791. The yes-man who worked for a boss who was always saying, "No."

792. The couple who tried to save their way to prosperity. They figured they would save enough on their food bill to pay for a refrigerator; they would save enough on carfare to pay for a car, and they would save enough on laundry to pay for a washing machine. It finally got to the point where they couldn't afford to save any more.

793. The man who approached a strange dog barking and wagging its tail. He didn't know which end to believe.

794. The fellow eying a pretty young blonde. She had something that would knock his eye out—a husband!

795. The fellow who had been unlucky all of his life. Finally, one day, things took a turn for the better. When they dug his grave, they struck oil.

AS MUCH CHANCE AS . . .

796. The fellow who went to Europe and called on three kings. Another fellow at the table had four aces.

797. The fellow who was traveling in Europe and picked up a little Russian. All she could say was "No."

798. The world has for peace when it has a bomb which will blow peace into pieces.

799. A person has trying to live a normal life in the world today. These days a person has to be crazy or he'll go nuts!

800. A fellow who took out a special kind of insurance. The policy provides that if you get killed by a railroad train, you receive an income for life.

801. The fellow who was married for ten years and didn't have any children. He had a strict mother-in-law.

802. The fellow who took out a $50,000 life insurance policy. It didn't do him any good. He died anyway.

803. The wife who had to get things fixed right around the house. Every time her husband attempted to fix something it would be like the time he worked on the cuckoo clock. When he had finished, on the hour the cuckoo would back out and ask, "What time is it?"

804. The fellow who lost his mind. He finally went crazy thinking about it.

805. Getting a dollar's worth of groceries for a dollar. The only money that goes as far as it did years ago is the dime that rolls under the bed.

AS MUCH CHANCE AS . . .

806. The motorist back of a woman driver who puts her hand out of the window of her car. It means only one thing—the window is open!

807. The fellow who asked the girl he admired if she could learn to care for a man like him. She replied, "Well, maybe, if he wasn't too much like you!"

808. A person living in our modern age. It's ashes to ashes and dust to dust. If cigarettes don't get you, the fallout must!

809. The housewife who tried to figure out the pattern of her furniture. It wasn't Colonial, and it wasn't Provincial. It was more likely Early Sears Roebuck.

810. The fellow who went to a doctor who believes in shock treatments—the first of every month!

811. The politician who tries to straddle an issue by staying in the middle of the road. It just makes it easier for him to get hit from both sides.

812. The football player who got fed up with the bad decisions of the referee and finally burst out in rage to that official, "You stink!" The referee stepped off a fifteen-yard penalty and asked calmly, "How do I smell from here!"

813. A diner in a restaurant trying to attract the attention of his waiter. No wonder, when one well-known waiter died they inscribed on his tombstone these words: "Here lies Tony, the waiter. God finally caught his eye."

814. The Russian who was up for deportation from the United States. The government said he was a Red Russian.

AS MUCH CHANCE AS . . .

He claimed he was a White Russian, and when he was deported he was a Blue Russian.

815.   The patron in a ritzy night club where the cigarette girl goes around calling out, "Cigars—cigarettes—small loans."

816.   The husband whose wife used to look over his coat lapels every night when he came home to see if she could discover any blond, black or red feminine hairs. For a few nights she found none at all and exclaimed in great irritation, "So it has come to this now. Even bald women!"

817.   The fellow whose father was real dumb, and he is a chip off the old blockhead.

818.   A truthful politician—one who would get up and ask the people to vote for him because he needs the job.

819.   The fellow who sat and waited for his ship to come in, when he should have given it a tug.

820.   The Hollywood man-about-town who complained that every time he met a girl he really liked, she was married or he was.

821.   The fellow who bet on a horse has to change his mind after the race is over.

822.   A salesman who tries to sell someone something he doesn't really need, to be paid for with money he hasn't got.

823.   The fellow who entered a battle of wits without any ammunition.

AS MUCH CHANCE AS . . .

824. The fellow who made a New Year's resolution to stop smoking and give up seeing girls. It was the most miserable afternoon he ever spent.

825. The girl who thinks no man is good enough for her. She may be right, but usually she is left.

826. The man in the moon when he tacked up a "No Visitors" sign.

AS PUZZLING AS . . .

827. The fact that so many Americans want to travel to the moon when you can't even get them to move to the rear of a bus.

828. The custom of many of our young married couples today who go to a friend's house to watch television all evening and pay a baby-sitter to watch it in their own homes.

829. How astronomers who discover new stars find out their names.

830. The Russians to the blond young girl who was drinking in the cocktail lounge. She couldn't figure out how the Russians do it because every time she drinks vodka she says "yes."

831. A cold in the head, which is both positive and negative. Sometimes the eyes have it and sometimes the nose.

832. The young man out on his first date with a girl who didn't know if he was a perfect gentleman or just not interested in her.

AS PUZZLING AS . . .

833. The reason why it is called a permanent wave.

834. The doorman who can open the car door with one hand, help you in the auto with the other hand and still hold out one hand for a tip!

835. A doctor's prescription written for a druggist. For all I know, it could mean, "I got my five dollars, now you get yours."

836. The store clerk who was telling a woman customer about the store's wonderful invisible hairpins. They are so invisible, he said, that he had just sold a woman five dollars worth—and the store had been out of them for two weeks.

837. The case of some delegates to a convention who had been doing some heavy drinking the night before and all showed up the next morning looking haggard and beat from the hangover except one. His friends couldn't understand it and one asked, "You look wonderful this morning! What's the matter with you—got an ulcer?"

838. The time a fellow who started to go home after a few drinks at the tavern and went into a bus. It didn't move for two hours, but he was really confused when people started to come into the bus and order hamburgers.

839. The problem presented the twelve-year-old girl who had been asked to baby-sit with a neighbor's twins. When the time came to feed the babies their formulas, one for the boy and another for the girl, the mother of the twelve-year-old baby sitter received a frantic phone call and her daughter asked in great concern, "Mother, which one is the boy?"

AS SAD AS . . .

840. The fellow who was born with a silver spoon in his mouth. All the other kids had tongues.

841. The man who finally became rich enough to sleep late but by then he was so old he would wake up early.

842. The patient who had just undergone surgery and learned that the doctor left a sponge in him. He didn't suffer any pain but he was terribly thirsty.

843. The millionaire whose daughter was in love with a penniless fellow. When the fellow asked the father for permission to marry, the millionaire replied, "Ask her if you want. I won't interfere. I've given her a good education and the opportunity to read newspapers and know what to do. If she hasn't enough sense by now to say 'No,' then she doesn't deserve any better luck."

844. The waiter where a diner kept complaining all through the meal. When it was all over the waiter asked politely, "Sir, was anything all right?"

845. The young fellow whose friend said he was going to dig up a girl for him, and he evidently did!

846. The man whose psychiatrist told him, "My friend, you do not have a complex. You ARE inferior."

847. The fellow who kept his nose to the grindstone. About the only thing he is any good for now is to cut bread with his nose.

848. The father who sacrificed everything to have his son become a doctor, and what happened? His son told him to give up smoking!

AS SAD AS . . .

849. The politician who dreamed that all the money he was spending was his own.

850. The middle-aged man who discovers everything he enjoys is either illegal, immoral or fattening.

851. The pilot who flew his airplane into a cloud before he realized it had a silver lining.

852. The chorus girl when she cut quite a figure sitting down on a broken bottle.

853. A pessimist who is always trying to find out how bad the world can really be.

854. The case of the girl who had two fellows and wished she could combine them into one. Jim was tall, handsome, amusing, gay and rich. Frank, the other fellow, wanted to marry her.

855. The case of the girl who bought imported perfume. It only attracted foreigners.

856. The man who made out his will leaving everything to his wife if she married within a year from the time of his death. He wanted someone to feel sorry he had died.

857. The time the girl backed into the airplane propeller— disaster!

858. The case of the young woman who called the police to report that she had been assaulted—last week. When the

AS SAD AS . . .

police asked why she had waited a week to report she had been assaulted, she replied, "I didn't know I had been assaulted until his check bounced."

859. The case of the young fellow who crawled under a tent to see a circus and discovered when he got in that it was a revival meeting.

860. The fellow who thinks everything is funny—as long as it happens to someone else.

861. The gambler who couldn't go to the race track because his wife had just blown all his money on rent and groceries.

862. The underprivileged fellow who had such little joy in his life that whenever he smells flowers he looks around for a coffin.

863. The fellow eating in a restaurant who complained about the soup tasting like dishwater. The waiter heard his complaint and returned in a minute with his apologies, "The chef regrets very much to inform you that it WAS dishwater."

864. The old man who was always giving good advice because he no longer was able to set a bad example.

865. A young fellow who spent a small fortune on expensive dance lessons to make him popular and discovered when it was all over that he wasn't popular with girls but he was extremely popular with the owner of the dance studio.

AS SMART AS . . .

866. The fellow who said his girl has two of the prettiest legs in the world. When asked how he knew he replied, "I counted 'em."

867. The boy who got the highest grades of all in his class who flunked.

868. The fellow who wanted to swap his troubles with a friend. It is always easy to solve the other fellow's.

869. The fellow who can describe a shapely girl without using his hands.

870. The fellow who believes in saying "nice doggie" until he can find a rock.

871. The fellow who wanted to join the police force but he was too short. He took stretching exercises. He would hang by his neck from a crossbeam and wear lead weights attached to his shoes. It worked wonders. He would have been the tallest cop on the force, if he had lived!

872. The girl who prefers beauty to brains because the number of men who see outnumber those who can think.

873. The small-town newspaper publisher who ran a contest for the biggest potato grown in the county. He didn't get any more readers but he got enough potatoes as samples to feed his family all winter.

874. The fellow who always made his New Year's reservations early. Then in case they didn't work out he could still change his plans and invite his wife.

AS SMART AS . . .

875. The woman who reminded the doctor that it was her boy who threw the rock and hit the rich kid down the street, giving the doctor a chance to earn some good fees.

876. The six Russians who came to America to study. The Russian government sent six Russians to England to study and six to America to study. The six who were sent to England were very smart and when they returned to Russia they were given high positions in the government. The six sent to America were even smarter. They stayed and never went home.

877. The two first-grade youngsters standing outside the school in conversation. Said one, "Do you think that the forces of gravity can best be overcome by thermonuclear projectiles?"

Said the other, "You have to figure the influence of radiation in the substratosphere. . . ."

Just then the school bell rang for the first grade to take up, and the first boy said to the other, "Darn it, there goes the bell. Now we have to go in and string beads."

878. My boy. He could recite the Gettysburg Address when he was eight years old. Abraham Lincoln didn't say it until he was fifty-four.

879. The fellow who figured out a system to bet on horses and he couldn't lose. By the time he figured out what horse to bet on, the race was over.

880. The fellow who claimed he could stay under water for twenty minutes. "You'll drown!" said a friend. "Shucks," replied this fellow. "You know the trick."

THINGS ARE SO TOUGH THAT . . .

881. People are no longer buying the giant economy size. They are buying the small, expensive size they can afford.

882. We now know why they say that charity should begin at home. That is where poverty starts.

883. Some parents never tell their children that other families eat three meals a day.

884. Even the race track gamblers are hoping they break even. They need the money!

885. What used to be weak coffee is now helpless.

886. If the average family man keeps saving for the next fifteen years at the same rate he has saved for the last six months he will be able to retire and owe $100,000.

887. One fellow in business lost one hundred dollars a week for three months. He couldn't afford to give up the business, though, because it was his living.

888. The fellow who can afford a Ford now buys a Ford instead of a Cadillac.

889. Keeping up with the easy payments is the hardest thing a person has to do.

890. You no longer hear the expression about a person being disgustingly rich. Nobody who is rich is disgusting!

891. People who spent this year's salary in advance last year are really lucky. They are not getting a salary this year.

THINGS ARE SO TOUGH THAT . . .

892. Families are roughing it on their vacations. They stay at motels which do not have TV and swimming pools.

893. People are driving in cars at least two years old to the unemployment office to pick up their compensation checks.

894. A person can't even afford taxes.

895. Even the Joneses are beginning to complain.

896. The only way most people can face bills is with pills.

897. Even the installment collector has a hard time keeping up with the Joneses.

898. When the preacher warns his flock to think spiritual things because there will be no buying and selling in Heaven, nobody cares. That isn't where business has gone, anyway.

899. The average businessman is like the fellow at the race track who had a great day—a friend borrowed fifty dollars from him before he had a chance to lose it.

900. Only the scissors grinder is happy. He has never seen things so dull!

901. Many people are going out and buying themselves a new car. If you ride on the bus, you have to pay cash.

902. One fellow out West is trying to sell snake oil to snakes.

903. Everyone could use a rich and generous relative. Those who have one usually do.

THINGS ARE SO TOUGH THAT . . .

904.   A restaurant owner, losing a fortune on the place, can't close because he hasn't got enough money to eat out.

THINGS ARE SO HIGH THAT . . .

905.   A person finds himself living in a much more expensive home—and he hasn't even moved!

906.   Making money is easy, but it is sure tough trying to make a living.

907.   You don't have to go away for a vacation any more. You can get the same effect by staying home and tipping every third person you meet.

908.   A dime is not what it used to be. We can truly say that dimes have changed!

909.   The Joneses are now having trouble keeping up with themselves.

910.   We have come to realize that buck-passing isn't anything new. It just passes faster these days.

911.   A person today can be broke with money in his pocket.

912.   A family's upkeep is a man's downfall.

913.   Finding a way to live simply is today's most complicated problem.

914.   A woman's face is no longer her fortune. It's the beauty parlor's.

THINGS ARE SO HIGH THAT . . .

915. The fellow on a job calls the money in the wage envelope take-home pay because he can't afford to go anywhere else with it.

916. Today two will live as steep as one.

917. When you go into one of our high-class stores and spend only five dollars they ring up "No Sale."

918. When I asked a hotel cashier to change a twenty-dollar bill she asked, "Change? What's that?"

919. The country would be satisfied to get even a *bad* five-cent cigar.

920. We can truly say we have never had it so good or parted with it so fast.

921. The only way you can doll up is on a dollar down.

922. A dollar saved is fifty cents lost.

923. We can truly say we are living in a land of plenty. Everything you want to buy costs plenty.

924. The only way today you can get more for your money is to weigh yourself at the penny scale right after eating a big meal.

925. You don't need a magician to cut a dollar bill in half without touching the paper.

926. Airplane fares have been increased. Even the cost of going up is going up.

THINGS ARE SO HIGH THAT . . .

927. The only way a family can hold the bills down is to get a heavier paper weight.

WAY BACK WHEN . . .

928. A woman could remember her husband's first kiss. Nowadays, a woman can't hardly remember her first husband.

929. The biggest worry of parents was that their son might take up tobacco chewing in his teens.

930. A person could go a whole year and not try to quit smoking or cut down on eating even once.

931. It was considered something unusual to be a neurotic. Today, anybody who is not a neurotic is underprivileged!

932. You had to pass a civil service test before you could work for the government. Now you can work for the government without a test, with taxes the way they are.

933. TV was in its infancy. Now it is in its second childhood.

934. Marriage was really considered a matter of give-and-take. Today, if a husband doesn't give his wife enough, she takes it!

935. You saw a boy with a lump on his head you knew that was where his father helped him with his school work.

936. You could not expect to get something for nothing. Now you can get nothing for something.

WAY BACK WHEN . . .

937. A child would say "thank you" if you gave him a penny instead of "what do you use it for?"

938. The game of love was played with clubs as trumps instead of diamonds.

939. You said a person had gone to his everlasting rest and didn't mean he landed a job with the government.

940. It was the help and not the boss who worked twelve hours a day.

941. Men used to lose their shirts in the Stock Market instead of the supermarket.

8

Favorite Stories or Anecdotes of Prominent Speakers

EVERY person has favorite stories. They are stories which they themselves enjoy and generally tell well because these stories are familiar to them. They are stories which have the ring of truth in them and a certain sincerity and straightforwardness, which comes only when a speaker is talking about something of intimate, personal knowledge to himself. Such stories are homely, ordinary conversation elevated one step up the ladder of human communication to reach the speaking platform.

Generally, the best stories are based on personal experiences of the individual, especially if they deal with situations encountered in public speaking. Next in order would be humorous and embarrassing incidents which other speakers have encountered. During the few brief moments when the speaker is standing before an audience, both he and the audience are transplanted into a separate little world all by themselves—the realm of visual and audio communication. In this sphere which they occupy they are intensely aware of the fact that they have departed from the normal range of their worldly contacts. They become interested in anything that pertains to the activity which has engaged their attention for the time—forming an audience to listen to a speech. It is like telling a fish story on a fishing trip, a golf story during a golf game or a courtroom yarn to lawyers. The audience becomes especially receptive to stories about public-speaking experiences, especially humorous situations and incidents.

Other favorite stories are those which may not deal directly with public speaking incidents but lend themselves well to platform use. They are stories which fit certain situations which confront every speaker, or they may be successfully tested stories which may be repeated with confidence and depended upon to go over well.

Every speaker knows the value of personal anecdotes and accounts of his own experiences, especially those which were humorous or proved embarrassing to him. A person who engages in speaking will do well to carry a notebook with him at all times and write down any foolish questions he may ask, any silly answers he may have received to some of his own questions, any misunderstanding of directions or instructions which caused him difficulty or embarrassment, any errors or mistakes which involved him in perplexing or disconcerting situations, any moments when he gives way to unwarranted pride or foolish vanity. All of these things are the crude, raw material from which the polished gem of a personal anecdote is manufactured. They are treasures to be collected as jewels for the speaker who desires a wealth of humorous material for his talks.

The stories which you will find in this chapter will be useful to you if you wish to relate them in your speech. However, their greatest value is the inspiration they offer for you to become a collector of personal anecdotes. See what others have done. Go, dear toastmaster, and do likewise!

942. Pride Before a Fall

Tom Wallace, Editor Emeritus of the Louisville Times *and past national president of the Izaak Walton League.* The following is an anecdote I have told from time to time in the course of an address:

I was present when a speaker delivered a fine talk about natural resources. I congratulated the speaker, who was applauded enthusiastically, saying I had often discussed the same subject, but never with as good results. I added, as a compliment merely, "I don't know how you do it."

The speaker replied quite seriously, "I appeal to the emotions of my audiences. I don't depend on merely appealing to their minds."

That meant to me use of oratory rather than argument without frills. I decided to try oratory. I worked on a speech till I believed it as eloquent as Robert G. Ingersoll's eulogy of his brother, Ebon, at the graveside, or at least as moving as Senator Vest's tribute to a dog, or Henry W. Grady's speech on cotton which made him famous.

I tried my oration on an audience in Columbus, Ohio. The applause was hardly more than courteous. I believed that the fault was not mine but that of a group (of sportsmen) who lacked appreciation of real oratory. I decided to deliver the same address to another Ohio audience. I did so with the same result. Faces in the front row expressed no emotion when I approached my climax. I was still convinced that my oratory was first-rate. I had an engagement to address an audience in Lexington, Kentucky. I decided to make the address for the third time where, I felt sure, the culture of my audience would be such that my art would be appreciated.

I felt vindicated and richly rewarded when the audience gave me an ovation. I had never witnessed a more emotional response except one evening in Paris when I saw some young men carry from the stage on their shoulders a famous Russian violinist at the end of a masterly performance.

When I was getting into a car with a friend with whom I was to drive home, he said, "Wallace, that was a good speech."

I replied with what I believed becoming modesty, and at

the same time sincerely, "That was a good audience, and a good audience helps."

Said my friend promptly, "It was the largest and most representative audience of its kind (meaning sportsmen) I have seen assembled in this state, but did you ever see an audience which contained so much whiskey per capita?"

Since then I have not attempted oratory.

943. How to Introduce a Complex Subject

Ruddick C. Lawrence, Vice-President, New York Stock Exchange. One day I gave an explanation to a group of educators of some rather complicated aspects of the Stock Exchange and the Specialist system. At the conclusion, an economics professor from Northwestern University related an experience which has since helped me many times in introducing a complex subject:

A student enrolled in an economics course. He attended the first lecture, but then proceeded to skip the rest of the classes. However, he did not withdraw from the course, and at its conclusion he showed up to take the final exam. The professor was upset, and looked forward with some eagerness to grading the exam paper. When the paper came in, he went over it carefully three times, but try as he might he was able to find only one small mistake.

The professor was amazed and decided to call in the student for an interview. He told him, "Joe, I went over your paper three times and I found just one small mistake."

Joe replied, "Gee, Professor, I'm sorry. I wouldn't have made that mistake if I hadn't been confused by your first lecture."

944. The Power of Words

Rev. Harry B. Schultheis, winner of the Freedoms Foundation Award for 1957, for the best sermon on the American way of life. In a church in Wyoming, where I pastored, I was prevailed upon to deliver a eulogy for an elderly, popular railroader. The church was crowded beyond capacity. The pallbearers brought in the body in the casket to the front. Then the six pallbearers retired to their respective pews on the side. The small pews would accommodate three smaller persons. But these three very large men decided to occupy the same pew. Hardly had the men got settled, and the signal had just been given for the soloist, when c-r-a-c-k, c-r-a-s-h, bomp, and down went the side of the pew, and the three big men fell in a heap on the floor! One red-faced man picked up the broken pieces, laid them gently to rest and then looked for another place to sit and be comfortable. Some in the audience screamed—and some just laughed. Well, that is the way I began that funeral.

I forget now what real words of comfort I said. However, when I was through, I slowly walked to the vestibule, just beyond the swinging doors. Shortly afterward, two lovely matrons walked out. They didn't see me. One said, "My, what a lovely funeral. I've used nine handkerchiefs!"

945. *A Long Talk*

Most Rev. Thomas K. Gorman, Catholic Bishop of Dallas–Fort Worth, Texas. Some years ago, when Bishop of Reno, in the state of Nevada, I spoke on a particular project in which I was very interested at all the Masses on a Sunday morning. The late Governor, Ted Carville, of Nevada, happened to be in the congregation that morning. After the Mass he attended, I met him outside the church and said to him, "Well, Ted, what did you think of that project?"

"Oh," he said, "it's fine, Bishop."

"I am very interested," I said. "Do you think I talked too long?"

"Oh no, Bishop," he said, "your sermon wasn't too long; it just seemed long."

946. When Time Stood Still

Ellis Arnall, Ex-Governor of Georgia. In this day of super-sonic speed, rockets and sputniks, I am reminded of the fact that some years ago while I served as Governor of Georgia, upon my recommendation, a law was enacted placing the entire state on Eastern Standard Time with a provision that there could be no Daylight Time in Georgia. Up until then, the Eastern and Central Time Zone divided the state and caused much confusion to our people. Our critics charged that we were undertaking to enact the rule of Joshua and make the sun stand still. Nevertheless, by law, the entire state was placed on Eastern Standard Time and so it remains.

Shortly after the time zone had been changed, an old Negro who lived in the country out from Dalton, Georgia, had occasion to go to Chattanooga, Tennessee, on the bus. Dalton was some thirty miles from Chattanooga, and Chattanooga was on Central Standard Time. The old Negro had not heard of the Georgia time change. He went up to the ticket agent at the Dalton bus station and inquired as to when the next bus departed for Chattanooga. The agent told him that the next bus left Dalton at six o'clock. "When does it get to Chatta-nooga?" the old colored man inquired.

"It gets there at six o'clock," the ticket agent responded.

The old fellow walked around an entire city block trying to analyze how it was that the bus could leave Dalton at six o'clock and get to Chattanooga at six o'clock. He was far from sure that he understood the ticket agent correctly. So after a while, the old Negro sidled up to the ticket counter and asked the agent, "When does the next bus leave Dalton for Chattanooga?" "It leaves here at six o'clock and gets there at six o'clock," the ticket agent replied. "I have told you that once before; now I want to know, do you want a ticket on the bus or not?" the ticket agent asked impatiently.

"I thought I wanted a ticket on the bus to Chattanooga,"

the Negro replied, "but if it's all right with you, I think I'll just stand around here and watch it take off."

947. *The Dangers of Perseverance*

Wren Jones Grinstead, co-translator from Greek to Esperanto of Gospel of John. The faculty of a college where I once taught gave a banquet in honor of the victorious football team of the Demonstration High School. As I had known the star player, Bill Crutcher, since his early childhood, I was asked to make a speech. I told the following true story.

As a child, Bill had been somewhat delicate. Hence his parents had rather babied him, and had not always insisted on minor points of manners. When he entered kindergarten, his teacher found that many of the children were not in the habit of giving a formal greeting, so she suggested that they say "Good morning" to her when they came into the room. All the others quickly took up this practice, but Bill would make no response to her greeting.

One morning when Bill came in a bit late, the teacher thought it an apt time to get some sort of response from him. So she stopped whatever the children were doing, and very pointedly said:

"Good morning, William." Bill merely stood and stared, so she tried again: "How do you do, William." Bill still stared. "Aren't you going to say anything to us this morning, William?" said she. Still no answer. "What do you say, William," she persisted, "when you first see anyone in the morning?" Bill made no response whatever.

This wouldn't do at all. Determined to get some sort of reply, the teacher said earnestly, "Now think hard, William. What was the first thing your mother said to you when you went into her room this morning?"

That registered. Bill's face lighted up and he answered, "Oh! Why, she said, 'Aw, go on back to bed, you little dickens. What are you doin' up here in the middle of the night?'"

948. Quiet, Please

George E. Hood, North Carolina attorney. This story was used by me in my campaigns for Congress. A former superior judge heard of it, and in the trial of a case at which time I talked rather loudly he called attention of the jury that this was my story and turned it on me: An elderly man was in the woods gathering firewood when a sudden storm came up unexpectedly. Everything became dark except when illuminated by sudden, vivid flashes of lightning, followed by deafening bolts of thunder. The old man knelt on his knees and prayed, "Oh, Lord, if it will be all right with You, please give me more light and less noise."

949. Alibi

Mary Hotchkin Hoag, lecturer on historical subjects. Returning to teaching during the demanding depression years, the best the educational field could offer me was a rural school. Poor in recompense but rich in experience were my two years.

I recall one incident which I have often referred to in my public speaking activities. Some of the youngsters had been romping and shouting happily during recess outside on the playground. Suddenly, en masse, they stormed into the schoolroom, crying out in unison accusingly, "John said a bad word!"

According to our custom, this called for careful consideration and the administration of justice. First, I must hear the defense. "How do you plead, John, guilty or not guilty?" I asked.

"Oh, Mrs. Hoag, I didn't say it on the school grounds," the boy answered quickly. He pointed to a neighbor's adjoining field and continued, "I just said it down by the fence."

When the time comes for me to use strong words or I am faced with a controversial subject, I do not try to avoid the unpleasantness of it by "taking my words down by the fence" or getting on the fence. Such an alibi merely evades the issue.

950. Against Stupidity

Albert D. Rosellini, Governor of Washington. One day, years ago, a very distinguished-looking gentleman came to my office and asked if he could help our local citizens' tax group by making a talk at a public meeting which was to be held that evening. He wished to expound his ideas concerning our revenue problems.

Upon inquiry, I was informed that he was now retired, but that he held a Ph.D. in economics and for years had been a professor of public finance at one of the major Eastern universities.

That evening he gave a very good presentation of his views and made some worthwhile-sounding suggestions; many of these suggestions impressed the audience. Just as the talk ended, we heard a disturbance in the back of the room. Two men were hurrying toward the speaker; the men wore white coats. In a very solicitous but firm manner, they took charge of the speaker, meanwhile explaining that he was one of their escaped wards and they had come to return him to the sanitarium. They said he fancied himself to be a learned professor of economics and public finance.

Several citizens at the meeting were amazed and very disturbed since his talk seemingly revealed him to be an erudite individual whose suggestions seemed helpful. Observing the agitation he had caused, the old gentleman drew himself up to his dignified best, looked over the advisory group at the head table and said, "Of course I have been able to give you some advice. I may be crazy, but I most certainly am not stupid!"

951. Embarrassing Moment

G. E. Tenney, past national president, Ohio State University Alumni Association. Some years ago, a Dayton, Ohio, company, which was a division of a big corporation, was having a very important sales meeting with their representatives from all over the country present in Dayton for several days. The executives of this company were put out when it was decided to have a spellbinder from another and larger division of this big corporation give a climax speech to end this important sales meeting. This good-looking spellbinder started out brilliantly and, as a promise of what was to come, he stated that if they would remember only the five simple things he was going to tell them, the sales meeting would be a huge success—and these five fundamental points were easy to remember and were essential to the success of the sales campaign. He then developed his talk and led up to the climax where he stated, ". . . and these five points are— these five points are—" (and he could not remember a single point, so had to pull his notes out of his pocket to see what they were).

Obviously, those present got considerably more pleasure out of his talk than they did benefit.

952.   *Too Late*

Dr. John Henry Grossman, gynecologist and obstetrician. For many years, I have been giving lectures on the sex education of children before interested parents' groups. I found the anecdote about to be recounted both educational and highly appreciated by my audiences. I wish that I could give proper credit to the originator, but I read or heard this story so long ago that I can't remember its source.

After a lecture of the type mentioned above, the usual question and answer period was being conducted, and a mother asked the sexologist if he thought her child was old enough to be given sex instruction. On inquiry, the doctor was told that the child was five years of age. Whereupon he said, "I advise you to hurry home at once, madam, since you have lost four years already!"

953.   *Another Point of View*

Orrin A. Bell, superintendent, Southern Reception Center, California Youth Authority. The following is a story that I have used for years. It has been very good with high school commencement classes, P.T.A. groups, service clubs, etc. I use it to show that one never knows the answers that the child will come up with to something that is perfectly obvious to most adults.

The fourth-grade teacher was just completing a discussion with her class on the evils of alcoholic beverages. In order to clinch her point she prepared a demonstration. She called the entire class to the front of the room around her desk. She said, "Now, children, in order to complete our subject, I want to make this demonstration for you. You will notice in this tumbler I am pouring pure, clear water." She then reached into her desk and brought out a little packet. She emptied the little packet into her hand, and there was a little vegetable worm. "Now, children," she said, "I'm going to drop this little worm into the tumbler of pure, clear, sparkling water." She did this. The worm swam around and enjoyed himself thoroughly. Then she said, "Now, children, I want you to watch this carefully. Into this second tumbler I'm going to pour alcohol." This she proceeded to do. The teacher then said, "I am now going to take this little worm which you have seen having so much fun in the water and drop him into this tumbler of alcohol." She did this, and the little worm shriveled up and died, much to the dismay of the youngsters in the class. After a proper pause, she said, "Now, is there anyone in the group who would like to tell me the lesson taught by this little demonstration?"

Volunteers came slowly, but finally the perennial Johnny held up his hand and said, "Teacher, I know the lesson that is taught."

"Very good, Johnny," said the teacher, "tell us what it is."

"The lesson taught," said little Johnny, "is that people who drink alcohol will never have worms."

954. *A Specialist*

James W. McClendon, Chief Justice (retired), Court of Civil Appeals and past Grand Master of Masons of Texas. The following occurred many years ago in a court trial in which I was an attorney, and I frequently relate the incident in my talks as an example of being a specialist.

It was necessary for me to use a witness of questionable reputation to establish a certain essential fact, all the other witnesses being barred under the "dead man's statute." When the opposing counsel, who had recently retired as a law professor, took the witness on cross-examination, this is what took place:

Q. "Bill Jones, how many times have you been convicted of cattle stealing?"

A. "Never was, Professor."

Q. "What? You swear before this jury you never have been convicted of cattle stealing?"

A. "That's right, Professor."

Q. "Bill Jones, you've been around the courthouse a lot, and you know they can put you in the pen for perjury. Now, do you tell this jury, on your oath, you have never been convicted for cattle stealing?"

A. "That's right, Professor. You've been up at the University for several years teaching law to these young law students and you haven't been keeping up with what's going on in the community at large. Let me set you right. *Horse* stealing is my specialty."

955. *An Apt Illustration*

Dr. Raymond Villers, lecturer in Industrial Engineering at Columbia University, and head of the firm of Rautenstrauch and Villers, Consultants in Industrial Management. At a New York hotel I was addressing a group of executives enrolled in the Management Course of the American Management Association.

I was talking about issuing precise instructions to organize activities in modern industry and warned the audience about going too far in this direction, because it is impossible to anticipate everything. Completely unforeseeable incidents are likely to happen. At this point, the door opened quietly and a janitor entered carrying a mop and pail. He started circulating among the audience of about one hundred executives. I tried to ignore this disturbance for a few minutes, but finally I asked him what he was doing here. "Looking for the gentleman who vomited," was the answer. After the laughter had died down, I had a hard time to convince the audience that this was truly one of those unforeseeable incidents and not something that had been prepared in advance to illustrate my point. Actually, the janitor had made a mistake. Somebody in another room had been sick.

956. Getting Down to Business

John A. Blume, consulting engineer. When declining an invitation from the chair to get up and deliver a few remarks, I often use this story:

Cherokee Charlie was about to be hanged. The sheriff asked Charlie if he had any last words to say before the end.

The outlaw looked at the sheriff and replied solemnly, "Cherokee Charlie come here to be hung, not to make speech."

957. Dangers of Overlearning

Recene V. Ashton, assistant professor of education, New Mexico Western College. At times I find myself before an audience pounding and hammering to clinch a point. Then I think of a teaching experience back in a fourth grade in Iowa, and I realize I may be going too far: Paul was having trouble with his spelling. I determined to help him individually in special fashion to build up some faith in himself. I chose the week when they were assigned the spelling of the days of the week. Leaving thirty-seven others to fend for themselves, I worked with Paul. We wrote all the days and then we practiced with lots of zest on the silent letters of *Wednesday.* By the time we were writing on Friday for a final grade, it seemed that sweet little Paul couldn't possibly miss a word. I pronounced them, and with great anticipation I picked up Paul's paper to see the results of my "hammer and tongs" method of teaching. Here is what his paper said:

> (Sunday)—Sunnesday
> (Monday)—Monnesday
> (Tuesday)—Tuesnesday
> (Wednesday)—Wednesday
> (Thursday)—Thursnesday
> (Friday)—Frinesday
> (Saturday)—Saturnesday

I concluded there are dangers in overlearning, so forgive me if I have hammered too hard on this project of mine.

958. *How to Combat Skepticism*

Harry E. Warren, advertising agency executive. I attended a meeting where a representative of the federal government was present in an effort to clear a number of misunderstandings. The speaker was of the opinion that this group would regard with some skepticism, or possibly disbelief, almost anything he might say. He opened his speech with this fairy tale:

A long time ago a young and extremely beautiful fairy princess, while walking through the royal gardens, was startled at a cry: "Be careful, princess, you might step on me." Upon observing the area most carefully, the only living creature anywhere in sight was a small frog. The princess was again shocked when the voice said, "It is I, princess, the frog, talking. You may think it strange that a frog can talk. However, you should know that once upon a time I was a fairy prince, but a bad witch caused a spell to fall upon me and I was turned into a lowly frog."

The princess asked sympathetically, "Isn't there something that can be done for you?" The frog gleefully replied, "Yes, I could be restored to my natural state of a fairy prince, nineteen years old and six feet tall, if a fairy princess would let me sleep under her pillow for just one night."

The princess took the frog home and put it under her pillow that night. Lo and behold, the next morning the fairy princess's godmother didn't believe one single word of the princess's story.

959. Warning

Edwin Z. Gabriel, professor in electric engineering, Villanova University. Unaccustomed as I am to public speaking, as well as being emotionally and sensitively inclined, I feel like the young minister who was preaching in his new church for the first time. He thought he had done a good job of memorizing his sermon and started out by saying, "The text of my sermon, ladies and gentlemen, is: 'Behold, I shall come to you again.'" To his consternation the new minister forgot the rest of his sermon. He thought to himself, if this time I lean heavily on my pulpit and repeat the text with more vim, vigor and vitality, it may help me remember the rest of my sermon. So he repeated his text and, as he did so, he leaned so heavily on the pulpit, he fell over and the pulpit after him. He fell right into the arms of an admiring lady parishioner in the front pew. The sensitive minister was as red as a beet as he tried to apologize. The lady comfortingly said, "It is quite all right, young man; you warned me twice that you were coming, but I did not suspect it was going to be quite so soon."

960. When Specialists Get Together

John C. Youngman, former district attorney of Lycoming County, Pennsylvania. A term of civil jury trials was being conducted in an upstate county. Usually these lasted only about three or four days. At this particular term, which had begun on Monday, there remained by Saturday morning one case to be tried involving a $250 automobile damage case.

Because court was usually over by Thursday or Friday, the local Bar Association had called a meeting in the courtroom of the courthouse for 9:30 A.M. Saturday morning. It developed that the judge had excused the jury panel on Friday, and it was necessary to call jurors from the audience which happened to contain nobody except lawyers. As a result a jury of twelve lawyers was picked to try the $250 automobile accident case.

The judge had a fishing date with a friend for 1:30 P.M. The case was very simple; the evidence was put in on both sides in less than one-half hour, and the judge charged the jury and the jury retired at 10:30 A.M. The judge was reasonably sure he would be able to keep his fishing appointment.

However, at 12 noon no verdict had been reached and the jury was taken out for lunch, returning about 12:30. By 1:30 no verdict was returned and the judge became nervous and impatient and requested the tipstaff to ascertain what was holding up the jury. The tipstaff listened outside the jury room and reported that the jury was talking and that no verdict had been reached.

By 2:30 the judge was in a real huff. He demanded that the tipstaff knock on the jury door and ascertain the true situation. The tipstaff went to the jury room and knocked on the door and it was opened. He said, "Has the jury reached a verdict?"; whereupon the lawyer nearest to the door said, "Verdict! I should say not. We are not even halfway through with the nominating speeches for foreman of the jury."

961. Pithy Summary

Max Band, internationally famous artist. The great philosophical debate was between two schools of thought: The materialists with the theory that everything is matter, soul included. The teachers of Reason and Idealism insisted that the mind and only the mind is the thing.

The arguments were so convincing that they weakened the conceptions of the adherents of both theories. When the turn came for a famous philosopher to make a speech, he said only one sentence: "Gentlemen, no matter, never mind."

962. On the Spot

Mrs. C. R. Joan Grant Govan, former concert singer. As Building Defense Director during World War II, I was asked to give a talk on "Fire Prevention." Several speakers who preceded me delivered their addresses, accompanied by the sonorous snoring of a man in the fourth row. When the program was over, the sound sleeper rushed forward, shook my hand vigorously and congratulated me on having given "such an inspiring and highly instructive talk." Finding it hard to believe that I alone had been able to capture such elusive attention, I put him "on the spot" by inquiring just what part of my speech he considered most helpful. Visibly embarrassed, the fellow stammered, "Er—er—that part where you told us to always get under cover as soon as the air-raid siren goes off."

"Well," said I, "you certainly have the right idea—getting under *some sort of shelter* in case of attack!"

963. A Man of Few Words

Carl R. Albach, consulting engineer. At a recent private school graduation exercise I was called on to say a few words. My remarks started something like this:

"I have been given permission to say a few words, but I was not told which few or how few, so I brought a few of my own—just in case. Words can be a problem, especially when you have to talk before so many English teachers as we have here tonight. I feel like the preacher who finally managed to save enough money to buy a secondhand car and then found he did not have the vocabulary to drive it."

964. *Importance of Every Detail*

Dr. F. W. Mohlman, director of laboratories, Sanitary Department of Chicago. I frequently use this true story to emphasize the importance of every small detail when delivering a speech:

Some time ago, the family was shopping downtown, glancing into windows here and there, reading the shopping signs idly and considering purchases. All were on the lookout for signs or ads of something new or unusual. Mary Franklin read them all.

Suddenly she stopped. Here was something new!

"Saint Warts," she exclaimed. "A new blend of coffee I never heard of before." So we stopped to see what she had discovered and read, "St-warts." The "e" had gone out. We still call it "St. Warts."

965. *Speedy Trial*

Charles H. Kirkman, North Carolina attorney. Whenever I think about the old phrase of suiting the action to the word, I recall a story told about an habitual thief who was on trial for larceny of a cow in the mountainous regions of North Carolina. During the course of the testimony in his own behalf the defendant said, "No sir, your honor, I didn't steal no cow, and that's the truth. If it ain't, I hope lightnin' strikes me right now."

The old man with a long police record had scarcely finished his statement when the witness chair collapsed with a loud bang, whereupon the presiding judge remarked, "Come down, old man. It appears that the Lord has seen fit to deal lightly with you." It's needless to add that the old man was promptly convicted.

966. Definition of an Economist

Robert E. Johnson, economist-actuary, Western Electric Co. An economist, wearing smoked glasses, recently appeared to address a group. He opened his talk as follows: "Let me explain these dark glasses. Economists have recently been characterized as a group of blind men feeling their way around in a nudist colony."

967. Prompt Action

Mary Hudson Brothers, writer and speaker on Southwestern history. A candidate for the office of senator in a Western state was making an impassioned speech concerning a big irrigation dam project, dear to the hearts of all present, regardless of politics. He brought out all the reasons why he had superior powers in that field, promising to have the project in working order first in six months, then three months and, finally, one month after he was seated in the house. There was a sudden scuffle, and one grizzled old farmer was pushing his way out, when someone asked, "What's wrong? Don't you want the dam built as soon as possible?"

"I sure do, but here I am fifty miles from home. At the rate he's going I am afraid that dam will bust, and I'll be drowned. I want to get home to try and save what I've already accumulated," and he fought his way out regardless of the disturbance he was causing in the meeting.

968. A Good Speech Opening

Dr. Howard S. McDonald, president, Los Angeles State College. The night before an important speech I was still dissatisfied with my opening lines—what I feel to be the seed of audience aspiration for further listening. To my further annoyance, a young scamp pulled into my parking spot just as I arrived. I honked my horn, believing that he would recognize me and vacate the spot. Instead, he thrust his head out the window and hollered, "Who in the Hell do you think you are, the President?"

I said, "I have aspirations." I also had the seed of a good speech.

969.   Running Over Your Speaking Time

J. Joseph Gribbins, editor and publisher, New Jersey Legislative Manual. This is a story I use when asked to limit my remarks to five minutes and discover I have exceeded my speaking time limit:

Many drifters drift into the State House newsroom in Trenton. Some of them are former newspapermen down on their luck.

One particular ex-newspaperman had been giving State House reporters the fast touch for some time, until his behavior became corridor conversation.

Recently, during a hectic session of the New Jersey Legislature, he pushed open the newsroom door, rushed over to my desk where I was busy pounding out copy and said:

"Can you let me have ten dollars for five minutes?"

Knowing the five minutes would probably last beyond my lifetime, I quickly said:

"Take a seat and rest for five minutes and you won't need the ten dollars." Needless to say, he made a hasty retreat.

970.   About Face

Neville Miller, past president, National Association of Broadcasters. I was Mayor of Louisville, Kentucky, 1933–37, when this incident occurred. During a session of the State Legislature, a member from Louisville joined with others to defeat a meritorious bill sponsored by the Governor. A motion to reconsider was made and those who had voted against

the bill, having had their satisfaction in defeating the
Governor, one by one arose and said how they loved their
Governor and for that reason would vote for the bill.
When it came to the turn for the Louisville legislator to state
his position he arose and said, "I love my Governor as much
as anyone else, but I am going to think a long time before
I fall in love with another Governor."

971. Afraid to Talk

*Rev. Russell Ayres Pavy, D.D., president, Conservative
Baptist Association of America.* There are times when it is
best for a person to keep his own opinion to himself. When
I want to illustrate this point to an audience, I tell them
this story:

A lawyer, talking with his client, reminded him, "After
the accident you stated you weren't hurt; now, you have
changed your testimony. How can I represent you in court,
having reversed your statement?"

"Your honor, it was this way. I was traveling down the
California highway, minding my own business, when along
came a big Cadillac, ran into my wagon and threw me, my
horse and my wagon into the ditch. Boy, were we a mess!
There I was on my back in the mud. I looked over at Jake,
my horse, on his back in the mud with his feet in the air.
The big Cadillac groaned to a stop; the man got out and
looked at my horse. When he saw that my horse had a broken
leg he went back to his car, took out his shotgun and shot my
horse. Then he looked at me and said, 'Say, are you hurt?' "

972. The Blind Leading the Blind

*Edward W. Hickey, retired president, Tarrytown National
Bank.* Back in 1947, a friend of mine, who had been born in
Switzerland but who was now a successful watch importer in
New York City, suggested that I accompany him on a three
weeks' flying trip to his native land.

I agreed, and early in July we landed in Geneva where his brother met us at the airport and drove us to his home in Solothurn.

My friend's name is Walter Kocher and his brother is Sylvain Kocher, president of the Eska Watch Company.

Two nights after our arrival, we were invited to attend a testimonal dinner to an employee who had served twenty-five years with the organization. As visiting *"Americanisch,"* we were invited to sit at the head table. Sylvain Kocher was master of ceremonies; I sat on his left; Walter on my left, and there were about twenty-five "important dignitaries" on the dais and over three hundred employees at the dinner tables in front of us.

As we were finishing the meal, Sylvain turned to me and asked me to make a speech. I said that I understood no German, but if he'd tell me the words for "ladies and gentlemen" in German, give me the name of the man being honored, I'd say a few words. He told me *"Damen and Herren"* for the salutation and the name I'd need.

Sylvain introduced me—I spoke for about five minutes on the beauties of Switzerland, the warmth of my reception, the friendliness I'd met with.

When I'd finished, a lean, lanky individual, sharp of feature and keen of gaze, who was seated about halfway down the room, got up and began speaking in German, unintelligible to me. The entire aggregation was shaking with laughter as he progressed; he must have been exceedingly funny.

After he'd been under way for about ten minutes, Walter Kocher poked me in the ribs and asked, "Do you know what he's saying?"

I said, "Of course not—I know no German!"

Walter said, "He's interpreting your speech."

I said, "But I only spoke for five minutes; he's been talking well over ten minutes, and he's still at it!"

"THAT's not the funny part of it," said Walter, "YOU don't know any German, but he doesn't KNOW A WORD OF ENGLISH!"

973. The Fate of After Dinner Speakers

John Goodspeed, the Baltimore Evening Sun *columnist.* These are my favorite opening remarks:

"If all the after dinner speakers in the country were laid end to end, they would be more comfortable."

Or—

"If all the after dinner speakers in the country were laid end to end, it would probably be because they were sick of creamed chicken."

974. Speech Instructor

Albert W. Holzmann, chairman, German Department, Rutgers University. A chicken farmer, dissatisfied with the productivity of his flock, decided to use a bit of psychology on his hens. Accordingly, he purchased a gay-colored talking parrot and placed him in the barnyard. Sure enough, the hens took to the handsome stranger immediately, pointed out the best tidbits for him to eat with joyous clucks and generally followed him around like a bevy of teen-age girls following a new singing star sensation. To the delight of the farmer, even their egg-laying capabilities improved. The barnyard rooster, naturally jealous of being ignored by his harem, set upon the attractive interloper, assailed him with beak and claws, pulling out one green or red feather after the other. Whereupon the intimidated parrot cried out in trepidation, "Desist, sir, I beg of you, desist! After all, I am only here in the capacity of a language professor!"

975. Double Jeopardy

Brooks Hays, former U. S. Congressman and past president of the Southern Baptist Convention. The official reporters of

Congressional speeches are among the most proficient in the world, but occasionally they attribute Members' speeches to someone else. This happened to me one time, and since I was particularly interested in my utterance on that occasion I was quite disappointed to see my speech credited to "Mr. Harris of Arkansas." I let the clerk know that I was provoked, and then I suddenly softened. "I am sorry," I said. "I should not have scolded you."

"Oh, that's all right, Mr. Hays," the clerk replied. "You should have heard Mr. Harris!"

976. *Turning the Tables*

Dayton E. McClain, vice-president, the American University. Perhaps the greatest applause ever given me was at a well-attended Grange Meeting held in the spring of 1914 in Milo, Maine. For five years I had been pastor of the Methodist Church there.

The speaker who preceded me told three stories and turned them all on me, and then sat down in a front row almost directly under the speaker's desk.

On arising to speak I told three stories and turned them on him. My third story was as follows: Near the town where I was reared on the Eastern Shore of Maryland was a section called Muddy Hole, and the post office then bore that name. No matter how dry it was everywhere else, there was a certain piece of road that was always muddy—so muddy that almost every day in the year the nearby farmers had to pull vehicles out that were stuck there.

It is said that one day a man going along that road saw a nice hat lying there, and in retrieving the hat he found a man under the hat. He marveled at the mud's being so deep; and the man under the hat said, "You needn't marvel. There's an ass under me." As I said this I pointed to the man who preceded me, sitting under me.

977. Well-chosen Word

Max Lerner. He appeared on the same program with Senator John F. Kennedy at a Cleveland Book and Author Luncheon. Senator Kennedy's talk was enthusiastically received with loud and generous applause. When things quieted down Max Lerner was introduced. He demonstrated a brilliant flash of wit when he explained that after listening to Senator Kennedy he should not have been introduced by his name of Max but rather as Anti-Cli-Max. This original and apt response to the introduction by the chairman was appreciated by the audience because of its originality and also because it was a most appropriate and gracious thing to say under the circumstances.

978. Oasis in a Sea of Speeches

Spencer Heath, LL. B., LL. M., president, the Science of Society Foundation. I like this as an after dinner speech, particularly at meetings where the preceding speeches have been uninteresting or long:

Mr. Chairman. At this juncture, I shall be brief:

To be seen, one must stand UP.

To be heard, one must speak OUT.

To be *appreciated,* one must SIT DOWN.

I thank you!

979. Modern Prayer

Dr. Dwight O'Hara, former dean of Tufts College Medical School. Years ago, after bidding a fond farewell to my family and leaving for a professional convention, I learned that my five-year-old son knelt to his evening prayers with the words: "Our Father, which art in Atlantic City. . . ."

980. Accepting a Speaking Engagement

Loretta Power Wilson, poet laureate of Society American Poets.

ON PUBLIC SPEAKING
(More Truth Than Poetry)

They say, "Oh, you're so poised, my dear, so natural,"
When e'er they want me for a poetry reading;
But if the truth were known, my knees keep knocking,
And butterflies, my tummy circle, feeding.
Some day I'm going to have my head examined,
This head that always warns me to refuse;
E'en when my heart dictates, "You should be gracious"—
HEART ever ruled *my* HEAD, in Win or Lose.

981. Bible Text

Carl Weeks, president of the Armand Company and trustee of Drake University and Edmundson Art Fund. Some years ago, one of our salesmen and a representative of another house were marooned in a small town in the deep South. Time hung heavy on their hands, so they decided to go to a colored church. They took a seat in the back row and waited and waited. Nothing happened until finally one of the elders got up and draped himself around the pulpit. Looking the congregation over, he said, "I guess the regular minister isn't going to show up, so I will preach the sermon. I takes my text from the Good Book. It is found somewhere between the first of the Generations and the last of the Revolutions, and it says, 'Where the hen scratcheth, there be the bug also.'"

982. Beating Them to the Punch

Marvin Davis Winsett, advertising writer. I was invited to a luncheon by a unique Dallas club composed of leading citizens. It is their custom to call on a visitor to make a speech when the time comes to adjourn. Then the members one by one get up and walk out on the speaker, making as much noise as possible. It is very disconcerting to anyone who does not know about the gag, but, knowing of their custom, I made my plan of action in advance in an effort to turn the tables on them. When they called on me to make a speech, I stood up and said, "Gentlemen, this occasion reminds me of what the great poet said . . . (long pause, as if trying to remember the poet's name) . . . I can't seem to remember his name . . . (another long pause) . . . as a matter of fact, I can't remember what he said either." With that I sat down, getting my speech over with before a single member could walk out on me. They gave me a big hand, and quite a number of them said that it was one of the best speeches they had ever heard.

983.   It Pays to Be Prepared

H. E. Rodgers, dean of Wilmington Law School. An old mountaineer was coming down the mountain road in western North Carolina one morning all dressed in his best clothes with the Holy Bible under his arm. A neighbor meeting him on the road said, "Elias, what does this mean?"

Elias answered him, "Well, I been hearing a lot about New Orleans. They say there is plenty of free-running liquor, plenty of gambling and some fine strip-tease shows. I thought I'd go down there and look around a bit."

The neighbor considered this thoughtfully and then spoke up, "But, Elias, why do you carry the Bible under your arm?"

"Well," Elias replied with a mischievous wink, "if it is as good as they say it is, I might stay over Sunday."

984.   Applause

Orion H. Reeves, Mayor of Easton, Pennsylvania. Before entering politics, I served thirty-five years as a junior high school principal. One day I invited a well-known local speaker to give an address in the school assembly. In order to have a record of the speech for the school paper, a sophomore commercial student was asked to take the address in shorthand. Throughout the discourse, there was applause which the student noted in her book. After the assembly, her article was transcribed and brought to my desk. I was amused, after reading the glowing account of the program, to discover her misinterpretation when she wrote, "The pupils thoroughly enjoyed the speaker, which was indicated by much 'applesauce.' "

985. Right in Style

Norman S. Weiser, newspaper syndicate columnist. I have found the following short anecdote most effective as an opening for a talk before a mixed (male and female) audience.

"A speech is much the same as a woman's dress. It should not be too short, or too long, but it should cover the subject."

986. Difficult Course

E. Stanley Howlett, Potsdam, New York, city official. The local college president was being introduced by the toast-master at a local banquet. He used this story:

A car of tourists was passing through the local countryside and the tourists saw a neat-looking group of buildings set back from the road, with a man busily mowing the spacious lawns near the roadside. The tourists stopped and inquired what the name of the college was, to which he replied, "This is not a college, but a state institution."

"Oh," replied the tourist, "the beautifully kept lawns and buildings look just like a college campus."

The man mowing the grass said, "There is one big difference between this place and a college."

"What is that?" said the tourist.

"You have to show improvement before you can leave this place," replied the man.

987. Misinterpretation

Reed A. Benson, son of Secretary of Agriculture Ezra Taft Benson. The little girl had just returned from her Mormon

Sunday school class, and around the Sunday dinner table asked her father when her little baby brother would be able to talk.

Her father said, "Well, when he gets to be two or three years old, because babies don't talk when they're small."

The little girl replied, "Oh, yes, they should. They did in the Bible."

Her father, being a good elder in the church said, "Well, then, quote me chapter and verse."

At this, the little girl turned to the Old Testament and read these words, "and Job cursed the day he was born."

988. A Question of Time

Andreas Bard, president, Evangelical Synod of Kansas and adjacent states. I had lectured on "Modern Ideologies" and, having failed to limit my subject to the allotted time, I noticed with alarm that fully two hours had passed since the beginning of my speech. Earnestly trying to ingratiate myself with the audience, and hiding my embarrassment, I ended my remarks and asked, "Now, is there anyone here who would like to ask a question?"

No voice was raised in response. Everyone seemed to be satisfied to let me leave the speaker's platform. I was about to finish with the usual "I thank you" when a voice broke the silence, saying, "I have a question, sir!"

Pleased with his thirst for knowledge, I replied "very good" and asked what was his question. Back came the reply, "What time is it?"

The audience roared.

989. Pithy Summary

Frank H. Lindsay, chairman of the board, Lindsay Brothers. I like to brag about Wisconsin and usually tell this story:

At a meeting in Green Bay a Milwaukee salesman made the following statement:

"Our early settlers in Wisconsin were men and women of outstanding character and ability. Our state leads the entire nation in the production of peas and cheese."

To sum it up: Wisconsin is noted for its

HE'S and SHE'S

and its

PEAS and CHEESE

990.   *What's in a Name?*

Riley H. Allen, editor, Honolulu Star-Bulletin. This is a story I use when I must introduce a speaker with a difficult name to pronounce:

At the outbreak of World War II and the bombing of Pearl Harbor and other Oahu military posts December 7, 1941, a visiting college football team was caught on the islands. It had played a Honolulu team December 6. The visiting players promptly signed up for military duty in various forms. Some joined the Honolulu emergency police force. They were called *malihini* (newcomer) policemen.

Not long after that a minor traffic case came up in provost court. One of the emergency policemen—from Oregon—had cited a car driver for a traffic violation. The policeman's written report showed that the citation was delivered on Smith Street. The defendant argued that he was never on Smith Street that day—he was on a nearby thoroughfare, Maunakea Street.

The Provost Judge asked the *malihini* policeman, "The testimony is clear. The offense, if any, was committed on Maunakea Street. Why did you write Smith Street?"

"Your honor," said the *malihini* policeman in some embarrassment—but frankly—"I couldn't spell Maunakea Street."

991. Hard of Hearing

Henry F. Misselwitz, writer and commentator. Over the years I have found it best when starting off a talk to any audience to help the listeners remember that, to many, rather odd name of mine. So frequently, when rising to speak, I congratulate the chairman on "pronouncing my name correctly, more or less," and tell this anecdote: When working as a newspaperman in Tokyo, Japan, some years ago, I attended a Japanese Imperial Garden Party, along with other foreign correspondents, diplomats, Foreign Office officials in Tokyo and so on. One such event included an elderly official who, when we were introduced, asked me to repeat my name. I did, and again he said, "Please, a bit louder in all this confusion at the reception." When I'd done this a couple of times, the old chap finally smiled sadly, cupped a hand behind one ear and confided, "I'm very sorry, I'm a bit deaf. Do you have a card? It still sounds like you're saying MISSELWITZ."

992. A Complete Introduction

Wesley I. Nunn, advertising manager for Standard Oil Company of Indiana. This actually occurred a half century ago. My father, the late W. R. Nunn, who was then superintendent of the Methodist Sunday school in my home town of Martinsville, Virginia, was called on to introduce the speaker at an evening church affair. Because of inclement weather, the audience consisted of only a handful of people. My father got up and spoke somewhat as follows:

"I have been asked to introduce our speaker to you this evening. This I am very glad to do. Ladies and gentlemen, this is Mr. John Brown. Mr. Brown meet Mr. and Mrs. Rucker, Mr. and Mrs. Witten, Mr. Stovall, Miss Stovall . . ." (calling the name of every member of the congregation).

When my father was called upon to introduce a speaker to an audience, he did so!

993. Better Left Unsaid

Keller H. Gilbert, judge of the Municipal Court, Philadelphia, Pennsylvania. The speaker of the evening, a distinguished judge, lingered behind the head table with other guests at the conclusion of the after dinner program, while a woman with vigorous stride and a determined look on her face approached him from the banquet floor. Arriving opposite him, she denounced his speech as the worst she had ever heard. The toastmaster, a law school classmate, came to his rescue. "Pay no attention to her, Judge," he said, "she's a half-wit; she repeats what everybody else says."

994. Compounded Mistakes

Ralph O. Keefer, vice-president, the Aluminum Company of America. In 1948, I spoke to the 7th District Conference of Purchasing Agents at New Orleans. Since I was national president of the National Association of Purchasing Agents that year, the N.A.P.A. Headquarters had issued my biographical sketch to all program chairmen where I was scheduled to speak during my term of office.

On this occasion, the chairman of the meeting obviously read from a copy of this biographical sketch when he introduced me—and he ended with the statement, "He is married, and has two children and a *daughter*."

When the audience laughed, he raised his head with a startled look and asked, "Did I say something wrong?"

Someone in the front row told him that the last sentence of my biographical sketch should read, "He is married and has two children and a *granddaughter*."

The M.C. then quickly looked at his notes, raised his head and told the audience, "Well, you know sometimes a secretary can make a mistake."

When the audience roared, he looked up, took off his glasses and asked, "Now what did I say wrong?"

That really brought down the house and the poor M.C.

was so bewildered that he was barely able to speak my name and sat down in utter confusion.

995. Fair Warning

Rabbi Jacob Philip Rudin, past president, Central Conference of American Rabbis. It is reported that the chairman gave the guest preacher a glowing introduction and concluded his remarks, saying, ". . . and before Dr. X preaches, the choir will sing 'Fear Not, O Israel.' "

996. 100 Per Cent Wrong

J. Robert Atkinson, founder of Braille Institute of America and past president of American Association of Workers for the Blind. All public speakers at some time have suffered embarrassment and some irritation when being introduced by a program chairman, and some amusement also. One such case is recorded as follows:

The occasion was a speaking engagement before a large church audience in a southern California city. On the program I was listed properly as J. Robert Atkinson, founder, vice-president and managing director of the Universal Press, Los Angeles. My theme was also properly listed as "Rehabilitation of the Physically Blind." My introducer, an elderly gentleman, had been furnished this information in writing. As we appeared on the platform I asked him if he had it available. "Oh, yes," he responded. "I have it right here in my hand written out."

His introduction, preceded by some impromptu remarks, went like this: "It is now my privilege to introduce to you as our speaker for the evening Mr. J. Robert Anderson of the University Press, who will speak to us this evening on the subject, 'Ree-hi-bel-ta-shun of the phiz-zack-ally blind.' "

997. A Compliment from the Heart

Alois S. Knapp, past president, American Sunbathing Association. A lawyer friend, who was also a minister and had a large congregation, invited me to talk to his flock. It was a colored church. We had been to law school together and were old friends.

He introduced me with these words: "Perhaps I should apologize to you today for having brought here one to speak to you who is not of our race. However, I have known Brother Knapp for many years and I can assure every one of you that although his skin is white, his heart is just as black as my own."

This was the best compliment I ever received.

998.   *Unconventional Introduction*

Noah Atler, Denver civic leader. When I served as district president of B'nai B'rith, it was my duty to visit all the lodges in the district and deliver an address. This duty brought me to a very small lodge in an isolated region of the West. After the dinner was completed, the man who was serving as president of the lodge and chairman for the dinner stood up and picked up a printed program, one of which had been placed at each plate at the table. The lodge president looked at the program intently for a moment and then remarked, "It says here that Noah Atler, the district president, will speak."

After this remark he paused. I did not know whether I should get up and start speaking or if a more conventional introduction would follow for me. There was an embarrassing pause and then the lodge president looked down over his glasses at me and said inquiringly, "Well?"

999.   *Entertainment Plus*

Dr. M. Eunice Hilton, dean, College of Home Economics, Syracuse University. Recently I attended a luncheon meeting of a career women's organization. The president asked the program chairman of the club to present the program for the day. The program chairman complied with the following startling introduction, "I don't know why I find myself in the position of introducing the artist who is going to entertain us today. I'm utterly unprepared to do so since I have not had time to find out anything about her. You see, the chairman of the day secured the artist and then called me and asked me to take over for her just before she left town! Mrs. _____ will now entertain us."

1000. Nice Recovery

Harry Apelman, past department commander, California Jewish War Veterans of U.S.A. Several years ago, I acted as master of ceremonies and the installing officer for the Department of California, Jewish War Veterans of the U.S.A. In the midst of my introduction as the installing officer, my dentures (which I had just received that day) kept slipping and making a clacking and whistling sound when I spoke. Noticing that some of the audience were looking at each other, and commencing to get a little disturbed myself, I broke off my talk to explain to the audience that I had just gotten a new set of "chinaware" and that it seemed that I could not get my "cups and saucers" to behave themselves. This got a big laugh, with big smiles on everyone's faces, and gave me the extra confidence which I needed so badly to continue. The balance of the installation and my acting as master of ceremonies turned out to be a huge success.

1001. Back to Work

Colonel Bernard L. Gorfinkle, personal military aide to former Governor Christian Herter of Massachusetts and former secretary to Bernard M. Baruch. The Governor of our state was requested to speak on culture before a particular organization. As he was previously engaged, I, as his military aide, a colonel in uniform, was sent with the organization's approval as a substitute for the Governor.

The program consisted in its first part of entertainment

of various sorts, and as I was next on the program, the presiding officer remarked, "Now that we have all had a good time, and been well entertained, I will now present our main speaker Colonel Gorfinkle, representing our Governor."

1002.   Good Mathematics

Arthur D. Graeff, author, lecturer and columnist. I was awaiting my turn, during the course of a banquet at which I was to speak on the topic "How Dumb Are the Pennsylvania Dutch?" A very active song leader was accepting request numbers from the members of the audience. Usually these requests were identified by a page of the songbook which all diners had at their elbows.

"Let's have Number 99," called out a voice. This was done to bait the enthusiastic leader because the last number in the book was 98.

With complete self-possession however, the Dutchman quickly declared, "Werry vell, ve vill sing serty sree (33) sree times."

9
Speaking Humor for
Special Purposes

THE fundamental purpose or objective of a joke is to entertain and create laughter. Nevertheless, laughter and entertainment should not in themselves become the primary aim of a toastmaster or speaker. If interested merely in laughs, he can wear an outlandish costume or paint clown markings on his face. The entertainment must be in keeping with the tone of the gathering. The joke must be suitable to the subject matter of the speech and fit the nature of the occasion. In other words, the joke must be apt and appropriate first of all and then possibly humorous. It should not be first of all humorous and then possibly apt and appropriate.

A large selection of this type of humor has been collected for this book and classified according to the most obvious characteristics or interests of the audience. That is, a toastmaster who presides at a meeting of a group interested in economic matters should have in his remarks humorous allusions that touch directly or indirectly upon situations and conditions related to the world of business and finance. This is also true for the speaker when talking on subjects of youth and education to groups of young people or parents, teachers and others interested in youth problems. The classified humor will be helpful in locating a large selection of apt and appropriate humor in keeping with the spirit of the meeting and catering to the special interests of the audience.

Among the groups of classified humor you will find some that are not so much concerned with the interests of the audience as with helping the toastmaster or speaker overcome obstacles to lucid communication with all those listening to his remarks. This applies particularly to the classification of club and lodge humor. Men and women attending meetings of this sort do not especially wish to hear about clubs and lodges. The humor found here is intended chiefly for the purpose of assisting the club and lodge officer or speaker perform some of the duties which may be his responsibility or meet situations which are indigenous to clubs and lodges. The individual who is elected president is required to say a few words before taking office, and a little humor will help him acknowledge graciously the honor and responsibilities conferred upon him. The individual retiring as president also must say a few words of thanks and deliver a report on the accomplishments during his term of office. A good story that fits neatly into the right place, like a square peg in a square hole, is always an asset to the report. Committee chairmen must give reports and urge members to volunteer help and support; members must participate in programs; the presiding officer must maintain order, welcome guests, adjourn the meeting and perform other duties regularly and monotonously from meeting to meeting. Apt and appropriate humor may be used to enliven what otherwise might become a hackneyed procedure.

The toastmaster who is asked to preside at a meeting would do well to classify to his own satisfaction the type and character of the people who will attend and seek to identify their interests with an established, recognized group, such as community affairs, church and religion, etc. He might start his search for suitable humor by reading through the collected humor for these designated purposes. Next, he may seek more specific humor for a particular part of a speech or remark by looking in the index. If he wants something inspirational which will offer food for thought, he should look to the section on inspirational suggestions. If it is to be a mixed group of men and women for an entertainment, such as a club ladies' night meeting, he will find, in the section devoted to men and women, a treasury of humor about the facts, fancies and foibles of the sexes and married life.

The toastmaster should use the references on speaking humor for special purposes to give the audience what they want, bearing in mind always that what a person wants is something he can understand and lies within the small, confined circle of his limited interests at this particular time and place.

BUSINESS AND FINANCES

1003. Complaints—We hear a lot of complaints about business these days. Some of the complaints are justified, some are merely pessimism and others are just uncalled for. Let me tell you about a fellow who has run a motel for years on Route 1 between Portsmouth, New Hampshire, and Portland, Maine. He complained bitterly about the effect on his business when the Maine Turnpike was put through, paralleling Route 1. Finally one of his neighbors tired of hearing about it.

"Look, Cal," said the neighbor, "I see a 'No Vacancy' sign out front of your place every night."

"You can't go by that," said Cal. "Before they put the turnpike through I used to turn away twenty-five to thirty parties a night. Since the turnpike, I don't turn away more'n ten or twelve a night."

1004. Bankruptcy—The fellow in business leads an exciting life. He never knows what is going to happen next. For instance, you've heard of instant coffee and instant tea. Now in Las Vegas they have introduced something new—instant bankruptcy.

1005. *Budget*—A family budget system works out just like any other way of living beyond your income—except, of course, you have a record of it.

1006. *Optimism about Future Sales*—From the way sales have been going the past few weeks I have the greatest encouragement and optimism for the future. I feel like the doctor who was treating a man with a serious ailment. The man asked his doctor what his chances were for recovery. "One hundred per cent," the doctor replied.

The patient was delighted. "I thought this disease was dangerous and usually fatal."

The doctor reassured him. "Medical records," he said, "show that nine out of every ten die of the disease you have. Yours is the tenth case I have treated. All the other nine have died, so you are sure to get well."

As I look over the sales records for the past weeks, it seems like the law of averages should start working and sales can't go anywhere but better.

1007. *Benefits of the Installment Plan*—When a couple gets married these days the first thing they do is try to make up a budget to govern their expenses. However, it seldom works. The trouble with most household budgets is that usually there is too much month left over at the end of the money.

As soon as the couple runs out of money they begin to live on credit and the installment plan. One recent bride was quite amazed when she first discovered the possibility of a charge account. She said enthusiastically to her husband, "Charge accounts are wonderful. They go so much farther than money."

Because of charge accounts we have what is known as prosperity. Prosperity to most people means getting credit to live beyond their income. For those who run out of charge accounts there is always the installment plan. The installment plan is wonderful for people but not for animals. If it were not for the installment plan, a lot of wild animals would have a better chance of wearing their own fur through the winter. The installment plan has created a great debt for the people of our nation. Even the government is beginning to be concerned about the growth of the installment debt. One government agency made a survey and reported, "Never before have so many owed so much to so few."

1008. Perplexed—You can't expect to make a success of things unless you know what you are doing. Otherwise you will be like the bride who went to a drugstore and somewhat hesitantly approached the clerk and asked about a baby tonic that was advertised. "We sell a lot of this baby tonic," the clerk replied. "It makes the baby big and strong."

"That's just what I want," answered the bride. "I'll take it, but tell me one more thing. Who takes it—my husband or me?"

1009. Payments—Business has been a little slow lately. Perhaps it needs the same thing that the auto industry has been waiting for. The auto industry brought out power steering, power brakes, power windows. All it is waiting for now is power payments.

1010. Prosperity Today and Yesterday—In the old days of our parents' generation there used to be a saying to the effect that most people cannot stand prosperity. You no longer hear this mentioned because most people today don't have to. In those bygone days, the man who saved money was considered a miser. Nowadays he would be regarded as a wonder.

Another old saying which was a favorite of our fathers was that a fool and his money are soon parted. Now it happens to everybody. The person who can save money these days is one in a million, and he can save in about this same proportion.

In the old days money would talk. Money doesn't talk these days. It goes without saying. Financial problems are driving people to drink these days. It is not unusual to see a disappointed salaried man going around most of the time half drunk. Poor fellow, that is all he can afford. Things have changed a great deal since the old days. In those far-distant days, the ambitious young man wanted to become a millionaire. This is no longer true today. The ambitious young man is satisfied just to live like a millionaire.

1011. Money-making Formula—You don't have to be a genius to make money. Just latch onto a good thing. Electricity was a great invention which required genius, but the guy who made all the money was the fellow who invented the meter.

1012. Evils of Money—One of my secret ambitions is to be able to enjoy some of the evils which go with having too much money.

1013. Importance of Car Ownership—Our present century will go down in history as the automobile age. You just aren't living today unless you have an automobile. When a young couple gets married today the first thing they look for is a home. Then they go out and buy a car so they won't have to stay in the place.

When the young married couple feels it has reached a point that they can afford a family, they buy a second car. No doubt by this time they will want one of the modern de luxe automobiles which keeps one strapped without a seat belt. It is better than buying a secondhand car at a bargain. A person who attempts to buy a secondhand car at a bargain soon discovers how hard it is to drive a bargain. Why should a person want to buy a secondhand car today when it is so easy to buy a new car without money? I have a friend who went into an automobile agency and wanted to pay cash for a car. The salesman studied the matter for a while and then told him, "Well, sir, it is very unusual. I am afraid you'll have to get two references."

1014. Flexible Figures—The old saying that figures don't lie but liars sure figure still holds true. A person can do just about anything he wants with figures to prove or disprove an argument. It's like they say, a youthful figure is something you get when you ask a woman her age.

1015. Getting Ahead—You don't get to the top in business by just being on the job. You've got to have something more than that on the ball. It's like the case of the young officer who was trying to get a promotion for an undeserving friend. The officer went to see the colonel and pleaded, "This man deserves a promotion. He has been through a dozen battles." The colonel replied by pointing out the window and saying, "Look at those mules. Every one of them has been through a dozen battles, but they are still jackasses!"

1016. Business Complacency—The way some of our salesmen have been going after business lately, it seems like they aren't worried about the way things are going any more than the henpecked husband of a woman who left on a short bus trip. The route of the bus led through the mountains, and a report was circulated that the bus met with an accident and went over a cliff. A friend heard of the accident and called the husband, who seemed to take it nonchalantly enough. "Aren't you worried about your wife?" the friend demanded.

"Not a bit," replied the husband. "I saw her get on the bus with my own eyes!"

Maybe this husband—and some of our salesmen—had better start worrying. If our business bus goes over a cliff, the crack-up isn't going to do anybody any good.

1017. Struggle—From the time an infant first tries to get his toes in his mouth, life is a continual struggle to make both ends meet.

1018. Money and Inflation—You have to have money these days if you want to get along. Of course, I admit there are other things in life besides money. For instance, stocks, bonds, travelers' checks and so forth.

Everywhere we go it becomes pretty obvious that money is important. For example, outside of Hialeah in Florida there is a sign which reads as follows, "Keep Florida Green. Bring Money."

Florida is a good example of how money goes these days. A Texas oil man drove up to the front of one of those fabulous Florida hotels in one of those new and expensive convertible automobiles. He handed the doorman a twenty-dollar bill and said, "Here you are, boy. Take good care of this car. I just bought it."

The doorman nodded understandingly and replied, "I know exactly how you feel, sir. I have one just like it."

You don't have to feel sorry for the hotel employees down in Florida. One guest asked a bellboy who had brought up his bags if he had change for five dollars. "Mister," the boy snapped back at him, "in this town a five-dollar bill is change!"

No wonder workers are always asking for more money. Still the majority of workers are satisfied with their income. All they ask is the same amount a little more often.

1019.   *Unemployed*—We have learned a great many things in the business downturn, recession or depression—however you wish to call it. During this time we have too many unemployed, but smart business executives also discovered that there were too many unemployed on the payroll.

1020.   *Born Too Soon*—There have been too many people who continue to live in the metallic age when we have already entered upon the space age. In this metallic age it was not unusual to find a man who had gold in his teeth, silver in his hair and lead in his pants. Many a fellow who thought he was a live wire was dead when he lost his connections. Then there were those like the salesman who lost his job and whose wife divorced him at the same time and both for the same reason. He could not take orders.

1021.   *High-pressure Selling*—Selling has become a talent and today a really good salesman is one who can put on so much pressure that the customer gets the bends. The man who succeeds in business must be awake. For instance, in a section of a large city where there were a number of hotels and struggling restaurants, one enterprising concern displayed a large electric sign bearing this information, "Open all night." Nearby was another restaurant, and soon a sign appeared over its door reading, "We never close." Nearby was a Chinese laundry in a small, run-down building. In keeping with the spirit of his neighbors he also put out a sign in large, scrawling letters, "Me wakee, too."

    If you want to get along well you must be awake and alert.

1022.   *Trying*—One reason we have trying times in business is that too many people stop trying.

1023.   *TV Advertising*—The only difference between times today and the depression of the thirties is that now we have TV to advertise things we can't buy.

1024. Work

> All things come to he who waiteth,
> If he worketh like hell while he waiteth.

1025. Be Prepared—A person should be fully prepared to do the task he sets out to accomplish. Otherwise he will be like the sailor who was following two girls when one of them turned around and said to him, "Now, look here! You either quit following us or get another sailor!"

1026. Warning Against Flawless Planning—I have always had a great deal of respect for making careful plans before a job is started. Every man who ever makes a success first has a plan which he must follow.

We have had some good plans presented to us. I hope they will do the job for which they are intended, but let me give you a little warning. You may have heard the story about the old hunter who was telling some of his friends about the most remarkable experience he ever had in his life. This was the time he saw a deer standing down in a gorge behind a tree. The only way he could hit the deer was to fire a bullet at the high gorge wall in such a way it would ricochet off the wall and change its course so as to go in the direction of the deer and kill it.

The old hunter as he told the story explained in detail how he gauged the wind velocity and calculated the speed of the bullet, the twist it had, the hardness of the bullet and the right angle at which it would have to hit the gorge wall so that it would bounce off and not be flattened out of shape.

After taking all of these things into consideration and making a careful plan, the old hunter took aim at the wall at the exact spot he thought he must hit it in order to make the bullet richochet off the gorge wall and hit the deer hidden behind the tree. It was a flawless plan. The hunter took careful aim and then fired. He missed the wall!

We have a wonderful plan here today, but it will do us no good if we miss the wall.

1027.   *Lawsuit*—When an irresistible force meets an immovable body, it is time to call in a good lawyer.

1028.   *Lack of Aggressiveness*—In these days of business aggressiveness, the only thing that comes to him who waits is second notices to pay on overdue accounts.

1029.   *Poor Sales Reports*—When I look over some of these reports and my salesmen tell me that they did their best I feel like answering them the same way a husband answered his wife when she started crying and said, "You treat me this way, and I gave you six of the best years of my life!" The husband answered, "Ye gods! Were those your best?"

1030.   *Consider All Angles*—You've got to work all angles—inside and out. If you think you can get by just by following a one-track course, you will be like the painter who parked his truck on a downtown street and left a note on it as follows: "Painter working on the inside."

When he returned to his truck after completing his work for the day he found this note on it with a parking ticket: "Cop working on the outside."

1031.   *Quick Thinking*—It is pretty difficult these days to keep any money. The cost of operating a business or a home is such that only good management makes it possible to have any money left after all the expenses have been paid.

The average person in charge of a budget is very much like the locomotive engineer who had a habit of bringing home his wages in cash every payday and turning it over to his wife to let her manage. One day this engineer was sick and unable to pick up his pay, so his wife went down to the railroad to collect it. She was surprised to discover that he was paid by check and not by cash, and also that the check was for a much larger amount than he was in the habit of bringing home and giving to her.

When the surprised wife returned home, she demanded an explanation from her husand. The dutiful husband replied, "I know my pay check looks big to you, honey, but after I pay my conductor and my fireman and the rest of my crew, there isn't much left."

1032. *Go-getters*—Some fellows who think they are go-getters are like the poor Mexican who couldn't sleep a wink all day.

1033. *Sales Calls*—A salesman need never be ashamed of his calling. He should only be ashamed of his not calling.

1034. *Talent Search*—What business needs today is young, fresh talent for this work. Most of the people you find in business are going to remain in it until they find some.

1035. *High Prices*—It is hard to figure out the price on some things—why it is necessary to charge as much as asked. For example, in an art gallery there is shown a painting with a price tag of $50,000—which is a lot of money, for only one coat of paint, too.

1036. *Spur to Action*—Necessity is not only the mother of invention but also it serves as a good spur to action. For instance, dogs in Siberia are the fastest in the world because the trees are so far apart.

1037. *Making Ends Meet*—There are a lot of people today who have troubles. Some troubles are real, some imaginary and some are like the fellow who made an appointment to see a psychiatrist.

When this fellow got into the office of the psychiatrist he said, "Doctor, I really have big problems."

The psychiatrist told him to lie down on the couch and tell him about his troubles. The fellow began a recital which brought out such facts as that he had a most devoted family and lived in one of the most luxurious homes in the suburbs. He belonged to several golf clubs and had three autos for his family. His house had a swimming pool in the back yard, and in addition he owned a winter home in Florida, a summer home in Canada.

The psychiatrist finally interrupted him and commented, "It doesn't seem to me with all the wonderful things you have that you should have any troubles."

"All these things are wonderful all right," replied this fellow, "but you see I have troubles. I only make one hundred dollars a week."

These kinds of troubles, on a smaller scale, are known to most of us.

1038.   *Importance of Money*—You don't have to go to Paris to discover what is the world's most beloved capital—American money!

1039.   *Money-maker*—He is a terrific money-maker. He has a verbal contract with his company for two thousand dollars a week. He is paid off verbally.

1040.   *Prices*—We may not be rich, but America is a land where everybody feels rich because they charge each other so much.

1041.   *Modified Proverb*—It may be true that time is money, but you don't get money unless you spend time.

1042.   *Money Talks*—Some people say that money isn't important, but don't let them fool you. The person who makes money makes other things as well.

Just to show you how this usually works, let me tell you the story about the young fellow who took his best girl to a dance at his club. It was a joyous night, and as the entertainment was drawing to a close, the young man took his girl by the arm and led her out onto the porch. There in a dark corner he held her tightly in his arms and whispered, "My beloved, I adore you. I may not be as rich as Henry Smith or spend money like Henry Smith throws it away, but I love you so much I would do anything in the world for you."

The young fellow felt his girl hold him tight and snuggle up as she whispered into his ear, "Darling, introduce me to Henry Smith."

1043. *Lack of Ambition*—One of our poorest salesmen owns a chair worth five thousand dollars. It is just a plain, ordinary chair, but last year it cost him five thousand dollars to sit in that chair instead of going out after business.

1044. *New Billing Method*—There is always something new being tried, in business or elsewhere. For instance, there is a psychiatrist who has hit upon a new kind of shock treatment. He sends his bill in advance.

1045. *In a Big Way*—There is still money around. For instance, a Texas oil millionaire and his wife dropped into a New York art gallery and bought all the Picassos, El Grecos, Van Goghs, Monets, Gauguins and others of equal reputation. "Well," breathed the Texan with a sigh of relief, "that takes care of our Christmas cards. Now we can start doing some shopping."

1046. *Which First?*—It is often a race to see if the rate of business decline will flatten out before the wallet does.

1047. *Threat*—In our business we don't have the hold over our customers that some people have. For instance, there was the psychiatrist who warned his patient that if he didn't pay his bill he would let him go crazy.

1048.   Mistake—With business conditions the way they are, it's easy to make a mistake these days like the fellow who showed up in town around his old familiar haunts. An old friend saw him and greeted him, "You back in town? I thought you was a farmer?" The sad fellow replied, "You made the same mistake I did."

1049.   No Competition—I don't know why some salesmen are so worried about competition. They are like the fighter whose manager told him not to be nervous. If the fellow he was going to fight was any good, he wouldn't be fighting him!

1050.   Money Worries—Money makes a difference. For instance, money determines whether you are the kind of person who worries over your next meal or over your last one.

1051.   Persistence—Success comes easy to the person who is persistent. It's the same as when a very wealthy Indian who owned a number of oil wells in Oklahoma was asked to explain his success. He replied, "Oh, it's very easy. I just kept on digging holes."

1052.   Selling Headache—The biggest problem of the salesman in any line is to make what he has to sell look attractive to the prospective buyer. This is not easy for many reasons. One reason is that the things the customer can afford never look good to him, and the things he can't afford are hard to sell.

1053.   Recession Cocktail—The public is pretty confused about the terms panic, recession, depression and the old familiar refrain—hard times. I admit I don't understand the difference myself but I go along with the wit who was describing a new drink called a recession cocktail—business on the rocks.

1054. **Contradiction**—What is true for the new cars seems to be true for everything today. The new cars are wider, longer, lower—and higher!

1055. **Keep Learning**—The things we learned about business during our early years of experience don't do us much good now. We've got to keep on learning all of the time. We can't be like the college graduate who returned to his alma mater and went to visit his favorite professor who was still there—a professor of economics. While he was in the professor's lecture room visiting with him he happened to notice on the desk a copy of an exam paper which was to be given to the students. He picked it up and looked it over and then exclaimed, "Why, Professor, these are the same questions you asked us on examinations twenty-five years ago!" "Yep," replied the professor, "the questions are the same, but the answers are different."

1056. **Courage**—In order to make a success in business you've got to have a fighting spirit. The man who smiles in the face of trouble is either courageous—or he's well insured.

1057. **Bad Deal**—I am afraid this might be a bad deal for us, like the customer who was advised to buy a new product. The store owner told the customer that if he wasn't satisfied he could return the unused portion of the product and the store would return the unused portion of his money.

1058. **Personal Satisfaction**—There is a great deal of personal satisfaction in rising from adversity to success. Those who have it easy in life never find this kind of happiness.

Wealthy people miss one of life's greatest thrills—paying the last installment.

1059.   *Odds 1 to 11*—There is a time and a place and a season for everything. Every business has its own best season. That is why they say that June is the best month in the year for preachers. Lawyers have the other eleven.

1060.   *Alert Salesman*—There is a sermon for the salesman in the story about the fellow who registered at a hotel. After his first night, he went down to the lobby and was approached by the hotel manager, who asked him how he slept. The guest complained that he did not sleep well. "In fact," said this unhappy guest, "I did not close my eyes all night."

The manager drew himself up to assume a haughty manner and observed, "Well, then, it is entirely your own fault. If you want to sleep, you must close your eyes." Just the reverse is true for the salesman. If he wants to be wide awake he must keep his eyes open and be alert at all times.

1061.   *Busy*—Busy people are successful people. That is why they say that the best way to get a job done is to give it to a busy man. He'll have his secretary do it.

1062.   *No Experience*—I won't say you people aren't trying hard enough, but may be that's not the answer. You may be like the young fellow who came to his boss the second day on the job and asked for a lot more money because he was so inexperienced. He explained, "It is so much harder when you know so little."

1063.   *Salad Recipe*—No matter what you call it, money is still money. And, furthermore, you can chalk this up for the truth: Tomatoes who know their onions usually marry men with lots of lettuce. So it doesn't make any difference if you are a man or a woman, lettuce is pretty important to you.

1064. *Agreeable*—When everybody agrees with you, it is a sign you are terribly brilliant or the boss.

1065. *High Prices*—All the talk we hear about high prices is merely propaganda put out by people who eat.

1066. *Tonic*—The best tonic for anyone is a vacation. A vacation is usually two weeks off which makes you feel good enough to go back to work and so poor you have to.

1067. *Surplus*—We're lucky money doesn't grow on trees. If it did it would be just another surplus commodity for the government to worry about.

1068. *Research*—Every business must devote a certain amount of time and money to research. Charles Kettering described research as an organized method of finding out what you are going to do when you can no longer do what you are doing now.

1069. *Tough Job*—Getting a tough job done is like getting up in the morning. It is a question of mind over mattress.

1070. *Experience*—Businessmen place a high value upon experience and they should. Experience is what you have left over when you have lost everything else.

1071. *Not Good Enough*—When somebody tells me that he did the best he could and I figure that it was not good enough, I put this fellow in the same class as the motorcycle cop who stopped a motorist and started to write a ticket.

"Officer," this motorist protested with great indignation, "I was not speeding! You are permitted to go fifty miles an hour, and I was only going forty."

"I know that," the motorcycle cop answered defensively, "but I can't catch up with the really fast ones."

When anybody tells me that he has done his best I figure that is not always good enough.

1072.   *Help Yourself*—We hear a lot about conditions, but conditions are different for different people and different circumstances. The aggressive, wide-awake salesman finds that conditions—like God and the mistletoe—help the man who helps himself.

1073.   *Business Brain*—The brain of the average businessman is divided into two parts, known as dollars and cents.

1074.   *Lazy Employee*—They tell a joke about a fellow who kept trying to get a job with the government. One day his brother was asked, "What's your brother, who has been trying to get a job with the government, doing now?"

"Nothing," answered the brother. "He got the job."

I wouldn't go so far as to say the same thing about some of the people who are employed here, but they shouldn't get the idea that getting the job is enough.

1075.   *Bright Idea*—In business, an idea isn't any good unless it is like sitting down on a pin. It makes you jump up and do something!

1076.   *Group Inactivity*—A conference is the salvation of business. It is the only place where a group of important men who can do absolutely nothing by themselves can save their faces by doing nothing as a group.

1077.   *Problem Solving*—We have a problem in our business. Like most business problems it can be solved in the same way that the psychiatrist solved his problem. A much discouraged and downhearted man was escorted into the office of the psychiatrist. He complained, "I have no desire to go on,

Doctor. Life for me is just too hectic and filled with tensions."

The doctor smiled cheerfully. "I understand," he said. "We all have our problems. I have my problems just as you have your problems. You will require at least six months of treatment at fifty dollars a week."

The downcast and discouraged man thought for a while and replied, "Well, Doc, that solves your problem, and now what about mine?"

1078. Nuisance—It is a long-standing rule in business that the customer is always right. He may always be right, but sometimes he's sure a nuisance.

1079. Legal Tender—Money is often called legal tender. I don't know exactly why unless it is tender when you have it and when you don't, it's tough!

1080. Success Motto—Times change and the rules for success which held true in the old days no longer apply. The motto for success in business today should be: "Early to bed, early to rise, work like hell and advertise."

1081. Changing Times—The terms used to describe business or economic conditions change with the times. For instance, there was an unfortunate class of people which we used to describe as being underprivileged. Today we still have them with us, but we now describe them as being over-financed.

1082. Luck and Skill—You have to have luck in order to make money. For instance, there was a woman whose husband was eating an oyster and swallowed a great big pearl. The pearl was so big and so valuable that she sold it and made money even after she paid for her husband's operation and the funeral expenses as well.

1083. Some Contract—I just ran into a fellow who signed a contract to ship a half-million dollars' worth of merchandise. The only trouble is that he can't get the firm he sold it to to sign the contract.

1084. Too Good for the Job—I have heard of cases where a person is too good for the job that is to be done. No doubt, there are such cases as this. I know of only one.

This was the case of the young bachelor who maintained a home for himself. He advertised in the newspaper for a cook. A beautiful young girl applied for the job, and this young bachelor turned her away with the remark, "I would never hire you."

The young girl demanded to know why he would not consider her for the job as cook. The young fellow replied, "Because in a couple of weeks I would have to get someone to cook for us."

1085. Business Gamble—Business today is a gamble. It's like the waiter who brought a man change of a fifty-cent piece and a dime from three dollars on a dinner which cost $2.40. The diner looked at the waiter sharply and remarked, "This should be a lesson to you. I am going to leave you a dime tip. If you had brought two quarters instead of a fifty-cent piece, I would have left you one of them."

The waiter shrugged his shoulders and remarked, "Don't worry about it, sir. I win more times than I lose."

1086. Take a Chance—The man in business must gamble all of the time. No wonder a businessman was not surprised as he was walking from his office to a restaurant for lunch when he was stopped by a stranger who said to him, "I don't think that you remember me, but ten years ago I came to this city broke. I asked you for a loan and you gave me twenty dollars because you said you were willing to take a chance to start a man on the road to success."

The businessman thought for a while and then he said, "Yes, I remember the incident. Go on with your story."

"Well," remarked the stranger, "are you still willing to gamble?"

1087. *Win, Place or Show*—The successful businessman must not only be willing to gamble but he must know what he is doing. He should be like Lady Godiva. She put all she had on a horse. She didn't win, but she sure showed.

1088. *Bankrupt*—If the businessman doesn't know what he is doing, it will be like the case of the store which went bankrupt after only two weeks in business. On the front of the store was placed this sign: OPENED BY MISTAKE.

1089. *Stock Forecasting*—The person in business who is willing to gamble must know what he is doing. Otherwise he will be like the well-known Wall Street analyst. A survey made of his stock forecast for a year showed that he was bullish two times, bearish three times and wrong six times. The moral of this for all businessmen is: Never change your mind and you will be wrong only once.

1090. *Choice*—In business today you have a choice. For instance, one very accommodating company I know will give you two years to pay or six years if you don't.

CHURCH AND RELIGION

1091. *Demands of Religion*—The work of God isn't automatic, as it requires the efforts of all who adopt religion— even though the demands are not too taxing. Yet even this little often brings complaints, like the case of the girl who was explaining to a friend about a new household appliance which was bought for the home. "It isn't automatic," she said. "You have to turn a switch."

1092. *Importance of Religion*—Most of us don't realize how bad off we would be if it were not for religion. We should be like the little boy who was saying his prayers and concluded with this remark, "Dear God, take care of Mommy, take care of Daddy, take care of baby sister and Aunt Emma and Uncle John and Grandma and Grandpa—and, please God, take care of Yourself, or else we're all sunk!"

1093. *Too Much and Too Little*—Some people seem to be very careful about the amount of religion they get. They are like the old colored woman who complained that she had just enough religion to make her contribute to the church and too much religion to enjoy the carousing she had been in a habit of doing.

1094. *Spiritual Dose*—The very environment of the church itself is spiritually stimulating and inspiring. It's like a fellow said on a crowded bus, "I'm so full of penicillin—if I should sneeze here in this crowd I am sure I'm going to cure somebody!"

1095. *Praying Fee*—Are the ushers in our church getting to be like those in a house of worship in the heart of a big city? In this church transients dropped in regularly and there were few contributing members. The income fell off so sharply that the pastor decided to place ushers at the door and suggest to each visitor that he leave twenty-five cents as pew rent. The ushers took their responsibility seriously, and when a man came in for the ten o'clock Mass and did not leave twenty-five cents at the door they became argumentative about it. The man protested that he had not come to pray. He had attended the eight o'clock Mass and was returning only to get his hat. As he started in, one of the ushers pulled his sleeve and whispered loudly in his ear, "Remember, now, you are only to get your hat—no praying!"

1096. **Flexible Conscience**—Conscience is that still, little voice within us that keeps us from doing wrong, and if we do wrong it keeps us from enjoying it. All of us at one time or another are troubled with our conscience.

A New York taxpayer sent a letter to the state comptroller's office in Albany saying that he had cheated on his income tax ten years ago and had not been able to get a good night's sleep since. He enclosed twenty-five dollars and added: "If I still can't sleep, I will send the balance."

Let's not be troubled by our conscience. Let's do what we are supposed to do and let's not have any halfway measures about it!

1097. **Vices**—A story is told about a teacher who was gambling at Las Vegas and having so much luck that she kept rolling the money in. She said to a friend beside her, "It's just like I keep telling my class. You don't have to smoke or drink to have fun."

I might add you don't have to gamble either or follow any of the vices of man. Fun can be had in a pure life and through religion.

1098. **Church Support**—Generosity to our church is often measured by the kind of standard which caused a druggist to remark to a man who rushed in the store on Sunday morning and asked for change for a dime, "Here's your change. I hope you will enjoy the sermon."

1099. **Church Budget**—A church is a religious institution, but even so it must consider practical affairs and have a budget. It is said that a budget is nothing more or less than a mathematical confirmation of your suspicions. If any of you have had suspicions that financial affairs are pretty rugged in our church, this budget will serve to confirm those suspicions.

1100.   *Two Sides to Helping Others*—We have heard and read a great deal about the importance of helping others and being a real friend of humanity. We have been told that we are foolish for working so hard to get money because money wouldn't bring you any friends. It will only get you a better class of enemies.

All of these things are true, and certainly I would be the last one in the world to encourage anyone to turn his back upon humanity and helping others. However, there comes a time in the life of every person when he reaches the same conclusion as the little boy whose mother was lecturing him about selfishness.

"You know, darling," she pointed out, "we are in this world to help others."

The little boy considered this for several seconds, then he asked with a great deal of seriousness, "Well, then, what are the others here for?"

This is a sensible question and deserves an intelligent answer. There comes a time when we can all ask this question. "Why are the others here?"

At this time, we need the help of others and I believe that they are indebted to us because our plea is just and deserving. Therefore, we need not feel embarrassed or self-conscious when we go forward and ask others to help us by participating in this special enterprise which we have undertaken.

1101.   *Birds of a Feather*—This is the church for me, and from what I know of most of the folks who belong I would say this church suits us to a T. Perhaps I had better explain to you what I mean. There was a fellow who moved into a strange city and started looking around for a church he would like to join. One morning he dropped into a neighborhood church and listened while the congregation repeated responsively after the minister these words: "We have left undone the things we ought to have done, and we have done those things which we ought not to have done!"

The newcomer to the town slipped into a pew and, with a sigh of relief, said to himself, "Thank goodness! I've found my crowd at last."

I think all of us are pretty much in the same boat, especially that part about leaving undone the things we ought to have done. This church and our minister can provide the inspiration and guidance for us to do now and in the future the things we have left undone in the past.

1102.   Brotherhood—We cannot expect to have tolerance and brotherhood here in our own homeland or peace and harmony throughout the world until everyone understands the fact that people differ and have different characters and ideas.

It is not so strange that members of the human family differ. We find this in nature as well. Even the lily family includes a cousin named garlic. We have our undesirable members of the human race but we must learn to live together in peace and harmony with tolerance and a spirit of brotherhood.

1103.   Hang on to Religion—A person should hang on to his religion—no matter what. No matter what he does, says or thinks if he can't help himself he should at least be like old Uncle Mose who said, "I'se never been what I oughta been. I stole chickens and watermelons, got drunk and got in fights with my fists and my razor, but there is one thing I ain't never done—in spite of all my meanness, I ain't never once lost my religion!"

1104.   The Limit of Prayer—There is an old Oriental saying which comes to us from Mahomet, and advises you to trust in God but tie your camel. There is a sermon in these words of wisdom.

The sermon which we find here is not that faith and religion are inadequate, but rather that we must call upon God for wisdom, inspiration and strength. But it is up to us to use these qualities for our own advantage if we are blessed enough to receive them.

If you need a helping hand in life, you will find it at the end of your arm. Religion will not fight your battles for you, but it will help you in fulfilling your purpose on this earth. We must search for God and find him for ourselves. Perhaps the biggest mistake most of us make is that when we are children we gain the impression that God takes a personal interest in the daily affairs of each one of us.

I recall a story about a seven-year-old boy who would not eat his breakfast cereal. His mother insisted that he eat the cereal or God would be displeased. The boy stubbornly refused despite this threat from his mother.

Not long after, a terrible lightning and thunder storm broke. The sky became dark and was filled with flashes of lightning. Thunder sounded like the roar of cannons. The young fellow went to the window and grew pale as he turned to his mother and said, "I am sorry. I did not think that God would make so much fuss over one small bowl of cereal."

As we grow older, we learn that God reserves his judgment for a life beyond our worldly understanding. It is our own responsibility to do well by ourselves and fellowmen.

1105. Universal Language—Religion is a universal language and it speaks to each person in a language he understands. It is like the case of the educated dog that went to college. When he returned his master asked what he learned. The dog said that he didn't do so well in mathematics and history but he was very good in foreign languages. His master asked the dog to say something in a foreign language and the dog replied, "Meow."

1106. *Virtue—*Virtue for some people consists of insufficient temptation.

1107. *Value of Church—*Attending church may not save a person's soul, but it will help preserve those things which make a soul worth saving.

1108. *Hard-working Minister—*Seldom do we realize how much burden we place upon our minister. Our minister is probably the most fully employed man in our community. He's working to beat Hell.

1109. *Wealth—*God does not place importance upon wealth. Sometimes He shows his contempt for it by the type of person He selects to receive it.

1110. *Christmas Spirit—*The true spirit of religion is best illustrated by the Christmas spirit—a spirit which inspires us to forget about guided missiles and concentrate on guided mistletoe.

1111. *Definition of Conscience—*Conscience is something like a wife. Sometimes you can't live with it and you can't live without it. Conscience has been described by a child as something that makes you tell your mother before your sister does.

1112. *Mix-up—*A person should avoid making mistakes in his life, because mistakes are easy to make but difficult to correct. It's like the case of the florist who sent a large basket of flowers to a store which had just moved to a new location and included the card, "Deepest sympathy." The owner of the store called the florist, who apologized for the mistake. "What really bothers me," said the florist, "is the flowers which were intended for you were sent to a funeral with a card, 'Congratulations on your new location.' "

1113.   Inaction—Religion for some people is like the love life of a middle-aged man. This man went to the doctor, complaining that he was always tired and all-in. The doctor gave him a thorough examination and then announced, "I do not seem to find a single thing wrong with you. I recommend that you give up half of your love life."

The patient thought this over for a while and then he asked the doctor, "Which half do you suggest I give up, Doc—thinking about it or talking about it?"

1114.   Sound Advice—Will Rogers left the world much good advice, but best of all I like his observation that what our country needs is dirtier fingernails and cleaner minds.

1115.   Faith—I think everyone will agree that the average man has faith. He must have faith, and you can tell by the way he drives an auto.

1116.   Don't Blame God—Cordell Hull put it in a nutshell when he said that war is not an act of God but a crime of man.

1117.   Slogan—The best slogan I ever saw for a church was this: Be square all week, and then come round and visit us.

1118.   Road Widening—The straight and narrow road could be broadened out a little if more people would walk on it.

1119.   Good for Nothing—In the United States there is a great opportunity for religious practice and observance, but unless we take advantage of these many opportunities they will do us no good. Too many of us think that we have special privileges, like the minister's son. A minister's son was talking with the son of a doctor. The boy whose father was a doctor said, "My father is a doctor. I can be sick for nothing."

The son of the minister replied boastfully, "That's nothing. My father is a minister. I can be good for nothing."

1120. *Rewards of Doing Good*—A person should do good for the unselfish pleasure of doing good and not with the hope or expectation of gaining some profit or benefit from his act. Those who do good with the expectation of gaining material advantage from their generosity are like the employee at a hotel where a woman guest of great wealth resided. This hotel employee showed this wealthy woman every possible consideration and did everything he could to be of help and service to her. He even appointed himself to take charge of her two ill-tempered and untrained dogs. He took them for their walk every morning and evening. Eventually, the old lady died and the hotel employee looked forward with great expectations to his reward. When the contents of the will were made public, the hotel clerk discovered that the old lady had left him, as a reward for his many acts of service, the two dogs.

1121. *Power of Prayer*—Sometimes we are skeptical about the power of prayer and then again there are occasions when we become convinced, like the little girl who prayed to God that she might pass her swimming test. Later she reported, "It took God two weeks, but He finally did it!"

1122. *Contributions*—A preacher (or fund raiser) is always ready to deliver a speech at the drop of a hat, and especially at the passing of a hat.

1123. *The Most Satisfying Moment*—A group of men at a stag affair engaged in a contest to see who could give the best answer to the question: "Where did you spend the most satisfying moments of your life?" A case of beer was to be the prize for the best answer. One fellow won the contest with the answer: "I spent the most satisfying moments of my life in the arms of my wife."

He came home late that night with the case of beer and explained to his wife that he had won a contest, but he didn't want to tell her how he had answered the question because he was afraid she would become so flattered and stuck up that there would be no living with her. So he told her he won the beer by saying that his most satisfying moments were spent in church.

The wife agreed that was a very good answer. The next day a friend was congratulating the wife and told her that she must be very proud because her husband won the contest with such a thoughtful and gracious answer. The wife replied, "Yes, I am very proud of him, but what I can't figure out is that he has only been there once in all the time we have been married."

1124.   *The Crux of the Story*—There are some facts which are important and some facts may be interesting but unimportant. For example, a preacher was telling his congregation about King Solomon, who had hundreds of wives and concubines. The preacher said that he fed all of these ladies ambrosia. This is an interesting but unimportant fact. The really important fact connected with this story was the information sought by one member of the congregation when he asked the preacher, "What did Solomon eat?"

1125.   *Punishment*—We are not always the best judge of what gives us pleasure or what might be regarded as a punishment. For example, I have always enjoyed the story about a minister who once sneaked away on a Sunday morning to play golf and left his assistant at the church to preach the sermon. He was quickly recognized by an angel that decided to give him a good lesson.

The minister started off on the first hole and drove the

ball nearly three hundred yards down the middle of the fairway. He proceeded in the same fortunate manner for the
entire course of eighteen holes and ended up with a remarkable 68. Considering that this was the first time in his life
that he had ever broken 100, the minister was overjoyed. He
was greatly elated with this pleasure until he realized it was
his punishment. The minister knew he would never be able
to tell anyone that he had played golf on Sunday.

1126.   *Unnecessary Advice*—It seems as if the wrong people
always get the right advice, and those who come to church
have to listen to sermons condemning others who stay away.
You can't explain these things any more than you can explain
Swiss cheese. Swiss cheese has all the holes when it is Lim-
burger that needs ventilation.

1127.   *Not Much of an Answer*—Today I happened to sit
close to a group of young people. There was one fellow who
seemed to be the center of attraction, and I tried to find out
why as he didn't impress me much. I heard one girl say to
another about the youth, "He's the answer to a maiden's
prayer." No wonder so few girls ever pray nowadays!

1128.   *The Hereafter*—People who think that all the life
they have to live are the days which they have on this earth
should change their attitude and be like the husband who
was leaving the office at the end of the day and said to one of
his co-workers, "Maybe we can stop off and have a drink
before I go home and explain to the wife."

His fellow worker was puzzled and asked, "What do you
have to explain?"

"How do I know?" replied this fellow with some disgust.
"I'm not home yet."

I think all of us should remember that we are not home
yet and we will not be until our days on this earth are over.

Then we will have to do some explaining about things we may know nothing about at this time.

1129.   Temptation—After four years on a polar expedition the group returned home, where they were immediately rushed to a press conference. The questioning went on until finally an unusually attractive feminine reporter asked, "During the four years you were out there in the cold, snowy, lonely wilderness, what did you really miss most?"

The leader of the expedition slowly looked her up and down, then said in a very deliberate voice, "Temptation, young lady, temptation."

1130.   Time and a Half—Temptation is something we do not have to worry about. There is enough for all of us at all times. They say that sin has many forms, which gives the individual at least some chance to be choosy. You can be sure that when the wages of sin are paid, a lot of people are going to get time and a half for overtime. So many are like the young lady with loose morals who hated to be poor worse than sin.

1131.   Sin—We always are aware when we sin. Our conscience takes care of that for us. Conscience is that still, small voice which tells us, when we are thinking of doing wrong, not to do it because it is wicked and besides we might get caught. Nevertheless, we all sin on occasion but there is hope for us regardless.

1132.   Forgiveness—We have the hope for forgiveness at all times. It is like the little boy told his Sunday school teacher. The teacher was giving them a lesson in religious rituals and she finally concluded the lesson by asking this question, "Can anyone tell me what you must do before you obtain forgiveness of sin?"

There was a long silence, and then from the back of the room a small boy spoke up and said, "Sin."

1133. *Sermon*—An old Hindu observation tells us, "Every sinner should have a future just as every saint has a past." In order to have a future, the sinner should attend his church as frequently as possible. Everyone should listen to a sermon now and then, including those who go to church.

CLUBS AND LODGES

1134. *Depleted Treasure*—Looking over our financial situation, I find our treasury in about the same situation as the fellow who went on a vacation to swim, play golf, fish and enjoy good food and rest. He came home looking wonderful with not an ounce of superfluous cash on him.

1135. *Squabbles*—We have a lot of arguments and squabbles but that only draws us closer together. We're like the couple of young kids who were fighting. A lady who was passing stepped in to separate them and proceeded to give them a lecture. "You should be ashamed of yourselves," she chastised them. "Don't you know that the Bible says you should love your enemies?"

1136. *Devotion*—I don't think we can get too devoted to our club or give too much time to our club activities. We do not have to worry about being in the same fix as the son of a mother who was talking with some other mothers who were bragging about their sons' devotion to them. The first mother said, "My son always brings me roses on every holiday."

The second mother, not to be outdone, bragged, "Well, my son brings me flowers every week."

The third mother seemed to swell with pride as she told them, "My son goes to see a psychiatrist two times a week and pays twenty dollars for each visit. And what do you think he talks about all the time he is there with the psychiatrist— me!"

1137. Uncompromising—The manner in which some members are insisting upon having their own way reminds me of the answer a young student gave to the question, "Why did the Puritans come to this country?"

The lad answered, "To worship in their own way and make other people do the same."

1138. Sticky Job—It seems that no matter how much I try to give up this job, I'm like the fellow who was arrested for stealing chickens from a hen house. He refused a lawyer and insisted on defending himself. He wished to question the policeman who arrested him: "Did you see me go into the hen house?"

"Yes," replied the officer.

"Did you see me come out?"

"No," the policeman admitted.

The accused fellow turned to the judge and remarked, "That's my case, your honor. I'm still in there!"

That's my case, too. I'm still in here.

1139. Tact—In my position I have to be impartial and diplomatic like the little runt of an umpire at a corner lot baseball game. A big, husky player was at bat and an equally enormous man was catching. The count was one and one. The pitcher threw and the ball sizzled across the corner. The diminutive umpire squeeked, "Two!"

The batter growled, "Two what?"

The tiny umpire looked at the batter, and also at the catcher who was glaring at him, and said, "Too close to tell!"

1140. Three-sided Argument—We've got to settle this one way or another. They say there are three sides to every argument, and we've got to take one of them in settling this proposition. We have three choices, your side, the other side or to hell with it!

1141.   Unpleasant Task—As chairman, I must report on the activities of my committee. I wish I could tell you how happy we are with this work but instead we feel like the prisoner who was accused of stealing ducks. His attorney went on at great length assuring the jury that the defendant was a man above reproach, that he had an alibi and it was never proven that any ducks were stolen in the first place. The prosecuting attorney then took up hours with wrangling and cross-examination. Finally, the judge turned to the weary prisoner and asked him what he had to say for himself. The exhausted fellow answered, "All I can say is I wish I had never seen those darn ducks in the first place."

1142.   Lack of Information—I would like to get a little more information and instruction about the job which we are expected to do. Otherwise, I may find myself in the same position as the city man who raised chickens.

When a city man moved to a farm, a neighbor presented him with a hen and a dozen baby chicks. A few weeks later, the man had to tell his neighbor that all the chicks had died, though the hen seemed perfectly fine. The neighbor wanted to know what type of feed he had been giving the baby chicks.

"What!" the city man exclaimed. "You mean the hen doesn't nurse her own chicks?"

It is surprising how many things a person can do wrong and that is why I feel when jobs such as this are given out, there should be more detailed information and instruction to accompany them.

1143.   Troubles—They say that a bore is a person who insists on telling you all about his troubles when you want to tell him about yours. This is the time when we can all be bores and tell our troubles.

1144. *Par for the Course*—It is not always how well you do a job, but also how quickly. Time counts, even in club work. As evidence of this, I recall the story about a noted golfer who was up before a court on a charge of beating his wife. The golfer's lawyer pleaded, "My client is a much maligned man. His wife constantly nagged and criticized him until finally, in desperation, he beat her into silence with his golf club."

The judge, taking unusual interest, interrupted to ask, "In how many strokes?"

1145. *Quick Settlement*—Let's get this matter settled quickly before it causes us a lot of trouble. It's like a fire in the home of one of my friends. They were lucky to get the fire out quickly before the fire department had a chance to do any harm.

1146. *In Good Standing*—I cannot emphasize too strongly how important it is for every member to maintain his membership in a manner that will keep him in good standing. Those who fail to do this may be very unhappy. I wouldn't go so far as to say they will be as unhappy as the fellow in this story about a playboy who was seen in a night club with the wife of a good friend. The one who saw him was quite shocked and went over to his table, got him aside and administered a short lecture. "I'm surprised at you," he said. "Don't you know that she is the wife of one of your brother lodge members."

"I know," replied the playboy, "but he isn't in good standing."

1147. *Quarreling*—Let's stop all further arguments and debates. If we are going to go on like this at our meetings we'll have to get some new furniture—something like the sectional love seats they now have for people who have lovers' quarrels.

1148. *Our Club*—Our club is like the letter Q. In order to spell anything the letter Q must have U. Our club also must have you in order to mean anything at all.

1149. *Friendship*—In our club we value friendship highly like the movie villain, Boris Karloff, who was once looking for a temporary place to live and told the rental agent, "My demands are modest. I just want a small place to hang my hat and a few friends."

1150. *Last Chance*—Our club is a meeting place for good friends. Here we can gather in a pleasant atmosphere and enjoy the fellowship of people we like. We regard these friendships like the friendship of the Bishop who was seriously ill.

This Bishop was so sick that the doctor said he could not have any visitors. Many of his closest associates were turned away from his room. However, one acquaintance, not a particularly nice fellow and a disbeliever in God, called to see the Bishop. Immediately word came from the Bishop's room that he would be permitted to enter.

The agnostic was admitted to the bedroom of the dying Bishop. As he was leaving, the agnostic asked the Bishop why he had been permitted to enter the sickroom while close friends were kept away. The rapidly fading Bishop replied, "I feel confident of seeing my friends in the next world. This is probably the last chance I will ever have of seeing you."

At our club, we can hope to see our friends in the next world and certainly we can see them often in this world. Let us take as much advantage of this opportunity for friendship and fellowship as we are able.

1151. *Questions for the Birds*—It seems like we are taking up a lot of valuable time asking questions when nobody seems to know the answers. It's like asking the woman a question about what flies over the Capitol Building. This woman was taking a citizenship quiz and had trouble answering a question about the flag. To help her, the clerk asked what flies over the Capitol Building. She replied, "Pigeons." Some of the answers we've been getting are for the birds. The questions aren't any better.

1152. *Downward Trend*—The way our club has been going lately it can be compared only to a prominent young actress who had a habit of trying to kill herself every time one of her many love affairs ended unhappily. When she was brought to a hospital after her sixth suicide try, a friend visited her and advised, "Honey, you've got to go easy on this suicide stuff, or the first thing you know you will ruin your health."

1153. *Acceptance on Election to Office*—I appreciate the honor which has been shown me by this selection for the office to which I have been named. However, I am afraid that my experience does not warrant so much responsibility. I feel like the bridge player who got in with some old hands.

Three bridge players were saddled with a fourth who proved after the first round of bidding that he was pretty new at the game. One of the three asked the beginner, "When did you learn to play contract, if I may ask?"

"Would you be surprised if I told you I began only today?"

"No, I just wanted to know what time today."

I hope you will forgive me for my mistakes and overlook ny shortcomings because of my lack of experience and ability to meet all of the requirements of this office.

1154. *Thanks for the Honor*—The truth is that election results are funny things. If you are fool enough to be a candidate for office, you are caught between the hope that you get it and a silent prayer that you won't.

But I owe you an explanation and here it is: It's a proverbially grand and glorious feeling to know that those you've learned to love and respect have—all the other eligible guys having held office—now turned the limelight on you. Yet every office—even a vice-presidency—entails some responsibility and usually plenty to keep you busy. You see, you're like the little girl with the kitten. You want to have it, and still you are just a little afraid of its velvet paws. So here I am, a very ordinary sort of fellow given preferment over many who are as capable or probably more so. I can see I'm in for a lot more homework than my children. For I'm also, remember, trying to make a living. And honors carry only the price tag of loyalty and devotion to duty. There you sit, you grand guys. And I hope, with your help and suggestions, to make you glad I'm the member you elected!

1155.   *Appreciation*—I certainly feel lucky to receive this (OFFICE, HONOR, AWARD, ETC.). I'm like the millionaire industrialist who came home one day and announced to his wife, "I took an aptitude test today." His wife gasped in panic-stricken horror, then quickly added, "Well, it's certainly lucky you own the company." I feel equally lucky to be in the position I'm in now.

1156.   *Time-consuming Questions*—I must place a limit on questions at this meeting. Otherwise we'll be like the case of the young woman who went to a fortuneteller. The fortune-teller charged her twenty dollars and said she would answer two questions. The young woman, after considerable hesitation, finally paid the money and then she said to the fortune-teller, "Isn't that a lot of money for only two questions?"

"Yes, it is," answered the fortuneteller. "Now, what is your second question?" I won't say all questions are useless, but they certainly are time-consuming and we do not have enough time for them today.

1157. Getting to Know You—The time has come for all of us to get better acquainted. We should get into the spirit of finding out more about each other—like the case of the wealthy and aged society leader who stepped out in the garden of his home during a party he was giving and discovered his young wife in the arms of another man. "What's the meaning of this?" shouted the outraged millionaire. "Who is this man?"

After a moment's embarrassing silence the young wife spoke up and said, "I believe my husband is perfectly within his rights. What is your name?" I think we are within our rights if we find out the names of everyone about us.

1158. Prepared—We know all the problems and the bad things to expect in the plans we are making. We are like the husband whose wife always seemed to lose her gloves wherever she went. In order to avoid his anticipated troubles this husband wrote as follows to a theater manager: "I am attending the performance at your theater the evening of November 21. I will be accompanied by my wife and we will sit in seats H–1 and H–2. This will notify you that my wife will lose a pair of gloves in your theater on that night and I will appreciate it if you instruct your ushers to watch for them."

1159. Hopeless Situation—There must be some way to explain this situation, although it seems as hopeless as the case of the soldier, walking down the street with his wife who had come to camp to visit him. He was greeted in a friendly fashion by a gay young blonde. The soldier's wife nudged him and asked him who was the girl. The distraught soldier snapped back at his wife, "Don't bother me! I'm trying to think of some way to explain you to her."

1160. Hard-working Officers—Things are certainly different in our club than they were in the Army. To explain what I mean, I want to tell a story told by a veteran who had a number of combat experiences to tell his children. He described an especially bad situation when the enemy trapped him out in the open and bullets were whistling all around and the field was a shower of fire and lead.

"Gosh!" exclaimed his young son. "Why didn't you hide behind a tree?"

"Hide behind a tree?" the veteran repeated. "I'll tell you, son, there weren't even enough trees for the officers!"

Now you can see why I say our club is different from the Army. In our club all of the tough jobs have to be done by the officers instead of the rank and file.

1161. Call for Workers—We need workers—members to serve on important committees. Alas, I know what the preacher meant when he said that many are called but few get up.

1162. Modesty—I feel very sad on this occasion when I take office as president. I cannot be like that distinguished American political leader, Salmon P. Chase, who once said, "I would rather that the people should wonder why I wasn't President than why I am."

1163. Getting Your Money's Worth—Spending money doesn't always mean we are going to get the best entertainment for our club meeting. The main thing is, we want something appropriate. Otherwise it will be like the case of the man who died and was put to rest with appropriate ceremonies. "He had a fine funeral," one friend told another. "The funeral cost five thousand dollars."

"Gee," the other fellow exclaimed, "for another thousand dollars they could have buried him in a Cadillac."

1164. Hash—At our club meetings we have the old stuff hashed up over and over again. Maybe our program chairman could take a tip from our member's wife who is a gem in the kitchen. She does an absolutely great thing with leftovers. She throws them out!

1165. For an Orderly Meeting—We don't mind having things called to our attention as long as it is done in a diplomatic and courteous manner. In this respect, I want to tell you a little story about a man who was interested in the rehabilitation of the mentally deranged. He visited the asylum one day and watched while one of the patients was laying a brick wall around the grounds.

He inspected the work closely and was pleased to see that the patient was doing an excellent, high-grade job. He spoke to the patient and complimented him on his work and then added, "I understand you will be getting out of here in the near future. Would you like to come and do some brick work for me?"

The patient was quite enthusiastic about this and told the visitor that he would be most happy to work for him when he was released from the asylum. "That is fine," replied the visitor. "I must leave now, but when I return next Monday I will talk to the superintendent about it."

The visitor turned to go and after he had walked a very short distance he was struck with a brick thrown at his head. Stunned, he fell to the ground.

When he was able to sit up and take notice, he saw the patient waving gaily to him and smiling as he shouted in a friendly fashion, "You won't forget about Monday, now, will you?"

1166. The Proper Spirit—Let's have a little more friendship spirit here. Things are getting as bad as at one club where if a member sneezes, before anyone can say "God bless you" they have to put it to a vote.

1167. *All Join In*—Some of our members seem to be afflicted by the ailment that prevents them from becoming active and joining in our many projects and undertakings. The ailment is sit-tightis. It frequently afflicts club and lodge members, although it may occur in other circumstances when a person sits in tight pants.

1168. *Not Enough Time*—I don't know how we find time to do all of the things we want to do. We're like the woman who had triplets. The happy mother was telling a friend that triplets happen only once in about sixteen thousand times. "Gosh," replied the friend, "I don't see how you have time to do your housework."

1169. *Not Interested*—It's time we think of other things, like the man who was celebrating his one hundredth birthday. Some newspaper reporters were interviewing him and one of them asked the man what he thought of modern women. "To tell you the truth," said the one hundred-year-old man, "I gave up thinking about women two years ago."

1170. *Talk and More Talk*—The question is now open for discussion and let us keep it reasonable. I don't believe in the definition of a discussion as an argument where you just keep talking and talking and don't throw anything.

1171. *In a Rut*—We are inclined to be suspicious and distrustful of anything which is different from what we have been doing in the past. This is particularly true of clubs and lodges, where there is a strong inclination to follow a set pattern.

Our fear of doing something differently reminds me of the story of the artist who had a bad headache and did not feel like working. His model came into the studio and prepared to disrobe so that he could continue his work painting her in the nude. However, he stopped her and told her that he did not feel like working, but intended to have a cup of coffee and then go home. The model offered to make the coffee for him and when it was ready they both sat down and started to drink, when all of a sudden there were familiar footsteps heard coming up the stairs. The artist hurriedly picked up the cup and saucer of coffee from which the model was drinking and shouted at her in excitement, "Good heavens! It is my wife! Get those clothes off fast!"

1172.   *Not Appreciated*—Somehow I think I fail to appreciate the members of this club. They treat me like a loving wife treats her husband. She will do anything for him except stop criticizing and trying to improve him.

1173.   *Good Job*—I want to compliment the committee on its excellent work. In the words of the medium when she saw the table begin to rise, I say, "That's the spirit!"

1174.   *Arguments*—Some of our members are like John Barrymore's wife. Of her Barrymore said that she was too beautiful for words, but not for arguments.

1175.   *Criticism*—I've been hearing a lot of complaints about our club and its programs and the like. I have no objection, but don't be like the woman who called a TV repair man. When he got there he asked what was the trouble and she began, "Well, for one thing, all the programs are lousy." If you think our programs are lousy, don't take it out on the club. Just try to help get better programs.

1176.   *Relax*—Some people want something going on every minute. They are not content to sit back, relax and enjoy the quiet contentment of things. They are like the man who was reading his newspaper and his wife interrupted him to exclaim, "George, don't you love to watch the sunset?" George didn't even look up from his paper as he growled back, "Why? What is it doing now?"

1177. First Name Basis—You will get along better here if you start calling everyone you meet by his first name. You should be smart like the little boy who was lost at a Sunday school picnic. His mother began a frantic search for him, and soon she heard loud sounds in a childish voice calling, "Estelle, Estelle!"

She quickly spotted the youngster and rushed up to grab him in her arms. "Why did you keep calling me by my name, Estelle, instead of Mother?" she asked him, as he had never called her by her first name before.

"Well," the youngster answered, "it was no use calling 'Mother' as the place is full of them."

1178. Completed Job—Doing this job for the club is like marriage. When all is said and done, you're done.

1179. Keeping Up Appearances—I do not think that we have to consider appearances and what would look best for our club in this matter. This is a case where we must consider ourselves and our own best interests. Those who urge us to do otherwise are like the American and his wife who were invited by an Englishman on a shooting trip on his country estate.

The American and his wife were not accustomed to the social graces of an English country squire and felt uncomfortable. Furthermore, their ability as marksmen left much to be desired. In fact, the American shot so badly that he almost hit the wife of his host. The Englishman became greatly angered and he exclaimed, "You almost shot my wife!"

The American, embarrassed and not knowing how to

properly atone for his error, replied, "I am truly sorry, sir. Here, have a shot at my wife."

1180. *Late Arrivals*—Maybe we would have fewer members coming in late if we could be like the psychiatrist who was so strict that if a patient came in late he would make him stand.

1181. *Success*—This sounds like it could be a big success, but I don't know for whom. It might be like the operation a man had at the hospital. The operation was a huge success— for the surgeon. He was paid a thousand dollars.

1182. *Fascinating Conversation*—I see now why they say that the only man who ever gets to talk without interruption is a married man who talks in his sleep.

1183. *Second Best*—We know what is the best thing for our club to do, but maybe we had better do the second-best thing. We can be like the woman who asked her friend, "What's good for a headache—besides a divorce?"

1184. *Fellowship*

> Is it true what they say about club meetings?
> Do club programs sparkle like a song?
> Does good fellowship prevail when members gather?
> If so, that's where I belong.

1185. *Imitations*—Some of our members seem to be expecting too much. They are not impressed with anything we have been doing. They remind me of the theatrical booking agent who thought he had seen everything.

One day a pathetic-looking little man walked into his office and announced that he had developed a new act for vaudeville. He wanted to have the opportunity to show it to the booking agent. After a great deal of argument the agent finally consented.

The would-be actor began his curtain speech by explaining that his act starts in where the Wright Brothers left off. He had discovered a way to fly without using any wings, motors, propellers or other mechanical contrivances. To prove this he began to wave his arms frantically and then suddenly his body rose into the air. At the same time he started to kick his feet. Thus waving his arms and kicking his feet, he proceeded to fly around the room for about five minutes. Then he made a graceful landing back on his feet before the booking agent and, swelling with pride, he said to the agent, "Well?"

The booking agent shrugged his shoulders and answered, "It's all right, I guess, but can you do anything besides imitating birds?"

1186. Good Report—The report which we have just heard seems to me to be a well-rounded report—like the course given by a professor at college. The students were asked to write on the examination paper what they thought of the course when they had finished. One student wrote, "This seems to be a well-rounded course. Everything not given in class during the semester has been included in the final examination."

1187. Behavior—I want you to keep order and be quiet while you are here. I'm like the farmer who was being interviewed by an insurance salesman. The insurance agent asked the farmer, "How would your wife carry on if you should die?"

The farmer answered, "I reckon it is no concern of mine—just so she behaves herself while I'm still here."

It is no concern of mine what you do when you leave, just so you behave yourselves while you are here.

1188. *Irreplaceable President*—I am your incoming president and I am here to succeed your outgoing president. You will note that I say I am here to succeed him and I do not say I am here to replace him. Anybody can succeed him, but nobody can replace him!

1189. *Latest News*—Some of our members don't seem to know what's going on around here. They are like the movie actress who was told that another movie queen was getting married again. "That's news to me," said the actress. "I didn't know she was even pregnant."

1190. *Support the Club*—Many people lose interest in our club because they may lose interest in some of our members, or they refuse to co-operate and give their support to some project because they do not care particularly for the person who is in charge of the undertaking.

People who adopt this viewpoint should try to realize that the club is one thing and certain members are something else again. They should be like the girl who broke her engagement because her feelings for the man completely changed. When a friend asked her why she continued to wear the engagement ring, this girl replied, "My feelings toward Jim have changed, but my feelings toward the ring are just the same."

Let your feelings toward our club always remain the same, regardless of how your feelings may change about some few of our members. After all, the club is the main thing and deserves your support.

1191. *Expecting Too Much*—I feel inadequate for this job I have been asked to do. I think you expect too much of me— more than I am able to accomplish. You look upon me like the little, frail old woman who was held up at a deserted street corner and robbed by a big, burly, ugly thug with a gun. The little old lady handed over her money but scolded him, "A big, husky fellow like you should be ashamed holding up a poor, old woman like me. You should be out robbing a bank."

1192. *Overworked Members*—I think maybe we are expecting too much and too often from some of our loyal members who have been the work horses of our organization and seem to fall heir to every job that comes along. I do not blame them if they begin to feel like the horse that was pulling a milk wagon.

The poor old horse, underfed and overworked, was standing hitched to its milk wagon when an old-time vaudeville entertainer, also looking underfed but not overworked, was walking down the street. The vaudeville entertainer stopped dead in his tracks when he heard the horse say to him, "Howdy, Jim, haven't seen you for a long time." When the unemployed actor got over his first shock of surprise the horse went on, "Don't you remember me—Gray Betsy—the talking horse. I've worked with you in vaudeville."

The old-time vaudeville actor was dismayed to see his old friend hitched to a milk wagon. "How come?" he asked.

"Well," explained the horse, "vaudeville got so bad and engagements so scarce that my owner finally sold me, and I went from one owner to another until here I am pulling a milk wagon. The guy who owns me is really mean. He beats me, makes me pull this wagon ten hours a day, never feeds me enough and doesn't give me the rest I deserve."

The vaudeville actor was indignant. "When he gets back I'm going to tell him just who you are!"

"Don't do that!" the horse pleaded. "If he finds out I can talk he'll have me hollering 'milk'!"

1193. *A Certainty*—In the old days, every boy was told he might grow up to be the president. Judging by the number of clubs, lodges and organizations there are in the country, I don't understand how a boy today can avoid it.

1194. Highest Authority—When I am called upon to criticize someone in a position of authority and responsibility, I feel like the rookie who accidentally bumped into the highest ranking officer on the post. The colonel shouted angrily at the rookie, "I'm the commanding officer of this regiment." The rookie replied with innocence, "Boy, are you going to catch hell. The first sergeant has been looking for you all morning!"

1195. Critics—After listening to this discussion, I know what they mean when they say that all the world is a stage and the people in it are merely critics.

1196. Friendly Greeting—We should try to be especially friendly with new members. It takes time to get acquainted and get used to a new member in any organization, but it takes time for the new member also to feel he is a part of our group.

This recalls to mind the story about a young man who was just married and his mother-in-law was to live with him. He didn't know exactly how he should address her and he was telling his troubles to a friend. "I don't like to call her mother-in-law," he explained, "because of all the comic paper jokes on that name, and somehow there is a certain sacredness about the word 'mother' that makes me hesitate to apply it to any but my own."

"Well," said the friend, "I can only tell you of my own experience. The first year we were married I addressed my wife's mother as 'say'; after that we called her 'grandma.' "

If we find ourselves using formal greetings and awkward expressions when trying to strike up a conversation with a new member, just have patience. In time he will be like one of the family, and while we won't call him "grandma" we will expect to be on close and friendly terms.

1197. Good Intentions—It seems to me that the program suggested may not bring us the favorable publicity and good opinion we seek. I am sure that those who suggested this project for our club are sincere, but others may regard it in the same light as the contribution made by a Texas farmer who struck oil on his property.

The oil millionaire contributed twenty-five thousand dollars to a political party. The boss of the party was both pleased and surprised to receive this gift and he hurried to the generous donor and asked the man if there was any favor he could do in return for this generous contribution. The new-rich oil tycoon replied, "I don't want you to do a thing for me, but you can do a favor for my wife and children. They would like to see me become a congressman."

In due time and a number of substantial contributions later, the one-time farmer found himself elected to Congress. Later, the same political party received from this man a check for nearly a quarter-million dollars. Naturally, the boss rushed over to see the millionaire to thank him personally for this very substantial contribution and asked, "Is there any favor that I can do for you in return for this valuable contribution?"

The generous oil man replied humbly, "There is nothing at all I want you to do for me as a favor. However, you can do a big favor for my wife and children. They would like to have me become a Senator."

In due time the local political boss was able to execute this request and the oil man became a Senator. As the presidential election began to approach near at hand, the political party received a check for a half-million dollars from this same oil man. Again, the party boss rushed over to see the millionaire and acknowledge this substantial gift. This time,

however, there was a great deal of apprehension in his voice
as he asked with alarm, "Are you again thinking of something
for your wife and children?"

In the same way, there are people who may question our
good intentions and think we have a selfish motive or are
seeking some glory or publicity for ourselves.

COMMUNITY AFFAIRS

1198.   Prosperous City—Why, in our city we are so prosperous that we even have drive-in unemployment offices.

1199.   Small Town—This town is so small everybody knows
whose check is good and whose husband isn't.

1200.   Point of View—These improvements are necessary.
It's just a question of making up your mind to it, like the
two roaches who got into a kitchen of a brand-new apartment
and found a piece of cake to eat. As they were nibbling on
it, they stopped long enough to look around and one commented to the other, "Everything is so bright and shiny—so
clean and sanitary—here." The other roach interrupted him
with, "Stop talking that way! Can't you see that I am eating?"

1201.   Pep Talk—We want to make a success of this campaign, and my message to the workers who have gathered
here on the eve of the drive is this: Let us celebrate tonight
and cerebrate later. To celebrate means to make festive, and
to cerebrate means to work with the brain. We've got to work
with our brains and everything else nature gave us to work
with to make a success of this undertaking.

1202.   Big Town—Our town is getting so big, pretty soon if
you want to make a telephone call from the east end to the
west side, you'll have to dial long distance.

1203. Last Resort—We've got to work out our own problems and try something different in our community. What suits the needs of one city isn't always suitable for another. It's like the case of a young executive's suggestion to his boss, who was suffering from a headache.

The boss showed up at work for the morning complaining of a splitting headache. All the help sympathized with him, until it came this young executive's turn. He said, "I had a headache myself not long ago. My wife pulled me over on the sofa beside her, hugged me and gave me a big kiss. Believe it or not, it worked—the headache went away."

The boss reached for his hat and started for the door. Then he turned to the executive and asked, "I've tried everything else so I might as well try that. Is your wife home now?"

1204. Crowded—Things are getting crowded in our city. Have you noticed the small lots they are building houses on these days? My grandfather was buried on a bigger plot than that!

1205. Examining the Proposals—There might be a lot more difference in these proposals than we see at first glance. It could be like the case of the psychiatrist who was questioning a patient and asked, "What would you say is the difference between a little boy and a dwarf?"

The patient thought a minute and answered, "There might be a great deal of difference. The dwarf could be a girl."

1206. Second Choice—This particular project is worthy of our support on its own merits. It shouldn't be a second choice like they say of the British—who are great tea drinkers. No wonder, you should taste the coffee over there!

1207. Unfriendly—In some communities people are so unfriendly that the only time a person ever gets to see his neighbor is when he takes him into court.

1208. Overdoing the Rules—Sometimes in our community we seem to be more concerned about following the rules than doing what is necessary and important for the welfare of all. It's like the case of an airline which had a rule every plane must fly the company flag at takeoff and landing. The copilot had the responsibility of looking after the flag, and any failure to follow this rule meant a fine of five dollars.

One day a new copilot was being taken on his first flight for the company by a veteran flyer. It was a bad night for flying, dark and stormy. The wings of the plane soon iced up. Then, all of a sudden the engines stopped. The young copilot was really frightened now and shouted excitedly to the veteran pilot who was acting as his instructor, "The way we are falling, we are practically on the ground!"

"Well," snapped back the pilot, "don't just sit there! Stick out the flag! Do you want to get fined five bucks?"

1209. Citizenship—A good citizen is a working citizen—one who does something worthwhile for his community. The Chinese sage, Confucius, had this to say: He who sits on end not always upright citizen.

1210. Planning for the Future—If we want progress and a good community in which to live, we should anticipate the future instead of waiting for troubles and unfavorable conditions to develop before we try to correct the causes. This attitude is like that of a father of three boys who never punished them.

If there was some trouble around the house and the father didn't know which one of three boys was responsible, he never tried to find out the guilty one. He just sent all three to bed that night without their dinner.

The next morning, he knew that the one with the black eye was the guilty party.

1211. *Crazy*—Some people think they can go around complaining and knocking our city and it is all right. In some parts of the country that wouldn't go. I know of one fellow who had to have his head examined. They figured something must be wrong with him. He was ashamed of Texas.

1212. *Different Types of People*—In our community, as elsewhere, people may be divided into three groups. First we have those few who make things happen. Then we have a larger and interested group who watch things happen. Finally we have the overwhelming majority who have no idea what has been happening.

1213. *Pride*—We should be just as proud of our community and have just as much confidence in the people who live here as the Texan who bought himself a solid gold automobile with diamond-studded hub caps. A visitor who saw this showpiece for the first time exclaimed, "Wow! Aren't you afraid to drive that around and leave it parked somewhere?"

"Naw, I'm too smart for that," replied the Texan. "I'll never drive it out of Texas."

1214. *Facing Reality*—In every community there are some things that the people who live there must learn to live with. We know what the problems are, but we do not always know how to correct them or have the means to do so.

This is very much like the case of an illustration used at a medical college. The lecturer showed the class a diagram of a man who had a deformity. The lecturer explained, "The subject shown here in the diagram limps because one leg is shorter than the other."

Then he turned to one member of the class and asked, "Now, young man, what would you do in a case like this?"

The young fellow thought for a while and then replied, "I imagine, sir, that I should limp, too."

When we are faced with certain realities of life, we must suffer the consequences. Sometimes it is better to live with these conditions than to stir up constant trouble and disturbance trying to bring public attention to them when a remedy is not practical or available.

1215. Perils of Progress—It is difficult to measure progress in what it accomplishes for the good of the individual. For instance, in the early days most city streets used to be so narrow that two cars could hardly pass without colliding. Today we have superboulevards and freeways where six and eight cars can pile up on top of each other at the same time.

1216. What Is Happiness—In our community we believe in living and enjoying the best things in life. The best things in life are not always the most expensive things. People who judge happiness by what money will buy are like the fellow who had worked hard and never made very much money. One day he was shocked to learn that he had a disease which would result in his death within a matter of a few months.

All his life this fellow had a desire to own a Cadillac. When he learned the verdict of the doctor, he took his money from the bank and bought himself a Cadillac. This he enjoyed for a few weeks, but as the time obviously grew close when he must leave this world, he went to a funeral director and arranged that he be buried and insisted that he should be buried in his Cadillac automobile.

Not long after the poor fellow passed away, and according to his instructions a large grave was dug and the fellow was put to rest inside the new and shiny Cadillac auto. One of the mourners present at the funeral watched the proceedings as the corpse was laid to rest in the Cadillac and said to his friend, "My, that's living!"

Those who have false notions about what is living may be disappointed in the things they are searching for and fail to find in our city, but those who know what they want can find real happiness and pleasure here.

1217. *Love*—The Bible teaches us to love our neighbors and to love our enemies. Often they are the same people.

1218. *The Value of Home*—Our part of the country may not have everything that you find elsewhere—those things which people seek when they travel away from home—but we have one thing in a most generous measure. I refer to the solid, substantial life that really counts. Those other things which some places boast about are merely surface qualities which usually do not mean any more than the healthy tan on the cheeks of the poor fellow who went to Florida to spend the winter and unfortunately died there. He was returned to his northern home for the funeral. At the funeral parlor, friends filed past his bier, and one said to another, "He certainly looks great, doesn't he?" The other responded with a touch of envy, "Why shouldn't he? He's been in Florida all winter." We may not always look great, but right here in our own home town we feel great because we enjoy that greatest feeling of all—the feeling of being at home.

1219. *Snobbishness*—Our community and all of the facilities which it offers is here for everyone to enjoy and use. In our community we do not adopt the same attitude as the wealthy woman who was frequently called upon for gifts. On this particular occasion she had prepared something special to be placed in the center of the public park.

A large celebration was planned at the public park when the object of her generosity was to be unveiled. At the proper moment, the covering was pulled aside, and a beautiful, large and expensively sculptured bird bath was revealed. There were some words beautifully inscribed around the edge. When the people drew close to read these words, they were startled to see, "This bath not to be used by sparrows."

1220. *Small World*—Local pride is a wonderful thing. I always have admired the Texan who said that he had made a round-the-world trip—from Houston to Dallas and back.

1221. *A New Twist*—We're not used to the good things in this city, and whenever we get something we should have had years ago we're like the fellow out in the wastelands of Texas. A long drought was broken when rain began to fall. One farmer was so shocked by the sight of rain that he fainted when the first drops hit him. They had to throw a couple of buckets of sand on him to bring him to.

1222. *Going in Circles*—Any belief that we have been going around in circles like a man lost in the woods is scientifically incorrect. Tests show that persons who are blindfolded or lost in the woods will not always walk around in circles. Some will take a zigzag course. Some here at this meeting haven't been going around in circles. They have taken a zigzag course!

INSPIRATIONAL

1223. *Expecting the Worst*—There is always something worse to think about. The thought that anything can happen isn't nearly as terrifying as the belief that it will.

1224. *True Measure of Success*—In our generation we are inclined to exaggerate the ability of any individual who happens to make a success. It is like in Hollywood where a genius is anyone who has ever produced, directed or authored a motion picture which made money. The time is coming when the ability to make money will no longer be a measure of success. A person needs something more than this one talent.

1225. On Growing Old—Getting where you want to go gets harder and harder as you put on the years. You find, as you get older, it takes you just half as long to get tired and twice as long to get rested. The iron in your blood has turned to lead in your pants.

1226. A Closed Mind—Don't have a closed mind. Be like the old maid who caught a burglar in her room. He pleaded with her, "Please, lady, let me go. I ain't never did anything wrong."

The old maid answered him, "Well, it is never too late to learn."

1227. Neurotic—We are living in an age when many people are confused, beset with fears and neurotic. A neurotic is a man with both feet planted firmly in mid-air.

There is a difference between a psychopath and a neurotic. A psychopath thinks two and two are five. A neurotic knows that two and two are four but he worries about it.

1228. How to Be Happy—Worry is the root of all evil in our modern life. So many live life today like the young fellow who was just taken into the Army. One morning during drill the sergeant was giving him a good bawling out, and concluded his remarks with this question, "What were you in private life?"

The rookie sighed deeply and replied, "Just happy."

Many people have forgotten how to be just happy. When a person's capacity to acquire outstrips his capacity to enjoy, life loses its meaning for him. They say that the person who keeps his mind on his work goes ahead. He who keeps his work on his mind goes crazy.

1229. Contentment—After a fellow finally reaches the age when he fully realizes that the world can get along fine without him and it doesn't matter much whether he lives or not; when he manages to throw away all his foolish fears, and when he has to admit he has no chance of becoming the big shot he long intended to be, he can then settle down to a life of comparative contentment.

One reason why there is no contentment for some people is because they worry and work hard and save for a future which they fear. Some people concentrate only on saving their money and good times in case there will be a rainy day. Very often they die before the deluge comes. I always sympathize with the man who worked hard and saved his money for a rainy day. At long last he took a vacation. It rained.

1230.   *Friendship*—Many a man who neglects his friends to make a name for himself is surprised when his friends tell him what the name is!

1231.   *Importance of Compromise*—Compromise, much like appeasement, is not considered a virtue by many people. To some people, compromise means a defeat.

People who think this way will probably always think along the same lines, so it would not do me much good to tell them a little story about the elm tree and the evergreen.

The elm tree is a stubborn tree which holds its branches rigid and refuses to bend or give way when a severe snowstorm piles weight upon its limbs. The elm tree bears this weight and doesn't yield until the branches break and the tree is injured or destroyed.

The evergreen is soft and pliable. When the heavy snows bear down on the evergreen, the branches move with the weight and compromise the situation. When the snow melts away, the branches spring back to normal position and are not injured. The evergreen has learned how to compromise with opposing and adverse circumstances and thus it has increased its chances for survival.

1232. *All for Himself—*You never know what you are going to like until you try it. It is like bathing beauties. You don't know whether you like bathing beauties until you bathe them.

1233. *Attention Please—*Sometimes even the best of people can be a bad influence. For instance, we have this story:

Pat was brought up before a magistrate for being drunk and disorderly. Asked what he had to say for himself, he replied that he had come up in a train with bad company. The magistrate asked who were his bad companions. Pat replied, "Four teetotalers."

"Well," said the magistrate, "I think that teetotalers are the best companions you could have."

"Oh, they're not," replied Pat, "for I had a bottle of whiskey with me, and I had to drink it all myself."

1234. *Too Perfect—*If you want to get the most out of our program, you must pay close attention. This is a voluntary gathering and not a marriage. By that, I am thinking of the observation once made to the effect that a husband who asks his wife's opinion on anything just hasn't been paying attention. Let's pay attention!

1235. *Evil—*A person should lead a good, kindly, helpful life of service to others, but at the same time he should lead such a life for his own personal satisfaction rather than praise or glory. Some people are so good in public they remind me of the story about the fellow who went to his doctor and complained of a severe headache. "Smoking too much?" the doctor asked. "Never smoked in my life," the fellow replied. "Perhaps you have been drinking too much." The patient said he never touched a drop of liquor. "Been stepping out with women too much lately?" The fellow with the headache answered, "Nope, never had a date in my life." The doctor finally arrived at the correct diagnosis. "I know your trouble. You are wearing your halo too tight."

1236.   Hard Traveling—The road may be hard and difficult, but remember that the route of all evil is Easy Street.

1237.   Self-made—Every man is self-made, but only the successful ones admit it.

1238.   Hard Work—They say that all the world is a stage, and most of us are bum actors. We need more rehearsals. There are so many people who go through life looking for horseshoes to bring them good luck when they should try using horse sense.

According to our Constitution, all men are born equal. It is what they do after that which makes the difference. Most people must go through life with the ordinary endowments of nature. Few possess genius. However, there is always hope. The willingness to work hard with persistence at a job you thoroughly enjoy doing is the best possible substitute for genius.

Some people never get anywhere because they do not want to pay the price. They may have heard that hard work never killed anyone, but they do not want to take a chance on being the first victim. Then there are the young people who dream of making good somewhere, but never try to make good where they happen to be. A person who wants to make good must begin where he is and not keep thinking of how much better it would be if he were somewhere else. Of course, there is the matter of good luck in success. Good luck is the usual result when proper preparation meets the right opportunity. Luck may bring about the opportunity, but only hard work and education can provide proper preparation.

1239.   Your Fault—When shooting to hit the bull's-eye, you don't blame the target if you miss. The fault lies with you.

1240.   *Just Cause*—There have been strong objections raised against everything good which has ever been accomplished. Objections are unimportant if the cause is just.

1241.   *Goal*—A person never gets anywhere in life unless he has a purpose—a goal to strive toward. Otherwise, he is like the woman who met a friend at the door of a psychiatrist's office. Her friend asked her, "Are you coming or going?"

This woman answered, "If I knew that, I wouldn't be here."

1242.   *Helping Others to Happiness*—Before a person gets too old in life he learns that he must do things which will serve to make other people happy. We all have a job of helping to bring happiness to others.

Sometimes this is not easy, and every individual must find his own way. Some may be like the mean-tempered old gentleman who possessed great wealth and a habit of being extremely stingy. Needless to say, he was not too much loved by his relatives, and one particular young nephew made very little effort to hide the fact that he was anxiously awaiting the day when the old man would pass along and he would inherit a substantial part of his uncle's fortune.

One day a member of the family approached the old man and announced, "Your nephew is going to be married soon. Don't you think it would be nice if you did something on this occasion for him to make the poor boy happy?"

The old man thought it over for a while and then replied, "Maybe you are right. On his wedding day I will pretend to be dangerously ill."

1243.   *No Cause for Gossip*—Reputation is important and we must always consider what other people are going to think of us. For instance, the football season is the only time any young fellow and girl can carry a blanket without being talked about.

1244. *Birds of a Feather*—A person should pick his companions carefully. The old adage about birds of a feather flocking together is still true, although we have a new version. It concerns a want ad which appeared in the personal column of a newspaper and read as follows: "Gentleman who smokes and drinks and carouses wishes to meet lady who smokes and drinks and carouses. Object: smoking, drinking and carousing."

1245. *Aim*—It's good to have the right aim in life, but you've got to pull the trigger!

1246. *All Work and No Play*—Life is made for enjoyment as well as accomplishment. When I get working too hard I think of what the undertaker said when he was asked what was the secret of his success. The undertaker replied, "Hard work—done by other people."

1247. *Vicious Circle*—When you worry it is like sitting in a rocking chair. The rocking chair will give you something to do, but it won't get you anywhere.

1248. *Cold-blooded*—We always hear a great deal about the advantages of being friendly and how a warmhearted person gets along better in life. However, we should be friendly for the sake of other people as well as for our own advantage.

I can't help recalling the story about a noted and hard-hearted banker who was being driven downtown by his chauffeur in his expensive limousine when suddenly a large truck came around the corner at a high speed and out of control. It struck the limousine and the chauffeur was seriously injured.

At the hospital it was determined that the chauffeur needed an immediate blood transfusion. The banker, suddenly becoming remorseful, offered his blood for the transfusion. The transfusion was performed without delay. It proved tragic. The shock of ice water in the veins of the chauffeur was too much for him. He contracted double pneumonia and died.

1249.   *The Wrong View*—Happiness must be earned. Those who think happiness can come easily do not understand the real meaning of happiness. They think that happiness is an agreeable sensation arising from contemplating the misery of another.

1250.   *Daren't Misbehave*—Some men and women are gentlemen and ladies from necessity rather than choice. They are like the boss who had a pretty secretary working for him. This pretty secretary confided to her friend, "My boss is a perfect gentleman. All you have to do is slap his face once in a while."

1251.   *Chip on Shoulder*—Being friendly for some people isn't as enjoyable as going around with a grouch. These grouches are like the little boy who asked his mother if he could go out and play with Timmie. "You know you don't like Timmie," his mother said.

"All right," replied this youngster, who has the makings of a future grouch, "then can I go out and fight with him?"

1252.   *Money vs. Love*—Money is the standard of success in our civilization, but money can never become the standard for happiness and contentment. There can be no substitution for love. Haven't you noticed that more girls marry for love than for money because, after all, there's more love around than there is money.

1253.   *Unfriendly*—Some people complain that it is very difficult to make friends. There was one such fellow who never seemed to be able to make or keep friends. He thought there might be something wrong with him, so he went to see a psychiatrist.

The psychiatrist was interviewing him but failed to catch something the man said and asked, "Would you mind repeating that please?"

"I said," replied the fellow who could never make friends, "for some reason nobody ever seems to like me. Why don't you pay attention to what I am saying, you fathead!"

You do not have to be a psychiatrist to understand why this fellow never made friends.

1254. Mistake Prone—Some people always manage to do things wrong. They are like a hot day in July when everything that's supposed to stick together comes apart and everything that's supposed to come apart sticks together.

1255. Nothing Stops Them—I have heard some people say that you should let nothing stop you if you want something badly enough. I do not subscribe to this belief. I think there are a number of things which should be permitted to stop someone no matter how badly they may want something.

To illustrate what I mean, I want to tell you a story about a woman who had waited for months to get tickets to the popular show *My Fair Lady*.

Finally the big night came and the woman, happy to finally get to the theater to see the popular play, entered and sat down. Later another woman came and sat nearby, but the seat between them was vacant. As the time drew near for the curtain to rise, this woman said to the one who sat on the other side of the vacant chair, "Someone is going to be late."

"No," responded the other. "The seat was for my husband, but he can't be here."

"How terrible!" exclaimed the woman who had waited so

long. "With these seats so difficult to get, couldn't you have invited a relative or a friend in his place?"

"No," responded the woman in a solemn voice. "I couldn't get any relative or friend. They are all at my husband's funeral."

She was a woman who wasn't going to let anything stop her from doing what she had set out to do. There are other instances just as drastic but less obvious than this.

1256. *Fear*—Sometimes we must take the chance and face danger. When we do this we call it courage, or maybe it is just fear of being ridiculed and called yellow. Maybe we are like the fellow who decided to give up hunting as too dangerous when he read about a hunter being shot for a moose by mistake. His friends ridiculed him and said that anyone who can be mistaken for a moose is better off dead.

1257. *Be Satisfied*—The person who is really successful in this life is one who knows what he wants and keeps after it until he gets it. Unfortunately, too many people do not know what they want, or they are too busy trying to get things that other people want and they think they should have also, even if they don't actually want or need these things.

All of us can take a lesson from a little story told by the famous prizefighter, James Corbett. Jim was doing road work when he stopped far out in the country to watch a man fishing. The fisherman was tugging at his line and pulled in a large trout. He took it off the line and threw it back in the water.

Pretty soon the efforts of the fisherman were rewarded and again he pulled in a large fish, a giant perch. The fisherman nonchalantly took the fish off the hook and threw it back in the water. The third time he brought in a small pike. This he put into his creel and started to get his stuff together to end his fishing. Corbett approached the man and asked him why he threw back two very large fish and kept the one small one. The fisherman answered simply, "Small frying pan."

How many people go through life with a small frying pan and try to catch big fish that are hard to get and of no real use to them! We should learn to know what we need and what we really want. When we understand these things and gain them, we are truly successful.

1258. *Business for Lawyers*—The only thing we can say in favor of bad people is that their badness makes good lawyers.

1259. *Cold Realist*—There are some people who do not believe in ideals and nobility of thought and action. They call themselves realists—practical people who want to see results and judge everything by cold, materialistic standards. They strike me as the same kind of person as the fellow who took his wife into darkest Africa with him on a trip he wanted to make. When he got deep into the interior he set up a tent and told his wife he would have to leave her alone but he left a bell and told her to ring it in case of danger. He started out into the jungle when he heard the bell ring and rushed back to the tent to find everything in order and his wife smiling. She explained, "I was just trying out the bell."

The fellow started back into the jungle when once more he heard the bell ring and rushed back frantically to the tent. Again his wife was there all smiles and no disturbance. She explained that she was dusting about and rang the bell accidentally. For the third time the man started out into the jungle but hadn't gotten far when he heard the bell ringing. He rushed back and he found the tent on fire and his wife lying on the floor with three arrows in her body. This practical realist surveyed the scene and exclaimed, "That's more like it!"

1260.   High Living—You never know what you can do until you try. Then you may be amazed, like the salesman who was being called on the carpet because of his large expense accounts. The sales manager shouted at him, "How is it possible for any human being to spend twelve dollars a day for food in Crossroads, Iowa?"

"Easy," replied the salesman. "Skip breakfast!"

1261.   Minor Detail—Sometimes we give a great deal of importance to minor things because we judge by outward appearances rather than the actual truth or facts in the case. We are like the secretary who was with her boss when suddenly they both looked out of the window and saw a man falling from a higher place in the building to the street below.

"Great guns!" the boss shouted with excitement. "That is Jim Bentley. He just got back from a vacation in Florida."

The secretary observed, "Well, Florida certainly must have agreed with him. Did you notice that tan?"

1262.   Conceit—They say that short men are conceited—just like any other kind. Conceit is a trait, or I might better call it a fault, which we find in many men and women.

They say that conceit is the most peculiar of all diseases. It makes everybody sick but the one who has it. Whenever people see success turning a man's head, they always wish it would go a step farther and wring his neck.

It is very easy to become conceited. In order to overcome a tendency toward conceit a person should learn to develop self-control. There are many ways to develop self-control, like the man who was playing golf. He told his caddy, "I took up golf to develop self-control."

The exasperated young man replied, "You should have taken up caddying, mister."

1263. *Chivalry*—This should be an age of chivalry instead of an age of chiselry.

1264. *Unnecessary Planning*—If, during your speech, you require an example of the futility or foolishness of looking too far ahead and examining all possibilities that the future offers in too great detail, you may drive your point home by the use of the following story:

"I'd like to know if I can get a divorce," asked the smartly dressed young lady.

"What has your husband done?" inquired the sympathetic judge.

"Is it necessary to tell that?"

"Well, we must, of course, make some charge against him. State what he's done."

"Well, as a matter of fact, he hasn't done anything. I haven't got a husband, but I'm engaged to a man and I just wanted to see how easy I could get a divorce in case of need."

Like this young lady we are perhaps too concerned about all the future possibilities and in our anxiety to make sure of everything we are really making ourselves ridiculous.

1265. *Improvement*—There is always opportunity for some improvement—like the case of Joe E. Lewis, who switched from Scotch to gin and carrot juice. He would get just as drunk, but he could see better.

MEN AND WOMEN

1266. *New Outfits*—They say that women's styles may change, but a woman's designs remain the same. Those who understand women best know that their designs are centered around new and expensive clothes.

They say a new outfit can be a tonic to a woman but it is always a bitter pill to her husband. Nevertheless, women keep getting new outfits and unless they are satisfied they will make life miserable for their husbands.

If a wife does not get the clothes she wants she will freeze up and become very cold. The best antifreeze from a woman's viewpoint is a fur coat. Experienced wives say that a good cry can be very helpful. It will get things out of your system, and out of your husband.

1267.   Clumsy—To hear the average wife tell it, a man is a clumsy creature. No doubt this is true. He can't slip a ring on her finger without winding up under her thumb.

1268.   Common Sense—They say common sense is necessary for a happy married life. Common sense would avert many divorces. As a matter of fact, it would avert many marriages.

1269.   Real Ladies—They say that a gentleman is a fellow who makes it easy for a lady to remain a lady. Members of our club feel like gentlemen tonight, because we believe it is easy for our ladies to remain ladies—not because of what we do or don't do but because they are real, high-quality ladies.

1270.   A Wife's View—The women—God love them—always have just the right word to describe the men they love. For instance, there was the wife who had a temporary disagreement with her husband and the man left the house in a huff.

Shortly afterward, a friend came by asking for him. When the friend wanted to know where he would find the husband, the wife said he went out fishing. "How will I find him?" the friend asked.

The wife, the soul of marital affection, replied sweetly, "Just go down by the river and when you find a fishing pole with a worm on both ends—that's him!"

1271.   Rest in Peace—We want everybody to have a good time tonight. I hope all of you have a good time like the

Hollywood dame who had divorced four husbands. It so happened that at one affair she attended all of her former husbands as well as her present one were there. She not only had a wonderful time but she was the "wife"of the party. It was shortly after this that the young lady passed on from too much wine, husbands and song. On her grave they erected a tombstone bearing this inscription: "At last she sleeps alone."

1272.   Peace at Last—Sometimes a speaker says things just because he thinks they will please his audience. It's the same situation as a man who buys his wife a mink coat—not to keep her warm but to keep her quiet.

1273.   Having Fun—We are pleased to have the ladies as our guests. They say that the best way to tell whether a man is having fun at a party is to watch the expression on the face of his wife. Judging by the expressions on the faces of the wives, I am sure that both they and their husbands are having a good time.

1274.   Hard to Understand the Feminine Mind—Men always complain that they do not understand the ladies. The women have a way of thinking which puzzles them. They can never get what they call a sensible answer, like the man who was talking to a woman who had just purchased ten dresses.

"What in the world would you possibly want with ten new dresses?" this man asked the lady.

Quick as a wink she replied, "Ten hats."

Things like this confuse the male. He wants what he considers a more logical answer to his questions. Furthermore, the male of the species is used to conducting his affairs on what he calls a businesslike basis. For instance, we can recall from the Bible which recorded the first direct-mail campaign in the history of publicity.

According to the Bible, the king sent letters to all his provinces stating that every man should rule in his own house. This proclamation or publicity by letter was the beginning of what we call direct-mail campaigns. This campaign was a flop because the Bible further tells us that Esther became the new queen and the Book of Esther convinces us that the king did not rule in his own house. Therefore, we must never underestimate the power of a woman and certainly none of us can expect her to act in a way which we understand or which makes sense to our manner of thinking.

1275.   *A Woman's Charms*—One of the fundamental differences between men and women is illustrated by the fact that a woman can go into raptures over a sheer pair of empty nylon stockings.

Smart women are aware of this situation and a girl's best weapons in the battle of love are her physical charms. No girl these days would ever be arrested for carrying concealed weapons. You don't see any more the old-fashioned girl who used to tuck her money in her bodice. The modern girl puts her money where it can't be seen.

The modern girl dresses this way because she realizes that a good woman may be worth her weight in gold, but it is usually the other kind who gets it. A girl who blushes today must admit that her blush is as big a bluff as a four-card flush in a poker game.

1276.   *The Brighter Sex*—A woman can do just about what she pleases. It is a well-known fact that a woman can make a fool of a man easily enough because she usually gets full co-operation. No wonder they say that heaven protects the working girl, but who protects the man she is working?

1277.   *Logical Latin*—The Latin word for woman is *mulier*. Most people think it is appropriate.

1278.   *Everything Is Wrong*—Many an experienced husband
knows that women are unpredictable. You never know how
they are going to make you miserable next. There was the
case of the wife who was reading her husband's fortune card
from a penny scale. She read, "You are a leader of men, with
a magnetic personality and strong character. You are intelligent, witty and attractive to the opposite sex!"

The wife then continued to add herself, "It has your weight
wrong, too."

1279.   *Henpecked*—Then there was the pathetic case of the
husband who got a set of new false teeth. He was showing
off his new teeth to the men where he worked, and he was
asked what his wife thought of them. The husband replied,
"I don't know. I don't dare open my mouth around the
house."

This fellow was as bad off as the husband who called to his
office and reported, "I am afraid that I'll be out from work
for about a week. My poor wife broke a leg last night."

His boss expressed his sympathy and then demanded, "And
just how does that prevent you from coming to work?"

"Evidently you do not understand," the poor fellow sighed.
"It was my leg she broke."

In spite of the fact that women have the upper hand in
love, courtship and marriage, men still retain one gratifying
source of satisfaction. Women are the sex which has to go
backwards when they dance.

1280.   *Differences Between the Sexes*—You have to figure
things differently for men or for women. It's like the case of
the teacher who asked a boy how old a person would be who
was born in 1920. He wanted to know, "Man or woman?"

1281.   *Hard to Please*—Sometimes you cannot please women
no matter what you do. There was the case of the wife who

hauled her husband into court for striking her, and he excused himself by saying, "I've always tried to be a good husband and do things with my wife. When she wants to walk, I walk with her. When she wants to play, I play with her. When she wants to sing, I sing with her. When she wants to do dishes, I do dishes with her. This time she wanted to mop the floor."

1282. The Stronger Sex—Doctors tell us that women live longer and are healthier than men. There are more men than women in mental hospitals. And who do you suppose put them there?

1283. Amibitious Women—We are indeed honored to have the wives of our members present at this meeting. We are all aware of how much we owe to our wives for whatever success we enjoy. Some fellows are born great—but most others marry ambitious wives.

1284. Dye—Here's a toast to our beloved wives. We'll love them when their hair turns gray. Why shouldn't we? We've loved them when their hair was all other colors!

1285. Divorce—In America one marriage in five ends in divorce. The others fight it out to the bitter end. Many fights between married couples are over finances. It really doesn't matter so much who wears the pants in the family as long as there is money in the pockets.

1286. Broke—When a young man is in school learning his lessons he is told that there are more important things in life than money. After he gets through school he learns that they won't go out with you if you are broke. Women prefer a man who has something tender about him—especially if it is legal.

1287. Employers—No wonder one sophisticated young man about town summed up his knowledge and experience about women by saying, "A husband is a man a girl looks for to spend with for the rest of her life. The young man who doesn't know this soon finds it out after marriage." For instance, a couple of old friends met after a long absence. One said to the other, "Well, Jack, who are you working for now?"

Jack replied, "The same people—the wife and three kids."

1288. Too Slow—Many a man has gone to the bank to get some money and has heard the teller inform him, "Sorry, my friend, but your wife has beat you to the draw."

1289. Joint Account—The worst case I ever heard about was that of the fellow who tried to borrow some money from a friend. The friend wanted to know why he didn't use his own money, and this fellow explained that everything he had was in a joint account with his wife. "You can draw money from this joint account," insisted his friend.

"Not this joint account," explained the financially destitute husband. "Our joint account is in the name of my wife and her mother."

1290. Domineering Wife—I always like the story about the timid man whose wife was very domineering and particularly tight with money. Every Friday she would insist on getting her husband's pay check and then give him back only enough for his daily lunches.

One day this timid little man came home quivering with excitement, "Helen!" he exclaimed, "you will never guess what happened. I have just won fifty thousand dollars on an Irish Sweepstakes ticket."

"Wonderful!" cried his surprised wife and then quickly added, "And just where did you get the money for the ticket?"

1291. Poor Taste—A husband is a much abused individual in his own home. It's like the case of the wife who was told that her husband was wanted by the police. "There is no accounting for tastes," she sighed.

1292. Hi-fi—In our home we have that hi-fi craze. Our radio is hi-fi. My TV is hi-fi. I have a tape recorder that is hi-fi, and you should see my wife!

1293. Intuition—Sometimes we must be guided by intuition. Intuition is that incredible sixth sense which tells a woman she is right—whether she is or not.

1294. Maiden Name—A woman's maiden name is the name she had before she was married. A husband's maiden name is "Darling."

1295. Marriage—Men do not understand women and women do not understand men. For instance, there was the married man who wanted to take a trip around the world, but his wife wanted to go someplace else.

1296. Perplexing—Then there was the wife who could not understand why her husband would go into a store and buy the first pair of shoes he tried on, just because he happened to like them.

1297. Which Million—When a woman goes into a beauty shop she thinks she looks like a million when the work is finished and she returns home. Her husband thinks she looks like a million—a million other women.

1298. Deep Freeze—Times may change, but the old rule about the way to a man's heart is through his stomach still holds good. In the old days, a man would come home tired from work and ask his wife what was cooking. Today the married man comes home and asks, "Darling, what's thawing?"

1299.   Early Victory—A humorist who lived during the last generation made a wise remark that was true of his times. He said that married life is like a game of checkers. The contest is to see which one will get into the king row. This is no longer true today. It is no contest. The young wife makes a couple of fast jumps at the beginning of the game and gets to the king row. She stays there for the rest of her married life.

1300.   Female Influence—Men may make fun of women and the great influence which they have upon their lives, but it is a fact that more than one man has had his life changed because of a woman. For instance, there is the case of a man who reached the age of forty years without learning to read or write. Then he married an intelligent young lady and for her sake he made a scholar of himself in two years. In another case, there was a man who was a profound scholar at the age of forty. He met a woman, and for her sake he made a complete fool of himself within two days.

1301.   Equality of Sexes—I'm in favor of equality of the sexes. The only thing is, if equality of the sexes is ever established it will take men some time to get used to their new rights.

1302.   Auction—Men appreciate their wives—they are so kind, thoughtful and considerate. It's just like one wife who was telling her friends at the bridge table that it was her husband's birthday. "What are you getting for him?" a friend asked. She quickly answered, "Make me an offer."

1303. Killing Pace—What would man be without a woman? Men often laugh at women and make fun of their wives and their mothers-in-law, but, when you get right down to it, women are not as bad for men as some men would have you believe.

I can prove what I say by telling you a story about a Sultan who maintained his harem five miles away from the house where he lived. Every day it was the custom of this Sultan to send over a certain servant to bring him a girl from his harem. The Sultan lived to be ninety years of age, but the servant died when he was only forty.

From this story we can see proof of the fact that it is not the women who kill you, but running after them.

1304. Lie Detector—I don't know if you ever saw the cartoon of a man being shown a lie detector. "Have you ever seen one before?" he was asked. "Hell," he replied, "I married one."

1305. Russian Paradise—The Russians maintain that they have given us the first of almost everything worthwhile. As a matter of fact, Communist scholars have now discovered that Adam and Eve were actually Russian. Here is proof. Adam and Eve had no clothes and no house. Apples were the only thing they had to eat. And they thought they were in Paradise.

1306. Firm Stand—When a man puts his foot down in his house it means that his wife has finished using the vacuum cleaner under his chair.

1307. Growing Older—Middle age is described for a man as that time when he stops growing at both ends and starts growing in the middle. For women, it is that time in life when her hair starts turning from gray to red or black.

1308. The Pleasure of Your Company—We are indeed pleased that the women are here with us tonight. Nothing gives a man so much pleasure and enjoyment as the association with attractive and delightful women such as our guests.

I always like to think about the story about the rabbi and the priest who were in a friendly mood and discussing some of their past experiences. The priest finally got around to asking the rabbi whether he had ever committed a sin against his faith.

The rabbi thought it over carefully for a while and then confessed that a long time ago, before he became a rabbi, he once ate a piece of pork. Then the two sat in silence for a while until the rabbi nudged the priest and asked, "Have you ever sinned, Father?"

The priest smiled a little shamefacedly and admitted, "Before I became a priest I had an affair with a woman."

There was more silence and then the rabbi spoke and said, "It sure beats pork."

1309. Prepared Foods—In these days of prepared cake mixes, canned and frozen foods and store-bought dinners, the little girls of the next generation will have no trouble baking pies, cakes and other foods like Mother used to make.

1310. Guilty Conscience—A man should always come home with a great big smile on his face. It makes his wife wonder what he has been up to!

1311. The Works—A robber demands money or your life, but a woman wants both.

1312. Prescription—Wives are called helpmates because they are always trying to do every little thing possible to help their husbands. For instance, there was Mrs. Brown who was concerned about her husband's health and went to the doctor to discuss his case. The doctor told her, "Mrs. Brown, what your husband needs is rest and quiet. Here are some tranquilizer pills. I suggest you take one every four hours."

1313. *Desires*—Before I got married I told my wife that I would fulfill her smallest desire. After we were married, I found out she didn't have any small desires.

1314. *Certain Winner*—Our men come from well-run households. This is the kind of home where the mother announced to her family that at the end of every week, on Saturday, a prize would be given to the most obedient member of the family. All the kids cried in protest, "That ain't fair! Daddy will win it every time."

1315. *Clothes*—That woman is a regular clothes horse. When she puts on her clothes she looks like a horse.

1316. *Modern Bedtime Story*—We're living in a new and different age. They are even telling the bedtime stories differently. Now the story goes, "Once upon a time there was a mama bear and a papa bear, and a baby bear by a previous marriage."

1317. *Custom*—Early American customs do not change as much as you think. The Indian is not the only one who sleeps with a battle-ax by his side.

1318. *Two Chances*—Women have the advantage over men. They have two chances for success. If they can't get it by being smart, they can try by appearing dumb.

1319. *Pleasing the Opposite Sex*—The way the young girls dress today they are out either to catch a man or a cold.

1320.   Be Alert—Women have to be pretty careful to look after the men they marry. Otherwise they will be like the wife whose husband was a second lieutenant. The first one got away.

1321.   Success Formula—If a husband wants to please his wife he should give her something which he made himself—like money.

1322.   Explanation—The reason most husbands are hen-pecked is that they come home from work with nothing but chicken feed.

1323.   Man's World—This is a man's world. It has always been a man's world, but these days you can be pretty sure it is in his wife's name.

1324.   Good Hosts—I hope the ladies will find us real good hosts as we want to do everything to please them. We can take a lesson from the story about a fellow who had been away for a while and arrived back in town wearing a long beard. His friends naturally kidded him about the beard and asked him how he happened to acquire the fur piece.

The fellow with the beard began to complain and curse the thing in no uncertain terms. His friends were amazed at the way he talked, and asked him why he continued to wear the beard if he didn't like it.

"I hate the blasted thing," this fellow told them.

"If you hate it, then why don't you shave it off and get rid of it?" one of his friends asked.

A devilish gleam shone in the eyes of the fellow with the beard as he answered, "Because my wife hates it too!"

No, we are not going to be like this bearded gentleman. We are going to try to do everything that we think our wives will like and enjoy.

1325. Married Bliss—Married life has its fights, troubles and hardships, but most married men, in spite of everything, love their wives still. Unfortunately, few wives are that way.

1326. Amateur—It really is amazing what some women can get away with and still keep their amateur standing.

1327. Advice—Jane Austen once gave good advice to women with these words: "A woman, if she has the misfortune of knowing anything, should conceal it as well as she can."

1328. Handling Women—A person can do anything if he just finds the right way to do it. For instance, there is only one way to handle a woman. It is too bad that nobody knows what it is.

1329. Sense of Humor—I hope the ladies like our entertainment tonight. I do not subscribe to the belief that women have no sense of humor. Some people say that God made women without a sense of humor so they could love men instead of laughing at them.

1330. Acting Like Gentlemen—We are pleased to have the ladies here and we will try to act like gentlemen while they are around. When I say that we will act like gentlemen, I do not mean it exactly the same way as the man who attempted to buy something on sale in a department store during the Christmas shopping rush.

This tall and dignified gentleman stood on the edge of the crowd in an effort to get up to the counter and buy a gift for his wife. In a polite manner he tried to work his way forward a little bit at a time, but after about an hour, he found himself no closer to the counter than when he started out. With a loud roar he lowered his head and used his elbows to try to force his way through the crowd and up to the counter.

The women looked at him with great annoyance and one said sharply, "Can't you behave yourself like a gentleman?"

"I have been acting like a gentleman!" this poor fellow protested. "From now on, I am acting like a lady!"

Since this is not a department store or a crowd of shoppers, I think we can all act like ladies and gentleman without disturbing anyone else.

1331. Changing Women—They say that women's styles change, but their designs remain the same.

1332. Love Song

That girl greets you with love and kisses
Until that girl becomes your Mrs.

1333. Tipster—I wish to say that the best advice I ever received was to marry the girl who became my wife. And I might add that she gave me the advice.

1334. Well Off—We are happy to have the ladies present with us today. We know that because they are here we are well off. In this respect, we are different from the young bridegroom.

It was not long after the wedding that the bride began to complain bitterly and condemn her husband. "You lied to me!" she charged. "Before we were married you told me you were well off."

"I was," the young fellow replied with sadness, "but I didn't realize it."

We have been married long enough to realize that we are well off with our wives and we are happy when they join with us as they do today.

1335. Showing Respect—I will say one thing about my wife —she never married me for my money. All she ever asked was that I treat her with respect. She says I can best show my respect by buying her a car, a nice home, a fur coat . . .

1336. *How to Live Longer*—Medical records show that women live longer than men, but no good explanation has ever been offered for this. The only logical reason seems to be that women don't have wives to contend with.

1337. *Changes in Motherhood*—In the old generation they used to revere Mother. Songs were sung in praise of Mother's hand that rocked the cradle. In our times, the hand that used to rock the cradle now wrecks the family car.

1338. *Good Listeners*—I'm pleased to see so many women in our audience. I have found women to be good listeners, and that is why I am always very careful about what I say when they are in the audience. I subscribe to the popular belief that the hardest thing to tell is a woman's age—especially if she' s listening.

1339. *Where His Money Goes*—It is by the woman he loves that a man is often judged. This is particularly true when we are told never to judge a man by his clothes. Judge him by his wife's clothes!

1340. *Men Are Necessary*—It always flatters men to let them think that they are pretty important people for the ladies. Even the children realize the importance of the man in our society.

A couple of little girls were playing and decided that maybe they would play mother and baby. "We can't do that," said one of the little girls. "You have to have a man to have a baby."

"You do?" replied the other in surprise. "Why?"

The other well-informed child replied, "Well, somebody has to pay for everything."

1341. Only One Fault—I should consider myself a lucky man. My wife has only one extravagance. She likes to spend money.

POLITICS AND GOVERNMENT

1342. In the Same Boat—A friend of mine has two sons. One is in politics, and the other is not much good either.

1343. Hard to See—The point our opponent makes is not easy to see. Perhaps it's like the time Charley McCarthy was showing the late and lamented W. C. Fields a small bird. "It is so small," Charley said, "that you need glasses to see it."

Fields looked and replied, "Yep, about three glasses."

1344. One World—Those who keep talking about one world have the right idea. One world is enough.

1345. Nepotism—One trouble with government is that the politicians always save the best jobs for themselves or their families. I always recall the story about some G.I.s who were having a bull session in their barracks. The conversation turned to friends at home who managed to escape the draft because of the influence of their family or personal pull with the draft board. It was generally agreed that sons of politicians were the ones who had the greatest pull with the draft board and escaped service in the Army. As the talk-fest grew hotter and everyone was adding a few words of condemnation for the sons of politicians a loud, clear voice rung out, "You fellows have got things all wrong. I'm a politician's son and I'm here in the Army just like the rest of you fellows."

Those who were doing the most talking turned around to get a view of this strange species and taking a quick glance said in unison, "Yes, sir, CAPTAIN!"

1346. *Personal Discussion*—Let's not get personal in this discussion. The situation here reminds me of the soldier who was called on the carpet for talking back to his superior—and not being very complimentary about it. The commanding officer was questioning the soldier. "Did you call him a liar?"

"Yes," was the answer.

"Did you call him a louse?"

"Yes."

"Did you call him a dirty, two-faced bum?"

"No—should I have?"

1347. *Abuse*—The abuse the public takes regularly can be compared only to the case of the owner of a big Cadillac who brought it to a garage in a badly battered condition. He explained, "A Volkswagen hit me." The garage man looked at the damaged car and asked, "How many times?"

1348. *Beyond Your Means*—We are living in the kind of country where we find the average citizen is one who as soon as he is able to afford a Plymouth buys a Cadillac.

1349. *Relief*—Today the government makes everything easy for a good and happy life. In the old days, if you had a headache you'd take an aspirin or just bear it and keep on working. Today you apply at your nearest unemployment office for quick, gentle relief.

1350. *Less Supervision*—The only satisfaction for the person who has to fill out a dozen government forms regularly and pay any number of a variety of taxes is that we are not getting as much government administration as we are paying for.

1351. *Elections*—Once more we are approaching an election and the country is looking for candidates with imagination.

Imagination is what makes some candidates think they are politicians and makes some politicians think they are statesmen.

A statesman is a man who helps to make a war. History shows that statesmen make wars, soldiers fight them and Congress investigates them. When a statesman needs help he calls for a diplomat. A diplomat is a person who tries to solve complicated problems which would never have arisen if there had been no diplomats.

The beginning of all this business is the election which gives the people a chance to name their favorite candidate. In our country it is a custom for the candidate to run for office. This is compared with the custom in England where the British candidates stand for office. In most countries many candidates will lie for office.

1352.   *News Story*—During an election campaign the public soon learns that the political timber offered is mostly bark. Speaking about bark reminds me that newspapers have changed their formula for a perfect news story. It used to be that the perfect news story would result when a man would bite a dog. Today, there has been a revision and the perfect news story happens when a bull throws a politician.

1353.   *Smart Politician*—The politician of today has come to realize that he has to be pretty smart to get elected. It is not enough to speak loud and carry an umbrella. Many a candidate who had little to offer except an itch for office has been scratched at the polls.

1354.   *Fall-out*—Each election makes it more evident that something must be done to control the fall-out from campaign speeches.

1355.   *Two Plans*—When you travel abroad you will like the European plan at hotels. Paid for by the American plan!

1356.   Proud to Be Known—I think every normal human being likes to know as many people as possible. It is part of human nature to extend our friendship in every way we can. Usually we find many advantages for ourselves in knowing people. However, there are some exceptions which prove the rule. For instance, there is the case of a young fellow who decided to enter politics and ran against an old-timer who was seeking re-election to office. When the results were all in, the young fellow was elected. He, along with a great many others, was considerably surprised at the results.

A friend was questioning him and asked him how he managed to get elected when the old-timer had been in office for so many years and the political party machine was back of the old fellow. The youngster frankly confessed that he didn't know except he presumed that everybody who knew the old-time politician probably voted against the old man. As the youngster said, he didn't know as many people as his opponent.

The only time we don't like to know too many people is if we are doing something of which we are not particularly proud. In this case, we would rather not have others observe us. In other usual cases, we like to have as many people know us as we can.

1357.   Truce—What the world needs is a truce, the whole truce, and nothing but the truce, so help us God.

1358.   Old Trick—It is an old political trick for a candidate who is weak and comparatively unknown to challenge a well-known rival to a debate. In this way, the unknown individual attaches himself to a well-known person and gains some publicity he could not otherwise get for himself.

All experienced politicians are aware of this old trick. Their view of it is best expressed by a noted United States Senator who refused to be drawn into a controversy with an insignificant opponent. He explained his reasons by telling a story about a skunk which once challenged a lion to a fight.

The lion refused to accept the challenge to fight with a skunk. He told the skunk that it would gain considerable fame by fighting a lion, while the lion would suffer. For a month afterward, everyone who met the lion would know he had been in the company of a skunk.

1359. *Working for the Government*—The government is in everybody's business and has a hand in every citizen's pocket. If you miss a day's work today the government loses as much as you do.

1360. *What You Get*—A dime today is actually a dollar with the taxes taken out.

1361. *Taxes*—All you hear these days is taxes, taxes, taxes. However, there is always a bright lining for every dark cloud. Now we can really say that it is better to give than to receive . . . and it's deductible!

1362. *Acrobat*—A good politician must be agile and acrobatic. He must be able to straddle a fence while keeping both ears to the ground.

1363. *Good Rule*—A rule for success in politics could be borrowed and used by a person who wants to make a success in any field. This good rule is: Pitch in and dig. But, be careful where you throw the dirt.

1364. *Government Belief*—The people who run our government evidently believe that the world is a big ball that revolves on its taxes.

1365. *Farm Problem*—No matter what our lawmakers do, it seems we keep on having the same old problems. For example, take the farm problem, which like death and taxes we always have with us. Almost every conceivable suggestion for preventing farm surplus has been made except that every third farmer be plowed under.

1366. Hidden Taxes—This year Congress intends to do something about hidden taxes. They are going to hide them better.

1367. Political Air—This is the political season of the year—which means the air is filled with speeches and vice versa.

1368. Pressure—The taxpayer no longer fears that Congress will let him down. He would be happy if it would let him up.

1369. Be an Extrovert—Psychologists tell us that a person should not keep too much to himself. The Bureau of Internal Revenue feels the same way about it.

1370. The Final Invention—There is one thing that can be said about the H-bomb. Unless governments do something about it, the H-bomb will be the invention to end all inventions.

1371. Economy and Taxes—There is something wrong with our language which still continues to use the term political economy. There ain't no such animal!

1372. Do Your Duty—Work hard and pay your taxes cheerfully. Thousands of government bureau workers are depending upon you!

1373. Russian Plan—We must never forget that the only satellites the Russians ever release are those shot into the heavens.

1374. The Politician's Personality—His political record shows that he can be depended upon to look twice before he leaps even once.

1375. Stumped—A politician never really stumps his state until after he has been elected.

1376. Cautious—He is one of those political candidates who refuses to answer any question on the ground that it will eliminate him.

1377. Public Interest—It is hard for a politician to get the public behind him because most people are less interested in a cause than a convertible.

1378. Inflation—Our political leaders tell us that we cannot afford to forget the serious international situation. In fact, there is very little we can afford these days.

1379. Red Tape—Politics are generally associated with red tape, and red tape is associated with confusion and delay. That is why they say that while the world was created in six days, we must remember that in those days they didn't have red tape.

1380. Progress and the Egghead—Today the egghead—the smart or intellectual person—is no longer looked down upon in politics. I can remember when the typical, average politician did not want to be associated with eggheads, and it wasn't surprising to attend a political meeting and hear some candidate make an announcement like this, so he wouldn't be misunderstood, "I ain't no egghead."

1381. Too Much of Everything—The trouble with this country is that there is a surplus of food, a surplus of manufactured goods and a surplus of people who know how to run the government.

1382. *Disappearing Magic*—We all know that you can't take it with you, but the real shock comes when the man begins to plan his will and arrange his estate. He discovers that, with taxes the way they are, you can't even leave it behind!

1383. *Simplified Form*—There is one thing about the Internal Revenue Department, they make tax collecting as painless as possible. I understand that a new simplified income tax form is being prepared for next year. There will only be three lines to be filled in, as follows: A. How much did you make last year? B. How much have you got left? C. Send B.

1384. *A Big Pile*—In politics it is always easy to make a mountain out of a molehill. Just add a little dirt.

1385. *Statesman*—When a candidate thinks of the next election, he's a politician. When he thinks of the next generation, he's a statesman. We need more statesmen and fewer politicians holding office.

1386. *Sheer Waste*—My son asked me if he should study political economy at college. I told him not to because he would be wasting his time. There is no economy in politics any more.

1387. *Skeleton*—Taxes, taxes, taxes! They are driving people crazy today. One man who couldn't stand it any more took a trip to Europe to quiet his nerves. He saw the Eiffel Tower in Paris and fainted. He thought it was the Empire State Building after taxes.

1388. *Uncertainty*—We can never be absolutely certain that crime doesn't pay unless the government takes over and runs it.

YOUTH AND EDUCATION

1389. *Still the Same*—Children today are just like they have always been in the generations before—boys and girls.

1390. *Good Excuse*—It is a wonder if the young people grow up to be decent men and women, considering what they are exposed to in our daily newspapers, on TV and in the movies. They can't know right from wrong any more than the little girl who drew a picture of a cowboy walking into a saloon. Her mother said that she didn't think it was nice for her to draw a picture of a man going into a saloon. The little girl replied hurriedly, "It is all right, Mother, he is not going in there to drink anything. He is just going into the saloon to shoot a man."

1391. *Privacy*—Kids get smart so young these days you can't fool them by spelling words out. The only way you can keep them from knowing what you are talking about is to pretend you are talking to them.

1392. *Electrical Failure*—In our modern homes we control everything with switches except the children.

1393. *Overcrowding*—The schools are so crowded today, no wonder so many kids flunk. They have to copy from their own papers.

1394. *The Knowing Age*—It is too bad that all of the world's biggest problems can't hit us when we are seventeen years of age. That is when we know everything.

1395. Different—This youngster wasn't like any kid of ten years. Maybe that was because he was eighteen.

1396. Benefit of Education—A good education is a wonderful thing. It enables you to worry about conditions everywhere in the world.

1397. Topsy-turvy—In school, our children get their lesson first and the test afterward. When they leave school and get out into the world, they get the test first and the lesson later.

1398. On Your Own—Your parents, your teachers and your friends can only do so much for boys and girls. About the time a young fellow starts growing up he begins to realize that he has to do his own growing—no matter how tall his grandfather was.

1399. Out and In—Vacation is a time when kids get out of school and into your hair.

1400. Environment—How you are reared is important. When you are reared a certain way you are going to be that way to the end of your days. For instance, there was the true son of Texas who—when he went broke in later life—hung himself with his money belt.

1401. College—There is nothing easier for a young person today than to attend college, and nothing harder than to get an education.

1402. Progressive Education—In the old days of the little red schoolhouse, if a kid hit a teacher they threw him out of school. Now we have progressive education, and if a kid hits a teacher it shows that he is aggressive and it would harm his personality to discourage him.

1403.   Same Meaning—I used to be blue and down in the dumps before I was educated. Now I am depressed and despondent.

1404.   Confused—Today we are worrying about the confused, miserable teen-agers. Just give them a few years and they'll settle down as confused, miserable adults.

1405.   Fast Thinking—You must learn to think straight—and do it fast the first time. The person who stops to think twice is usually too late.

1406.   Grown-up—Youth is a state of mind—something we can have with us throughout our lives. For example, we hear these days about the new adult or mature Western pictures. The only difference I can see is that they must use older horses.

1407.   Juvenile Delinquency—We hear these days a lot about juvenile delinquency, but nobody is exactly sure just what makes a juvenile delinquent. I've heard juvenile delinquency defined as a situation when the youngster stops asking his parents where he came from and starts telling them where they can go.

1408.   High-class Kids—They say that kids are smarter these days than they used to be. This is true, especially when it comes to doing things they shouldn't. I just read about a new gang of juvenile delinquents who are too young to drive, so they only steal automobiles with chauffeurs.

1409.   New Generation—I am among the last of what the world has known as the rising generation. This new generation believes in keeping its seat.

1410. *Study Courses*—It is difficult to say which course of study is most important for young people. With a girl, we know her history isn't as important as her geography.

1411. *History Repeats*—Newspapers are full of stories about juvenile delinquents, and history books are filled with stories of ancient delinquents.

1412. *Quite an Art*—Our younger generation have learned to read books the hard way—while watching TV.

1413. *Very True*—Young people have a fresh and original viewpoint. Their minds are not cluttered with old time-worn thoughts and old ways of doing things. I think this is best illustrated by the story about a student. He was asked by his teacher this question: "What do you suppose Julius Caesar would be doing now if he were alive?" The student's frank and forward answer was: "He'd be drawing an old-age pension."

1414. *Pleasure of Youth*—I hear old people say that youth wastes its time. How sorry I feel for these oldsters who cannot remember that that is what youth is.

1415. *Punishment*—We've had a lot of talks and a great many studies on the subject of juvenile delinquency, and after all the smoke clears away we must realize that juvenile delinquency is still with us. I think maybe it is about time we come to an end in that period of our thinking when everybody and everything is blamed for crime except the fellow who commits it. Maybe the kids themselves are to blame. Maybe we should stop excusing and start punishing juvenile delinquents.

1416. *What a Difference*—Dad and Mom can't always advise their children with as much authority as they used to.

Things are so different at school now. For instance, I keep thinking of the college football star who just finished reading a letter from home and complained to his friends, "I wish Dad would stop writing me for money every week."

1417. *Character Building*—Young people must through their lives create for themselves both a character and a reputation. Their character will be judged by what they stand for; their reputation by what they fall for!

1418. *Latest Invention*—They have everything for children these days. I just heard of the latest invention. Some company has come out with reversible roller skates for backward children.

1419. *Frank Answer*—A father I know asked his son how he liked school, and the lad shouted back, "Closed!"

1420. *Comfort*—They say that children are a great comfort in your old age. And they help you reach it.

1421. *On Target*—The great love which most children have for their teachers is well illustrated in this story about some youngsters who were playing war. With their imaginary planes and atom bombs they were destroying enemy soldiers and enemy war plants. As the war progressed, they started to bomb enemy schools. Mother heard them shout in glee as they announced, "A direct hit on the first grade! Here's one for the whole school."

The mother was shocked. She reprimanded them by saying, "Don't you know that, even in war, bombs are directed against soldiers and factories. Gentlemen fighters never bomb schools where there may be children."

Little Johnny was quick to explain. "It's all right, Mommy. We weren't bombing the children. We were bombing the teachers."

1422. **Times Change**—What happened to the old ways and the old games we used to play when children? You never see any of these young delinquents playing hopscotch any more. If they do, they use real Scotch!

1423. **Exclusive**—The way some of our high school children act, you would think they are trying to get into a very exclusive school. You know the kind I mean—you can't get in unless a judge sends you!

1424. **How to Win Friends**—A friend of long standing once said to Winston Churchill, "Do you know, Sir Winston, I have never told you about my grandchildren."

Sir Winston nodded in agreement and answered, "I realize it, and I cannot tell you how grateful I am."

1425. **Parent's Problems**—In spite of this warning I am going to talk to you about my children and your children. We are all interested in children because we have the same problems rearing them. In order to help us with this job we employ what we call psychology. Psychology is a word of four syllables which a parent throws into a discussion to distract attention when he has himself cornered and cannot explain his way out. Being a parent is really discouraging. It is always a great shock to a mother after she struggles for years to civilize a son to see a little five-foot-two girl with a sweet face tame him in a week.

1426. **Up to the Keeper**—Children are very difficult to manage, and we can sympathize with the father who was asked by his wife to take Junior to the zoo. "I should say I will not!" the father replied. "If the zoo wants him, let them come and get him."

1427. **Best Helper**—Only a mother can appreciate the story about a little girl who went to her first meeting of the Brownies. Each little girl present was asked to tell what she had done at home to help her mother since she first joined the Brownies. One told how she had made beds, others had washed dishes, some had dusted their rooms and performed other duties around the house. Finally the troop leader came to one little girl sitting near the outside edge of the circle and asked what she had done to help her mother. This little girl replied very solemnly, "I kept out of her way."

1428.   Miraculous Words—A mother was having a great deal of trouble with her young son in a department store. The floorwalker and several bystanders tried to help her quiet the boy down and get him to behave. It so happened that a noted child psychiatrist was walking through the store at that critical moment and the mother recognized him. Eagerly she went up to him, explained the situation and pleaded, "Can you do something with this child?"

The noted psychiatrist nodded in a scholarly fashion. He took the child by the hand and walked him aside, then bent down and whispered a few words in the boy's ear. The youngster immediately quieted down. The mother was amazed and asked the learned man what he had said which worked such a miraculous cure. The psychiatrist, pompous and dignified, answered slowly, "I told him if he didn't behave I'd spank the stuffings out of him!"

1429.   Quick to Learn—The youngster found out the facts of life during his first day at school. When he returned home his eager mother was waiting at the door to greet him and asked, "Well, did you learn anything at school today?" The lad was quick to reply, "You bet I did. All the other kids get an allowance but me."

1430.   New-style Furniture—Young people depend more on their parents than they think they do. For instance, when a young couple was married and moved into their home some friends visited them and asked about the furniture—what period it was. The bride informed them the furniture was early matrimonal—"Some given by his mother and some by mine."

1431. Reform School Material—Some of the kids in my neighborhood are so delinquent they could go to reform school on a scholarship. Honestly, though, don't we use the term delinquent too loosely these days? I'll go along with the preacher who said that a juvenile delinquent is someone else's bad boy.

1432. Honor Students—We read a lot these days about the honor students in our schools. With them, it's "yes, your honor" and "no, your honor."

1433. No Happy Medium—Youth must learn to take orders and also how to give them. Cyrus Curtis said that there are two kinds of men who never amount to much: Those who cannot do what they are told, and those who can do nothing else.

1434. Protection—In the old days, they used to say you had to understand children. Now you have to protect yourself against them. Just the other day, I heard one little boy say to his playmate, "What are you going to be, if the neighbors let you grow up?"

1435. Unemployed for Years—Young people should start early in life to be useful. Jascha Heifetz, the noted concert star, earned a living for himself with his violin ever since he was six years old. Before that he was a bum.

1436. Children's Advantages—Young people today have more advantages than their parents. I know even today my own son does things I feel I can't afford to do because he is lucky enough to have a well-to-do father and I never had one.

1437.   Continuous Study—A young man and a young woman should understand the importance of study after they leave high school. If a person will study diligently from the age of eighteen until he is eighty years old, he will be able to learn about half as much as he thinks he knows at the age of eighteen.

Index

Throughout the book, most of the items are numbered. In the Index, the numbers shown refer to these numbered items except in the cases of unnumbered material. Then a page number is given, and the abbreviation "p." precedes the number.